THE WORLD OF NUMISMATICS

GENERAL EDITOR: PETER A. CLAYTON, F.S.A.

ANCIENT GREEK COINS

by G. K. JENKINS
Keeper of the Department of Coins
and Medals in the British Museum

G. P. PUTNAM'S SONS
New York

First published in the United States of
America in 1972 by G. P. Putnam's Sons,
New York, N.Y. 10016

Copyright © 1972 by Office du Livre,
Fribourg.

Published simultaneously in Canada
by Longmans Canada Limited, Toronto.
Library of Congress Catalog Card Number :
70187894

Printed in Switzerland

CONTENTS

5

NOTE ON ABREVIATIONS

The abbreviations that appear in the captions to the illustrations are, in the main, self-explanatory as they are linked to the Select Bibliography and to the list of special studies under that heading. Under the name of the place of issue of a coin in the list of special studies will appear the full title and date of the work cited against the author's name, e.g. illustration No. 28, a coin of Knidos, has the reference Cahn 33; turning to the heading of Knidos under Special Studies, Cahn is revealed as H. A. Cahn, *Knidos*, Berlin, 1970 and No. 33 is a coin of similar type to that illustrated here.

The other abbreviations commonly used but that are not found listed under Special Studies are :

BM and a date, which indicates a British Museum coin and the date of its acquisition.

BMC and a number, indicates the number of the coin in the relevant volume of the 29 volumes of the *British Museum Catalogue of Greek Coins*.

Lloyd and a number, refers to the coin in the *Sylloge Nummorum Graecorum*, Great Britain vol. II, Lloyd collection.

PCG and numbers, is a reference to the plate and number of the coin in the *Guide to the Principal Coins of the Greeks*, British Museum, London, 1932; 2nd ed. 1959.

RPK after a coin citation indicates that the coin formed part of the Richard Payne Knight collection acquired by the British Museum in 1824.

PREFACE

The appeal of ancient coins—and especially of Greek coins—as collectors' pieces has never been greater than it is today. It is eloquent of this that fantastic prices are often realized in the sale room for choice specimens. This is, of course, partly due to the extreme rarity of some of these coins, which in some cases may be the single survivor out of an original issue of many thousands. But an even more important factor is that such coins are objects of beauty in their own right, as well as having their historical interest and curiosity.

It is only in fairly modern times that collectors have begun to specialize seriously in Greek coins, but the taste for collecting coins as such, both as objects of beauty and of curiosity, is by no means a purely modern one. We have plenty of reason to think that in ancient times too, fine coins were capable of being appreciated, over and above their value as currency, as objects for presentation and for adornment, often mounted in jewellery; and likely enough they also had a place in ancient art collections. The emperor Augustus, it is related, was himself fond of old and foreign coins and gave them to friends.

The history of serious coin collecting, however, began at the time of the Renaissance and the rediscovery of classical antiquity. A notable figure in the early days of collecting was the poet Petrarch, and his example was followed by numerous scholars and humanists as well as by princes, popes and emperors; the Medici rulers of Florence were prominent collectors, as was the humanist Pope Paul II. At a somewhat later date Queen Christina of Sweden in her exile in Rome included coin collecting among her pursuits; later again, the Hapsburg Charles VI, father of Maria Theresa, was so devoted to his coin collection that he had it carried with him even on the battlefield. Several of these former royal collections survive in national museums.

In the early days of collecting, it was Roman coins and medallions to which most attention was given. At first only a very limited range of Greek coins was known, and these were sometimes strangely misinterpreted. Thus the coins of Rhodes with the rayed head of Helios were in medieval times held to be the Biblical thirty pieces of silver and to represent the head of Christ wearing the crown of thorns, and even in the sixteenth century it was possible for the river-god of Gela to be thought to represent the Minotaur. Italian medallists of the same time could, without any obvious sense of incongruity, invent entirely fictitious portraits of many ancient worthies. By the eighteenth century, at least, it may be said that a more realistic conception of Greek coins had been attained—a concomitant of that fuller and more systematic study of Greek (as distinct from Roman) antiquities typified by the work of Winckelmann. By this time the range of ancient Greek coinage which was known had become quite comprehensive, as can be seen, for example, from the splendid collection made by Dr William Hunter now preserved in the University of Glasgow. At the same epoch came the encyclopaedic works of Eckhel and Mionnet which put Greek numismatics on modern foundations.

To the early nineteenth century, when the passion for Greek antiquities was in full spate, belongs a collection from which many examples are illustrated in this book; that of Richard Payne Knight, a noted English dilettante and connoisseur, surprising in his day for a signal lack of enthusiasm for the Elgin marbles. It is, however, of more positive importance that he had succeeded during his travels in forming a priceless collection of Greek coins, which he bequeathed to the British Museum; his own catalogue, written in Latin, was published after his death, in 1830. Other magnificent collections which have been permanently preserved are those of the Duc de Luynes in Paris since 1862, and that of Baron de Hirsch in Brussels since 1899.

There is no doubt of the enormous progress which has been achieved in Greek numismatics during the nineteenth century and after; an important landmark being the first publication in 1887 of Barclay Head's *Historia Numorum*, a new and masterly synthesis of the whole field of knowledge. Since that date, there has been a proliferation of a whole vast literature of specialist studies on every aspect of Greek numismatics. But in all this, it is clear that the roles of the scholar and of the collector are necessarily inseparable in ensuring true progress; and in this respect we may think of the great Swiss master of numismatic study, Friedrich Imhoof-Blumer, or again of Sir Arthur Evans, who was not only the discoverer of Minoan Crete but equally one of the great names in Greek numismatics, or again of Edward Newell in the United States, the most brilliant figure in the numismatics of the Hellenic period.

In recent times there has been a tendency for Greek coin collections to become more specialized and concentrated; thus, another distinguished collection from which many of our illustrations are drawn, that of Dr A. H. Lloyd, bequeathed to the British Museum in 1946, is devoted entirely to Sicily and Magna Graecia, while Michael Vlasto spent his whole life collecting the coins of a single city, Tarentum. But such a degree of specialization implies no sort of limit to the manifold and varied interest afforded by Greek coins nor to the number of those who, in one way or another, experience their perennial fascination.

I. INTRODUCTION

It was the nineteenth century French numismatic scholar François Lenormant who said, 'Greek coins are like so many fragments taken from the Parthenon frieze.' It is not really an exaggeration, for it soon becomes clear when handling such a coin that it is not merely an object of historical and curiosity value—though it is likely enough to be both at the same time—but a genuine and original work of art revealing beauties that one is hardly prepared to find on so small a scale.

First impressions of Greek coins are sure to be conditioned to some extent by contrasts—in the modern world we are accustomed to a coinage which comes at the other end of a long tradition, and which is now regarded as necessarily a purely utilitarian artifact, mechanically reproduced in vast quantity to stereotyped patterns, offering few real attractions to the senses. The contrast seems the sharper when we reflect that it was the character of coinage as the Greeks conceived it which has determined the general pattern of almost all subsequent coinage in the European tradition. It is of course not the only possible tradition, as is clear for instance from the older civilization of China where coinage developed—probably at about the same time as it did in the Mediterranean world—on a radically different pattern, with nothing but lettering for the design and showing no tendency towards becoming a work of sculpture; and much the same is true of Islam, whose iconoclastic urge determined a development of coins relying entirely upon patterns of calligraphy, and often attaining very beautiful and complex results. To the Greeks, however, it was from the first apparent that the nuggets of metal which were to serve as coins could be brought alive with truly sculptural forms. It was in fact the opportunity to create an entirely new class of object which had not existed in the older Near Eastern civilizations in Egypt, Babylonia and elsewhere. Those older cultures had of course a long experience of money in various other forms, including the use of precious metal by weight; but the coin as such, implying the stamping of such nuggets with recognizable designs, together with a standardization of the weight, was a new invention, and not known until the seventh century B.C.

The first steps in the development, which occurred in the area of Ionia–Lydia, are 4-12 attested by finds from the Ephesos excavations. Whether the concept of coined money is to be credited precisely to the Greeks or to the Lydians can hardly be determined with certainty, but at least there is no doubt at all that the evolution of coinage was an achievement of the Greeks and that it spread rapidly into all the corners of the world which they inhabited. The coins give at once a vivid and varied picture of the rich multiplicity and individualism of the city-state civilization, with its many centres of political and cultural life, each pursuing its own aims in accordance with an intensely local character and tradition. [The coin devices were usually composed of figures or heads of the chief gods or heroes, of animals and typical products, and of themes from local mythology.] Many of the devices correspond to the official civic emblem employed for other purposes such as the design of the public seal, of weights and measures and of proxeny decrees (conferring certain diplomatic privileges to foreigners). [A considerable number of designs form a punning allusion to the

301* city's name; we have the rose (*rodon*) of
137 Rhodes, the wild celery (*selinon*) of Selinus,
183, 106 the apple (*melon*) of Melos, the goat (*aix*) of Aigai, the elbow (*ankon*) of Ankona, the table (*trapeza*) of Trapezos, and many other such. By no means all coin types are so simple and obvious as these, however, and there are plenty of cases in which we cannot be sure, in spite of the best efforts of modern scholarship, precisely why a certain design was chosen for a particular coin.]

46*, 47* [Sometimes, as on the coins of Kyzikos,
58-60 we have a repertoire of devices which may

have a personal rather than a strictly civic significance, as the emblems of the mint-official rather than of the city as such.] Generally such personal emblems when used are inserted as a subsidiary 'symbol' beside the city emblem, sometimes with somewhat bizarre reversal of scale, as when for instance on a coin of Metapontion a huge 489 corn ear is juxtaposed with a minuscule club, the former being the civic device and the latter the personal one. On the classical city-state coinage, such a symbol of a mint-official, or his name, is normally the only sort of allusion which we find to an individual person. Important rulers or kings, like Gelon or Dionysios of Syracuse, Polykrates of Samos or Arkesilas of Kyrene, leave no trace of their existence on the coins of their respective cities, [and names of rulers are to be found only on the fringes of the Greek world, as in Macedonia, Lydia or Cyprus.] In the Hellenistic period however, the vast eastward extension of the Greek world by Alexander the Great's conquests has its counterpart in the prolific coinages of the various empires established by his successors, and there is a general adoption of the practice of portrait coins exhibiting the features of individual rulers, thus taking us a step nearer to the character of coinage as we know it.

The coinage of Rome developed as a special offshoot on the Greek pattern, and culminating in a vivid portrait gallery of imperial figures laid further foundations for what was to become the mainstream of European coinage.[But the general tradition of Greek coinage was taken up in antiquity by many non-Greek peoples who came more or less under the spell of Greek culture and adopted their coinage from the same source; most of this coinage is by convention included in the scope of what is called Greek coins. Coins of the Semitic races especially, the Phoenicians, the Carthaginians, the Jews, the Nabateans and Himyarites of Arabia, often show a close adherence to Greek models, though there is also a considerable admixture of other styles of art, and inscriptions are added in other languages and scripts. The Parthian empire is a special case where the Greek style of coinage was taken over direct from the Seleukids. At the other end of the Mediterranean, Carthage forms an important offshoot of the Greek tradition, which still, though more remotely, underlies the indigenous Iberian coinage in the Spanish peninsula. Again in the Balkans and across Central Europe the prototypes of Greek coinage served to inspire a whole range of highly individual stylistic variations in the coins of the Celtic peoples, from the Black Sea to Britain.

Although the spread of coinage was comparatively rapid, and most of the more important Greek cities were minting by about 500 B.C., some time must have elapsed before the use of coins for all normal purposes was fully established. It seems probable that coins were made at first for specific and limited purposes, such as for payments to mercenary soldiers, rather than for general trade or daily shopping. Indeed in some cases even well after the establishment of coinage, other and more primitive types of money lingered on, such as the iron bars or spits once used in the Peloponnese; in Sparta in fact there was a rigid and typically puritan prohibition of the use of coined money which persisted until the third century B.C.

In the early phases coins were made only of precious metal, gold or electrum (gold alloy), and silver, and were normally of such a size that only rather large amounts could be paid with them. This aspect of early coinage is one that is hard for the modern mind to grasp easily, as if one could buy for instance a whole sheep but not a cabbage. By and large this situation was fairly quickly surmounted as small change came more into use, but the evolution to a monetary economy, though rapid in some places, may have been very slow in others. In Ionia there were almost from the first many small subdivisions of the standard electrum coin, and by the middle of the sixth century there is even the first instance from Ionia of small silver pieces which probably gave as flexible a range of possibilities as the coinage of fifth century Athens; and even there the smallest silver coins, the obol (one-sixth of a drachma) and the half-obol, must have been extremely trying for daily use, being at once too small and easy to lose and at the same time probably not small enough in value for the smallest purchases.

Bronze coins representing smaller values, however, did begin in the fifth century, apparently first in Sicily, where an *onkia*, in value only one-sixtieth of a drachma, was the smallest value so far represented in regular coinage, unless the tiny Athenian *kollyboi* really belong to the fifth century. Both at Athens, and elsewhere generally in the Greek world, it was only during the fourth century that bronze coins finally appeared in significant quantity; and it is a fair surmise that they must represent values which are fractions of the silver obol (e.g. the *chalkous* was at Athens one-eighth of an obol). The lack of explicit marks of value on most Greek bronze coins is indeed tantalizing to us though, as they were normally used only at the city of origin, the relative value would be known and agreed.

The scope even of coins of greater value such as the silver tetradrachm (four drachma) and didrachm (two drachma) may, in the classical period, have been somewhat restricted by the fact that different cities used different weight standards; in this respect the Hellenistic period brought about much greater uniformity. However, it was probably not too difficult to reckon relative values since precious metal everywhere had its intrinsic value on the scales. It seems that a coin possessed an extra value as legal tender in its own territory, since the issuing authority can always place its own valuation on its own coin (and can refuse to accept other coins, for instance, in payment of taxes); and this enables the issuing authority to cover the cost of production and even to make a profit on the issue. A coin deprived of its character as legal tender by being exported or demonetized would revert to its metal value, sometimes with the result that it was worth restriking as a new coin.

The technical methods employed for the production of Greek and other ancient coins were essentially very simple, and involved nothing but hand-work. There was in fact little change in the procedure until the seventeenth century of our era when for the first time minting machinery began to be commonly used in Europe. There is first the preparation of the flan, or blank piece of metal, and then the conversion of this blank into a coin by striking it between two dies or metal negatives on which designs have been cut. As we shall see, the earliest coins did not even have a design on both sides, the reverse being stamped with a more or less rough punch.

The metal to be made into blanks must first be heated to a molten state and then cast in moulds into suitably shaped pieces for striking; at the same time the weight must be adjusted. Some practical experiments carried out in recent times have shown that this is by no means an easy process to achieve successfully, and it is still not fully understood how the ancient mints managed to obtain an accurately weighed blank—and the accuracy of their weighings could be considerable, especially for gold coins, though silver is often less exact and bronze quite often most irregular. For bronze coins this probably did not matter, as their value was not closely related to the weight and pieces of nearly enough the right size would pass. On occasion it was not necessary to make new blanks, as existing coins, usually of other cities, might be available for restriking, which would partially or wholly obliterate the former design.

Having prepared the blanks, the next step was to stamp them with the intended designs which had been prepared on the dies. The dies themselves were normally made either from a specially hardened bronze containing a high proportion of tin, or else of iron. A few ancient dies survive to attest this. The lower die, with which the obverse face of the coin was to be struck, would be fixed in an anvil, the upper die which would strike the reverse of the coin being held in the hand. The blank of metal,

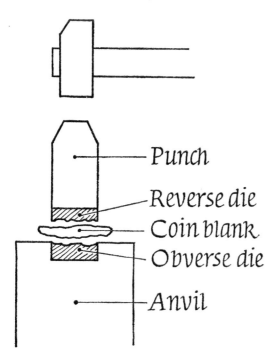

Punch

Reverse die

Coin blank

Obverse die

Anvil

heated to make it malleable, was placed on the lower die, while the upper die was stamped into it with a hammer. This single operation leaves the impression of both dies

simultaneously on the blank, which in the process has been turned into a coin.

This is a bald description of the ancient coining process, as tested by the actual modern experiments. The results of the striking do of course vary very much with the skill of the striker, and there are all too many examples of ancient coins with badly-shaped flans, of the flan not really fitting the dies, and the designs from the dies being badly struck and only partially coming out on the coin. But given skill and application, the ancient methods were capable of producing great quantities of well-struck specimens, while the effective life of an ancient die made of hardened bronze compares not too unfavourably with that of a modern hardened steel die. The recent experiments proved that a die of the ancient kind can be used for striking at least ten thousand specimens—and probably the maximum would be much higher—without damage or wear to the die. The rather irregular shape which most ancient coins have is of course the direct result of their primitive technique. But this is also one of the attractions of ancient coins as objects; their appearance would not be enhanced by being regular and smoothly circular. It was this irregularity which was rightly estimated by one of the most notable scholars of Greek coins, Charles Seltman, when he spoke of them resembling some irregular living organism.

What of the preparation of the dies? Here we are concerned with the artist, and it is here that there has been much controversy about the exact methods used in

Poseidonia

Metapontion

Tarentum

Herakleia

Sybaris

Kroton

Terina

Kaulonia

Eryx
Zankle-Messana

Panormus

Lokri

Segesta

Himera
Rhegion

Selinus

Naxos

SICILY

Katane-Aitna

Akragas

Leontinoi

Gela

Syracuse

Kamarina

MAC

Zakynthos

Pantikapaion

BLACK SEA

Sinope

Populonia
ETRURIA

ARMENIA

see main map

BITHYNIA

Ekbatana

PHRYGIA

Aspendos

Aphrodisias

Smyrna

Tarsos

PISIDIA
CILICIA
Antioch

Athens

LYKIA

Seleukia Pieria

PAMPHYLIA
Side
Soli

Seleukeia

SYRIA

Salamis

Babylon

MEDITERRANEAN

CYPRUS
Byblos

Carthage

Sidon
Damascus

Tyre

PHOENICIA

SEA

Kyrene

Alexandria

EGYPT

0   800
0   500

ONIA

DERRONES

ORRESKIOI

Aigai

Pella

Amphipolis

Lete

Akanthos

Potidaia

Skione

THESSALY

THRACE

Neapolis

Abdera

Dikaia

Thasos

Ainos

Byzantion

Lampsakos

Kyzikos

AEGEAN

Peparethos

Tenedos

MYSIA

Pergamon

LESBOS

Mytilene

Phokaia

Kymai

LYDIA

Chios

Smyrna

Sardis

Klazomenai

Erythrai

IONIA

Kolophon

Samos

Ephesos

Miletos

Delphi

Haliartos

Khalkis

Eretria

Thebes

Sikyon

Athens

Pheneos

Corinth

Elis

ARKADIA

Argos

Aigina

Olympia

Sparta

Seriphos

Naxos

Delos

Siphnos

Melos

Thera

Kalymna

CARIA

Halikarnassos

Kos

Knidos

Ialysos

Rhodes

Lindos

RHODES

polis

A

Knossos

Itanos

Gortyna

Phaestos

CRETE

AEGEAN SEA

0   250 Kms

0   150 Mls

antiquity. Coin designs are almost always rendered in relief, so that the die must be in negative : though in rare cases it is the design on the coin which is in intaglio or negative, and in these cases of course the die must be in positive relief. But normally the dies were in intaglio, like the design on a carved gem. On the whole it seems most likely that the designs were carved directly into the die face, and to a craftsman accustomed to working in negative this would be a natural way of proceeding. This is not however, the only way possible of obtaining a die cut in intaglio. It is possible to build up the design in positive relief, as it would eventually appear on the coin, on a punch which would then be used as a master tool for preparing the die by striking, in the same way that the die would strike the eventual coin. This double process of preparing the die from a master punch and then the coin from the die, is basically that used in modern minting procedures and can produce a number of dies from a single master punch. Punches were used too in medieval times to form the lettering on the dies. But so far as Greek coins are concerned, it has not yet been possible to prove that this indirect way of preparing dies by means of relief punches or 'hubs' was much used, if at all. Great care and trouble often seems to have been taken, where we can trace the life of a particular die from extant coins, to repair and re-engrave the die, whereas from a master punch it would theoretically have been possible to have another new die at a single blow. But the question whether direct

cutting was the only method used must depend also to some extent on our idea of what kind of craftsmen were employed to make coin dies.

We have already mentioned gemstones, and no one can fail to notice the similarity in general terms between ancient coins and carved gems; the repertoire of designs used in both spheres is often remarkably similar and it is natural to wonder if there may not be also a close analogy in terms of technique. Gemstones must inevitably have been carved direct in negative, and many gemstones are moreover much harder and more difficult to work than the hardened bronze from which coin dies were made. Gem carving is, in any case, an older art than that of coinage. The early Ionian coin displaying the signet of Phanes is so much like a gem impression as to suggest that the technique as well as the concept of coining owed much to the gem engraver. Again there are close analogies for the coining process in the technique of jewellers and goldsmiths. Much ancient jewellery is made up of small pieces, each the product of repetition work produced from die matrixes. This could often be deduced from extant examples of ancient jewellery and it is fully confirmed by the existence in the Ashmolean Museum at Oxford of a metal die prepared in negative and evidently destined for the making of jewellery or jewellery components. This die was closely studied from the technical point of view by Stanley Casson in connection with both gem-cutting and coin die-cutting, and he concluded that in both cases the tools and procedures employed are very similar. Moreover, technical examination of certain other classes of ancient metalwork, such as the silver bowls with a border of chariot designs in the Metropolitan Museum, New York, has revealed that these bowls too were made by the method of hammering the silver into a die engraved in negative. This is a particularly suggestive analogy for our purpose as, although these silver bowls are much larger than any coin (with a diameter of over 20 cm.), not only is the technique involved very similar but in many cases the designs are extremely close to those which are found on many of the best Sicilian coins of the fifth century B.C. and strongly suggest the same artistic milieu. Thus we find that with gem-cutting on the one hand and metalworking on the other, the technical means for the production of coins existed ready to hand when the concept of making coins was originated.

The degree of minute and finished detail which it was possible to achieve in the engraving of coin dies is certainly remarkable, but there is not on that account any reason to believe that either gem-cutters or die-cutters in antiquity performed their work except by the naked eye. The existence of optical aids such as magnifying glass in ancient times remains very problematical, although there are references in some ancient authors to suggest that the principles of optical glass were being explored; for practical purposes, however, these aids did not exist. That such fine work was nevertheless possible to execute should not occasion too much surprise, since those who take up such work often have a kind of eyesight which is specially adapted to the small scale, and it is a fact that many modern workers in this field prefer to work by the naked eye.

The Greeks themselves clearly had a definite feeling for their coins as works of art. We can deduce this from the many imitations of specially impressive coin designs which were made not only on other coins but also in other works of art. It is also significant that during the most creative phases of coinage, in Sicily and elsewhere, we have a number of artists' signatures, in the same way that we find them on painted pottery or on gems. Such signatures remain rather tantalizing, for unlike the great names of Greek art the artists of the coins are quite unknown from our ancient sources; yet at the same time they are in a way more real to us than many better-known names whose work is lost. The main incidence of signatures is in fifth century Sicily, at Syracuse and elsewhere, and in Italy in the fifth and fourth centuries, though we also have some examples from the Peloponnese, from Thessaly, Ionia and Crete. In a number of cases we simply cannot be sure that a name appearing on a coin is that of an artist rather than of a mint-official. It is interesting to note that two names—Phrygillos and Olympios—are known both from coins and gems, though it would be rash to conclude too much from this. While it is a legitimate object of study to try to isolate the work of individual artists, within certain groups of coins, there seems little prospect of making the sort of comprehensive attributions to artists which have been made in the field of vase-painting.

Yet Greek coins cannot be considered only as works of art, though it may well be as such that we feel first attracted to them, for they are other things as well. They are also official state documents and as such can afford useful evidence on political and historical questions, not to mention economics.

Before we can assess the historical significance of any coin, we need to know not only its place of mintage but also as exactly as possible its date. Explicit dates hardly ever appear on Greek coins before the Hellenistic period, and when they do, the equivalent must be deduced indirectly. The presence of a magistrate's name on some series of coins would have given to a contemporary the equivalent of a date but for us this remains something to be discovered. The coins of Alexander at the mints of Sidon and Ake in Phoenicia are marked with the dates of local eras, and such local reckonings begin to appear more often in later Hellenistic times; on Seleukid coins of the second century, for instance, there begin to appear dates by the dynastic era of 312 B.C., and this is paralleled by the kings of Pontus and Bithynia who reckoned from an era of 297 B.C. The Ptolemies on the other hand dated their coins by the years of each reign. Not only years but even months of issue were marked on the Parthian coins, giving an even greater precision; and months also appear on the later coins of Athens where, however, the years are only indicated by magistrates' names and the precise

equivalents are still the subject of much controversy.

More often, where coins do not bear explicit dates, or at least, as usually with Hellenistic coins, the name of an identifiable and datable ruler, it is necessary to rely largely on the criterion of style; and fortunately the evolution of style in Greek art generally is well enough understood to serve, in combination with other factors, as a reasonably reliable basis for any chronology. In a few cases there is documentary evidence, as for instance the testimony of Aristotle that coins showing a mule-chariot were minted by Anaxilas of Rhegion to **380** mark the occasion of his Olympic victory; a more notable case is the Syracusan 'Demareteion' dekadrachms of the early **357, 358** fifth century which have long been regarded as the coins mentioned in our Sicilian sources as being minted after the victory of Himera in 480 B.C., though here a profound controversy has recently arisen. We have good ancient evidence that Athens produced an emergency issue of gold coins in **153-6** 406 B.C., and a set of inscriptions from Delphi furnishes a sure date of 336 B.C. for the Amphiktyonic silver coins. There is **268, 269** always the search for fixed points whereby— with or without explicit documentary support—coins can be related to known historical events.

Side by side with such criteria, it is the characteristic and basic method of modern numismatic study to reconstruct as accurately as possible the precise sequence in which the coins of a given mint were issued. This is often possible, where the material extant is sufficiently comprehensive, by means of the technical fact that obverse and reverse dies of Greek coins did not normally last for exactly the same length of time; the identification of the dies used will reveal overlaps between the life of obverse and reverse dies in such a way as to reveal the sequence of striking. A typical example might be described thus (with capital letters for obverse and small letters for reverse dies); Aa Ab Ac Bc Bd Cd Ce. The use of coins which might have been thought to be produced at a number of different mints were in fact all produced at the same mint— a notable example of this is the identification of the profuse issues of the chief mint of Alexander the Great at Amphipolis. A considerable part of modern numismatic study is devoted to the establishment of such coin sequences based on study of the dies and their successive connections, and is fundamental to our understanding of the

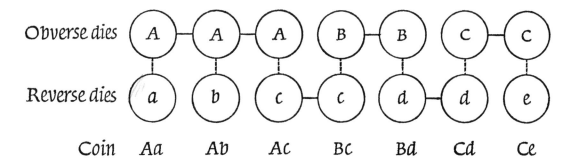

Obverse dies A A A B B C C

Reverse dies a b c c d d e

Coin Aa Ab Ac Bc Bd Cd Ce

reverse c with both A and B, and the use of reverse d with B and C at once establishes a chain of connections which can be doubly assured if, as is often the case, there are signs of some progressive wear to be observed on some of the dies—if, for instance, reverse c appears more worn when used with B than with A, and reverse d more worn with C than with B, then B is certainly after A and C after B. By the study of such minutiae vastly extended over a great number of specimens from a given mint, the coins can be arranged in a definite sequence. Sometimes indeed the same line of study can reveal that certain groups of way in which any given series of coins came into being.

The chronology of coins can be further confirmed and elucidated from the evidence provided by hoards. Such groupings of coins, buried together in the earth simultaneously, can afford a vast amount of information of several kinds. It can for instance inform us as to the directions in which certain classes of coin tended to circulate, often far from the place of origin—one of the most fruitful sources of Athenian coins of the classical period, and of archaic coins of the Macedonian region, for instance, has been the large hoards discovered in Egypt, while hoards from Sicily are one of the chief sources of Corinthian coins of the later fourth century. From the chronological point of view also, the presence of sufficient datable specimens in a hoard can often help to determine at least in broad terms the probable date of associated specimens whose date would otherwise be uncertain; here we may instance some groups of Syracusan coins both of electrum and of silver formerly assigned to the time of Dionysios I (405–367 B.C.) but which from the evidence of hoards can now safely be placed much later, in the reign of Agathokles (317–289 B.C.).

Another phenomenon of great importance in Greek numismatics is the study of 'overstriking'; where a coin is struck not on a newly prepared flan but on another, already existing, coin. This process of reminting is apt to leave some traces, often still quite legible, of the old coin; and this can afford very valuable and sometimes surprising indications as to which must have existed first. Overstriking was usually performed either on foreign coins or on coins which had been withdrawn from circulation and demonetized. A particularly remarkable series of such overstrikes occurs in the late fourth century in Crete, re-using a large stock of coins from Kyrene which had come back with returning mercenaries; in this case important modifications have had to be made to the whole chronology of Cretan coinage. Another interesting case occurred at Alexandria in 312 B.C. when Ptolemy I decided to introduce a coinage of a new and lighter standard, much of

1 ▶

2 ▶

3 ▶

1 Ionia: *Stag with inscription of Phanes*, c. *600 B.C. (stater, 14.02 gm; diam. 21 mm., PCG 1.9, found at Halikarnassos)*

2 Ionia: *Ibex, 600-550 B.C. (stater, 14.28 gm.; diam. 17 mm., PCG 1.8)*

3 Ionia: *Lion's head, 600-550 B.C. (stater, 16.09 gm.; diam. 19 mm., PCG 1.17)*

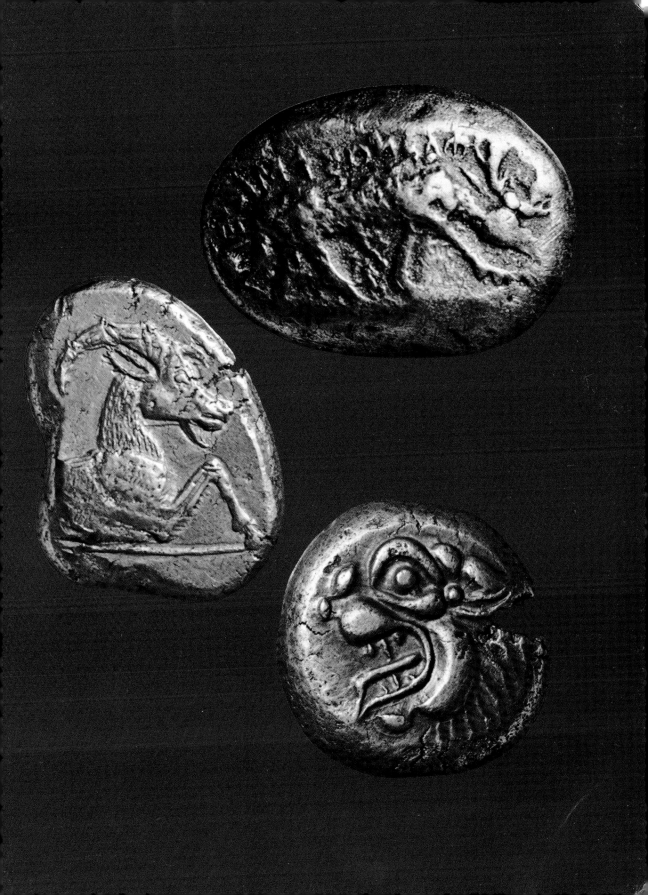

4, 5 Ionia: *Striated surface/Incuse, 650-600 B.C. (sixth, 2.39 gm., diam. 13 mm., BMC Ionia I.9 ; similar specimens from Ephesos ; Robinson 4)*

6, 7 Lydia: *Lion head/Incuse, 650-600 B.C. (third, 4.73 gm., diam. 13 mm., from Ephesos ; Robinson 56)*

8 Ionia: *Goat head, 650-600 B.C. (half, 7.24 gm., diam. 11 mm., from Ephesos ; Robinson 32)*

9 Ionia: *Two cocks, 650-600 B.C. (half, 7.15 gm., diam. 12 mm., from Ephesos ; Robinson 36)*

10, 11 Lydia ?: *Inscription between lion's heads, c. 600 B.C. (thirds, 10: in private possession ; 11: 4.71 gm., diam. 13 mm., from Ephesos ; Robinson 60)*

12 Ionia: *Human head, c. 600 B.C. (twelfth, 1.18 gm., diam. 6 mm., from Ephesos ; Head 75)*

13 Ionia: *Swastika, 600-550 B.C. (eighth, 1.24 gm., diam. 8 mm., BMC Ionia II.9)*

14 Ionia: *Winged daimon, 650-600 B.C. (half, 7.04 gm., diam. 15 mm., BM 1906 ; possibly from Ephesos ; Robinson 67)*

15 Ionia: *Stag with inscription of Phanes, c. 600 B.C (third, 4.75 gm., diam. 14 mm., PCG 51.3)*

16 Ionia: *Warrior's head, 600-550 B.C. (eighth, 1.30 gm., diam. 8 mm., BM 1953)*

17 Ionia: *Boar's head with inscription, 600-550 B.C. (sixth, 2.33 gm., diam. 10 mm., BMC Ionia III.17)*

18, 19 Ionia (Miletos ?): *Lion looking back/Three punches with stag's head, fox and star, 600-550 B.C. (stater, 14.01 gm., diam. 18 mm., PCG I.7)*

20 Lydia ?: *Lions' heads confronting, 600-550 B.C. (stater, 14.26 gm., diam. 19 mm., BM 1928)*

which was restruck on specimens of the older and heavier standard, whose weight had been suitably adjusted for the purpose (with consequent profit to the state). Sometimes too, in the Hellenistic period, overstriking was a deliberate means of obliterating the coins of a defeated enemy, as when the Seleukid king Demetrios I (162–150 B.C.) reminted virtually the whole stock of coins of the usurper Timarchos.

Of the direct value of coins as historical documents, we must here be content with a few examples. Naturally the precise amount of the contribution which coins can make to historical knowledge must vary very widely from one case another, and according to the extent to which such evidence fits in with other kinds of evidence. The mere existence of coins of a given city or ruler is a fact from which usually at least some historical deduction can be made. Considered collectively, coins offer considerable illumination not only on questions of commerce and economics but even on political events. During the Athenian empire under Perikles, for instance, there was an attempt to suppress all non-Athenian coin and to make the coinage of Athens the universal currency of the Aegean; it was a political act of great importance, and the evidence of the surviving coins has been carefully surveyed to see how far the policy was in fact carried out and what difficulties were met with in its enforcement. The history of other cities—in some cases their very existence—can rest heavily on coin evidence, as in the case of the vicissitudes of the Sybarites after the destruction of their city in 510, or the temporary revival of Zankle under its original name in 460 after it had for a generation been called Messana. Coins give us the only evidence for the formation of a league of the cities of Euboia in 410, and for the alliance of a group of cities in Asia Minor early in the fourth century. Sometimes theories based too confidently on material so far known can be demolished dramatically by the appearance of a new coin, as in the case of King Demonikos in

324, 325 Cyprus who was previously held to have been an Athenian-born ruler of Kition, but thanks to the discovery of a new coin with an explicit legend it is now known that he was in fact king of Lapethos. Then there is a series of coins of Karystos in the third century B.C. which furnish the only evidence for a tyrant of that city, while the coins of the various Hellenistic monarchies are often of the greatest value historically—the most notable example being the magnificent series of coins produced by the Greek

613-25 kingdom of Baktria and India, which preserves for us the names and portraits of an important line of kings most of whom are quite unknown to the meagre historical sources : here are coins primary and indispensable evidence for the reconstruction of a 'lost' dynasty. Even the later phases of the Seleukid empire of Syria, though better

attested by other sources, remain in much obscurity, some of which it has been possible to dispel by systematic study of the coin evidence. Here we may note specially the history of the city of Susa during the period of Seleukid decline and Parthian conquest; the only continuous commentary is that provided by the coins—many of them previously unknown—which fortunately were discovered in great quantities during the excavation of the site, and on their showing, the course of events at Susa has proved to be far more complicated than had ever been supposed.

In short, the wide range of investigation which is being focussed on Greek coins to-day is ample proof that they are in no danger of being overlooked as a rich complex of historical and artistic material. Even the quality of metal used is being put under closer scrutiny by various methods of physical science. In any case, there is much still to be found out and plenty of room for future study of every kind; many of the techniques and lines of research briefly touched on here have as yet only been applied to a comparatively limited range of known coins. And the totality of the coins known is constantly being enlarged by the discovery of fresh specimens, raising new problems and throwing fresh light on old ones.

II. THE ARCHAIC PERIOD

The invention of coinage was in antiquity credited to various Greek cities or else to the Lydians, though this question cannot be decisively resolved. The beginnings of coinage in the Greek world were at least provided with an archaeological setting by the excavations at the temple of Artemis at Ephesos. The work carried out at that site under the direction of D. G. Hogarth in 1904–5 produced the vital evidence, restudied more recently by Robinson, which has enabled us to set the earliest coins securely in the latter half of the seventh century B.C.

There were two groups of coins from Ephesos which are crucial: the first was a group of coins forming a foundation deposit below a 'basis' structure which itself underlay the foundations of the temple built by Kroisos (Croesus); the second group were found hoarded in a pot buried not far from the same place.

The coins from the basis deposit include some of the most primitive type, small globular pieces of metal with no design but 4, 5 sometimes with a rough striated surface and in any case stamped on the back with a punch mark from which developed the characteristic reverse of most archaic Greek coins. Another type represented has a design in the form of a lion's head whose 6, 7 general characteristics agree with those of typical lions in Near Eastern art of the seventh century and in particular show a strange nose-wart like Assyrian lions. The reverse is punch-marked as before. These lion coins are considered, with great probability, to be an early issue of the kings of Lydia marked with their royal device; this is confirmed by the distribution of the coins, which have turned up widely over Asia Minor and most notably in a hoard discovered at Gordion in Phrygia.

The second group of coins from Ephesos, the hoard found in the pot, is of a somewhat different character; the 'striated' type was represented, but also others which show simple figures superimposed on the striated surface, such as a goat's head or two cocks, 8, 9 as if to suggest the first evolutionary stage towards a coin with designs. It must be added however that the basis deposit and the pot hoard are virtually of the same date —which, as is indicated by Jacobsthal's thorough study of all the other objects found in the same archaeological levels, is very close to 600 B.C.

By this date, then, but not very long before it, the first steps had already been taken in the production of the coin as we know it. Clearly Lydians as well as Greeks were involved, and if Lydians are to be regarded as the true inventors this would scarcely be surprising in view of the fact that the precious metal used in the early phases of coinage was a gold-silver alloy known as electrum. This metal occurs naturally in the silt of the river Paktolos which flows through the Lydian capital, Sardis; the precious silt was probably dredged with sheepskins, a practice which may have given rise to such legends as that of the Golden Fleece. It is not certain how we should understand Herodotus' statement that the Lydians were the first to mint gold and silver coins, for this may refer to the later bimetallic coinage of Kroisos; but he also tells us of gold bricks dedicated by the Lydians at Delphi, noting that some were of pure gold but others, of 'white gold' (i.e. electrum), were of the same dimensions but weighed less—a correct observation, since the density of electrum is less than that of pure gold. Such was the metal of which the earliest coins were made.

The precise reasons for the invention of coins as a measure of value are still rather elusive, though it is to be doubted whether the invention was designed specifically to facilitate trade or commerce; more likely it was thought up as a convenient way of regularizing official payments such as the hire of mercenaries or other public employees, and to constitute an official medium for the payment of taxes. Once in existence however, the uses of such a medium could obviously be extended widely as smaller subdivisions came into being. At first, many of the pieces would be of too high a value to effect any but large payments; a stater, the standard coin in electrum weighing about 14–16 grammes, according to its local weight system, could, as we know from Xenophon at a later date, represent the wages of a mercenary for a month. But at a very early stage small subdivisions were already being made; the Lydian lion-head coins from Ephesos are mostly one-third of a stater, and the smaller fractions range through the sixth, twelfth, twenty-fourth and forty-eighth down to the ninety-sixth, which is a very tiny crumb of metal indeed (about 0.13 grammes), probably equivalent to no more than two silver obols. The discovery of more and more of these tiny electrum coins, and also of silver pieces no bigger, is beginning to show that the use of coinage in daily life may rapidly have become a practical possibility.

In the development of the early electrum coins in Ionia we are at once struck by the great diversity of designs; from the Ephesos finds alone we have coins not only with the goat, the cock, the lion, but also the stag, the human head, the bull's head, the horse's 12 head, the beetle, the griffin's head and the seal. There exist many others besides, and this very variety makes it difficult to answer the question, of which city or authority are they the coins? Apart from the Lydian lions, and a few other types such as the seal of Phokaia, attribution remains a very difficult problem. One of the earliest Ionian staters has the device of a feeding stag, 1·

which in later times is well attested as the sacred animal of Artemis on the coins of Ephesos itself. But the early stater gives also an inscription above the stag saying, 'I am the badge of Phanes' (the third of a stater has merely 'Of Phanes'); who this man was, we do not know, and while he may have been an Ephesian we cannot assume it. The formula of the inscription, so reminiscent of gem-inscriptions, compels us to think that here we are concerned with an emblem of the individual and not of the city. A similar question can be asked re-18 garding a stater showing a recumbent lion looking backwards—a device typical in later times for the coins of Miletos as the 689 emblem of Apollo of Didyma. On the 19 reverse of this stater it is interesting to note a first attempt to incorporate some device in the punch marks, which contain respectively a stag's head, a fox and a star-shaped ornament.

Similar uncertainty of attribution attends numerous other electrum coins, many of which can only be intelligibly grouped by their weight standard or by the character of their reverse punch. Possibly associated with the excavation finds from Ephesos is a half-stater of very primitive aspect, depict-14 ing a winged daimon with beard and wig-like hair, set on a striated background like the Ephesian goat and cock types. A group of pieces of quite another character, mostly of rough and knobbly designs, came from a hoard found in the island of Samos; this seems to reveal the origin of another independent local coinage as primitive as that from Ephesos, but of a different weight standard, the 'Euboic'. Of yet another weight, the 'Phokaic', are two eighth-staters, one with a swastika pattern and the 13 other with a helmeted warrior's head. 16 Among many diverse animal types is a boar's head, which, like the stag of Phanes, is accompanied by some lettering, hard to 17 read. This last forms an interesting comparison with certain pieces which were once regarded as among the earliest of Lydia; 10, 11 engraved on the die between two confronted lion's heads are letters reading *walwei*, formerly interpreted as the name of Alyattes (*c.* 615–560 B.C.). It is typical of the primitive technique of these coins that the whole design is not preserved complete on either specimen—one of which shows one lion and the inscription, the other the inscription and the other lion. Probably the die was made for a stater, and these pieces are only thirds. The significance of the name can no longer be regarded as at all certain, owing to the recent discovery of other closely related pieces with a name which cannot be that on any of the Lydian kings. A stater which might be Lydian 20 shows two confronted lions' heads, with a suggestion of something else above and below.

Not all lions were Lydian, however, and one of the Ionian cities can surely claim the splendid snarling lion's head which is one 3• of the most vivid and impressive of all early coins. Here the weight standard is the heavier 'Phokaic' one used in northern Ionia, and the coin is tentatively attributed to Smyrna. Another magnificent stater, showing the forepart of an ibex, is on the 2•

lighter standard used both in Lydia and at Miletos. Neither of these, however, has an explicitly civic device, one of the first of which was a stater of Phokaia with the type of a seal accompanied by the initial of the city's name.

The varied repertoire of early electrum coinage is constantly being increased by new discoveries, and although intelligible attributions of all these coins remain beyond reach, it seems clear that many groups of them must belong to the great Ionian cities such as Phokaia and Miletos; possibly the latter may claim a number of early sixth-century types, and perhaps also a series closer to 500 B.C. which has sometimes been regarded as a federal issue of the Ionian cities in revolt against Persia. This group includes some types also known as civic 45* devices, such as the sphinx of Chios and the winged boar of Klazomenai, but the other 61 types such as the boar-sow, the Athena head, a pair of lions, a horse, a cock, a cow 62 forepart, are not so easy to accept as civic devices. It would be quite in keeping with the general character of Ionian coinage if in fact such a group of coins of different types were the product of a single mint, which might well be Miletos.

In the later archaic period important centres of electrum coinage certainly existed at Phokaia, and at Mytilene on the island of Lesbos. Around 500 B.C. both these mints began a series of small hektai (=sixths of the stater) which maintain the characteristic Ionian tradition of a coin series with constantly changing types, and continued it down to the time of Alexander

21 Phokaia: *Head of goddess*, c. *520-500 B.C. (diobol, 1.37 gm ; diam. 10 mm., BM 1927)*

22 Kolophon: *Facing head of Apollo*, c. *520-500 B.C. (stater, 5.62 gm ; diam. 15 mm., BM 1894)*

23 Erythrai: *Horseman*, c. *500 B.C. (didrachm, 7.01 gm. ; diam. 18 mm., BM 1949)*

24 Klazomenai: *Forepart of winged boar*, c. *500 B.C.(didrachm, 6.99 gm. ; diam. 18 mm., BMC 6)*

25 Lesbos: *Calves' heads*, *500-480 B.C. (billon stater, 11.14 gm. ; diam. 21 mm., BM 1964)*

26, 27 Methymna: *Boar/Athena head*, c. *500-480 B.C. (didrachm, 8.39 gm. ; diam. 21 mm., BMC 2)*

28 Knidos: *Aphrodite head*, *520-495 B.C. (drachm, 6.16 gm. ; diam. 15 mm., BM 1947 ; Cahn 33)*

29 Lindos: *Lion head*, *520-500 B.C. (stater, 13.80 gm. ; diam. 20 mm., BMC 2)*

30, 31 Kalymna: *Warrior head/Lyre*, c. *520 B.C. (stater, 10.51 gm. ; diam. 24 mm., BMC 2)*

21

22

23

24

25

26

27

28

29

30

31

32

33

34

35

36

37

38   39   40   41   42   43   44

the Great. The Phokaia series includes several pieces with groups of seals, *phokai* 49
alluding to the name of the city, but more often with the head of a deity, in one case a charming and elegant head which is perhaps Aphrodite and which is a small mas- 51
terpiece of Ionic art, like the Herakles head which is ascribed to Erythrai. The Pho- 52
kaian electrum hektai continue to use a typeless reverse throughout; the Lesbos coins differ in this respect, as they have a 53-7
reverse type from the beginning, and combined with such obverses as the winged boar, the winged lion or the ram's head, we have reverse types which appear in intaglio on the coin—a Herakles head, a cock's head, a lion's head. This unusual technique, which continues at Lesbos well into the fifth century, is hard to parallel unless we think of the curious reverses of the 'incuse' coins of southern Italy (p. 64).

A third important centre of electrum coinage in the late archaic period is Kyzikos, a Milesian colony on the sea of Marmara, whose great series of electrum began only in the second half of the sixth century and, like those of Phokaia and Lesbos, continued until the fourth. It is a coinage of the same general pattern, inasmuch as we have a continual change of type, and for the two hundred years which the series lasted there are well over two hundred types known; each type—perhaps a personal badge—is accompanied by the civic emblem, a tunny fish, which seems inconspicuous beside the main types of which typical examples are the Gorgon, the kneeling Herakles wielding 58, 47*
club and bow, the head of Athena in a

32, 33 Aigina: *Turtle/Incuse, 600-550 B.C. (stater, 12.11 gm.; diam. 22 mm., BM 1947)*

34 Andros: *Amphora, 550-520 B.C. (stater, 11.94 gm.; diam. 18 mm., PCG 5.41)*

35 Seriphos: *Frog, 550-520 B.C. (stater, 12.25 gm.; diam. 19 mm., PCG 5.46)*

36 Thera: *Dolphins, 550-520 B.C. (stater, 11.85 gm.; diam. 24 mm., BM 1841)*

37 Naxos: *Kantharos, 500-490 B.C. (stater, 12.12 gm.; diam. 20 mm., PCG 5.44, RPK)*

38 Naxos (?): *Satyr head, 550-520 B.C. (stater, 13.60 gm.; diam. 21 mm., RPK)*

39 Melos: *Gorgon, 550-520 B.C. (stater, 13.60 gm.; diam. 20 mm., BM 1953; probably found on the island of Melos)*

40 Delos: *Lyre, 525-500 B.C. (didrachm, 8.21 gm.; diam. 18 mm., RPK)*

41, 42 Siphnos: *Apollo head/Eagle, 480-470 B.C. (drachm, 3.66 gm.; diam. 15 mm., BMC 1950)*

43, 44 Thebes: *Shield/Reverse with initial, 550-500 B.C. (stater, 12.31 gm.; diam. 18-19 mm., BMC 2)*

winged helmet, another helmeted head facing, or a head presumably of an athlete
59 superimposed on a discus (in the manner of an Athenian sculpture of the sixth century). The reverse remains plain throughout the series, as at Phokaia, and the precise sequence and chronology of the Kyzikos coins still remains somewhat conjectural. Nevertheless, the rich variety of the types and the often superb execution of the dies—not unfortunately always matched by care in striking the pieces—afford a splendid microcosm of Greek art both in the archaic phase and later.

If the electrum coinage of the Greek East represents the main line of development there in archaic times, the beginnings of silver coinage seem more spasmodic. There is also some contrast, for as against the apparently bewildering variety of types exhibited by the electrum coins, the design of silver coins tended to emphasize a constant and predominant civic emblem. Already in the archaic period there were established such types as the bee of Ephesos, the sphinx of Chios or the lion scalp and cow of Samos, though the more characteristic examples of these are to be seen in later phases. At the same time it is remarkable how some types, such as the winged boar or the griffin, tend to recur from one mint to another so that the distinction of mints can often seem blurred, especially as in the early phases there are no inscriptions as a guide. As in the electrum coins, there is some variety of local weight standards.

One important feature of silver coinage among the eastern Greeks is the comparatively early appearance of very small coins, some of which, of uncertain mintage, and only a quarter the size of the later Athenian obols, seem to be as early as *c.*550 B.C. These must represent only a fraction of the value of the smallest electrum coin. No silver coin larger than a drachm (and most were smaller) was minted at, for instance, Miletos or Phokaia during the archaic period. To Phokaia probably belong some attractive pieces, very closely paralleled in 21 Phokaian electrum, showing the head of a goddess wearing a cap or helmet and a rosette ear-ring. These were mere diobols, one-third of a drachma; specimens were found along with Persian coins in a hoard from old Smyrna, but it is eloquent of the Phokaians' far-reaching voyages of colonization that coins of this same type, though of more provincial style, were found far away in southern France, at Auriol near Marseilles, the ancient Phokaian colony Massalia. Another piece, probably of Kolo- 22 phon, which also finds an echo in some of the small coins found at Auriol, presents a curious facing head of Apollo—one of the earliest instances of this kind of representation; its weight seems to conform to the Persian standard.

In cases where the same city was minting both in electrum and in silver, we cannot be sure that there will be any recognizable correspondance either in theme or in form between the two coinages. Silver of Samos, for instance, in the time of Polykrates (*c.*532–521 B.C.) bears not the slightest relation either to the earlier electrum coins of the island or to the strange gold-covered lead pieces, simulating electrum staters—of which some survive—with which the tyrant bought off the Spartans. At Erythrai, there is a silver didrachm showing a horseman whose mount tosses its shaggy mane in elegant movement, while the rider has the typical late archaic posture with shoulders in frontal view and the stomach in profile; but the same mint is credited with a fine electrum third with a Herakles head of typical Ionian style. There are good reasons for regarding both as of the Erythrai mint, yet there is no apparent connection. On the other hand, the winged boar didrachm assigned to Klazomenai is almost identical with one of the electrum staters of the 'Ionian revolt' group; yet it is uncertain how far this winged boar can be considered a civic emblem since it also occurs on silver coins of Samos and of Ialysos in Rhodes.

On the island of Lesbos, side by side with the electrum coinage we find an archaic issue in base silver—perhaps the first of its kind, for most coins of the archaic and subsequent periods are of good metal; here is the motif of two confronting calves' heads with a tree between, which must have some special local significance as it is picked up on a later electrum coin. The mint was probably Mytilene, for the other city of Lesbos, Methymna, has simultaneously a distinctively double-type silver issue displaying a lively boar on the obverse, and on the reverse a head of Athena wearing a helmet decorated with a Pegasos and set in a square frame. This head set in low relief on the reverse of a double-sided coin recalls the technique of several Dorian mints, most notably Corinth but also, in Asia Minor, Knidos.

Knidos was the most important among a group of Dorian cities on the southwestern corner of Asia Minor, an area which falls outside the limits of the electrum coinage. Here, during the latter part of the sixth century was inaugurated a remarkable series of drachms on the weight standard of Aigina and showing the head of the goddess Aphrodite. There could hardly be a stronger contrast with the luxurious elegance of Ionia, such as in the Phokaian goddess, for at Knidos the head has all the severity of character which marks the Dorian art of the Peloponnese and which finds further expression on the coins of Kyrene and of Syracuse. The obverse of the Knidos coins consists of a lion's head that has many eastern parallels—one of these is the type of Lindos, on the neighbouring island of Rhodes where prior to 408 B.C. separate coins were minted by the individual cities, Lindos, Kameiros and Ialysos.

Among the somewhat sporadic issues of silver coins on the eastern side of the Aegean, an outstanding example comes from the island of Kalymna; here the human head is forcefully depicted on the obverse, a ferocious warrior with a huge staring eye and wearing a helmet with bristling crest, which in some ways makes the same impression of primitive grandeur that is given by some of the early Athena head coins of Athens. The warrior is likely enough Ares, if he is not some unnamed local hero, and the head recalls an early electrum coin of uncertain origin. Added to this powerful head is a reverse which has a peculiar technical interest; a seven-stringed lyre with its tortoise-shell sounding box (whose thematic relevence to the warrior is not clear) is here not set in the usual square or circular field but in a deep depression of a shape more or less following that of the lyre. The strange effect of this is impossible to parallel at such an early date but recalls technical features of some Cypriote and Phoenician coins. The warrior head and the lyre occur again on later inscribed coins which surely belong to Kalymna, confirming the attribution of this piece.

Many of the typical features of the archaic Greek coinages in Asia Minor can be paralleled in that of Lydia and of the Achaemenid empire of Persia down to the fourth century. Some of the first Lydian coins, especially those represented in the Ephesos finds, have already been considered; but a new type came into being in the time of Kroisos (560–546 B.C.) who abandoned electrum as the regular coinage metal in favour of a bimetallic currency of pure gold and pure silver. Both metals bore the identical design, the head of a lion confronting the head of a bull. It has been speculated that the significance of the confronting lion and bull may be connected with the ancient symbolism of sun and moon. Apart from the metal and the weight, the gold and silver pieces are indistinguishable; their relative value one to the other was fixed, as we know from the

45 Ionia, Chios (?): *Sphinx*, c. *550-500 B.C.* *(stater, 14.06 gm.; diam. 17 mm., PCG 1.11)*

46 Kyzikos: *Facing head of Athena*, c. *500-480 B.C. (stater, 16.04 gm.; diam. 17 mm., PCG 2.23; Fritze 68)*

47 Kyzikos: *Herakles kneeling*, c. *520-500 B.C. (stater, 16.02 gm.; diam. 19 mm., PCG 8.4, RPK; Fritze 107)*

48 Lesbos: *Winged lion*, c. *480 B.C. (sixth, 2,54 gm.; diam. 11 mm., BMC 25)*

49   50   51   52

53   54   55

56   57

58

59   60

61   62

49 Phokaia: *Three seals,* c. *520 B.C. (sixth, 2.57 gm., diam. 10 mm., BM 1924)*

50 Phokaia: *Two seals,* c. *520 B.C. (sixth, 2.55 gm., diam. 10 mm., BM 1935)*

51 Phokaia: *Head of goddess,* c. *500 B.C. (sixth, 2.57 gm., diam. 10 mm., PCG 8.11)*

52 Erythrai: *Head of Herakles,* c. *500 B.C. sixth, 2.62 gm., diam. 10 mm., BMC 7)*

53, 54 Lesbos: *Winged boar/Herakles head incuse,* c. *500 B.C. (sixth, 2.49 gm., diam. 10 mm., BM 1922)*

55 Lesbos: *Head of cock incuse,* c. *480 B.C. (sixth, 2.54 gm., diam. 11 mm., BMC 25) reverse of 48*

56, 57 Lesbos: *Ram's head/Lion head incuse,* c. *480 B.C. (sixth, 2.53 gm., diam. 10 mm., PCG 18.12)*

58 Kyzikos: *Gorgon,* c. *500–480 B.C. (stater, 16.15 gm., diam. 16 mm., BM 1892; Fritze 129)*

59 Kyzikos: *Head with diskos,* c. *520–500 B.C. (stater, 16.09 gm., diam. 14 mm., PCG 8.3; RPK; Fritze 105)*

60 Kyzikos: *Athena (?) with winged helmet,* c. *500–480 B.C. (stater, 16.06 gm., diam. 19 mm., PCG 2.24; Fritze 65)*

61 Ionia (Miletos ?): *Boar-sow,* c. *500–490 B.C. (stater, 14.00 gm., diam. 19 mm., PCG 1.15)*

62 Ionia (Miletos ?): *Cow looking back,* c. *500–490 B.C. (stater, 14.06 gm., diam. 19 mm., PCG 1.12)*

subsequent Persian value-ratio, at $13^{1}/_{3}$:1 (or more simply, 40:3) and the weights of the coins were so arranged that one gold piece was worth twenty of silver. There is some distinction in style between the original coins of Kroisos himself and the subsequent continuation of them by the Persians after their conquest of Lydia in 546 B.C., which are of a somewhat cruder and more formal style. In fact the bulk of the extant coins of this type are later than Kroisos and were still being minted in the time of Darius I (521–485 B.C.) as is shown by a foundation deposit from Persepolis, datable to 515 B.C.

At about this time, however, the Lydian type was superseded by new Persian types depicting either a running archer in the archaic kneeling position or a half-length figure of an archer; a hoard found at Smyrna in 1950 shows that these were the earliest Persian types and that they existed by about 500 B.C. During the fifth century the type of the running archer was introduced both for the gold daric and the silver siglos, and remained the standard Persian coin until the end of the Achaemenid empire. The archer usually carries a spear as well as a bow, though this is sometimes replaced by a dagger. Once the bearded archer is beardless, and this coin which is exceptional and has been thought to be of Cyrus the younger, has also a small intaglio of a satyr's head of purely Greek style on the reverse on the right of the normal plain incuse punch. But the attribution of specific variations of the type to particular kings is not practicable, although we can observe a

110•
113
116
117
111•
119, 120

general development both in the obverse and reverse from the early fifth to the later fourth century. The latest pieces of all 112* were double-darics minted at Babylon in the time of Alexander the Great.

It was long supposed that the archer on the coins represents the Great King of Persia, but recently doubt has been thrown on this assumption, and it has been pointed out that the spiked crown which he wears is not in fact the Persian king's typical head-dress. Possibly, therefore, he is rather a mythical or national hero or deity, 333 with a close likeness to the figure who appears on fourth century coins of Sidon. The artistic merits of this prolonged and conservative currency are perhaps small by comparison with the regular coins of the Greeks, but the Persian money was of great importance in the ancient world and played a considerable part in influencing events and personalities in Greece itself, especially at the time of the Peloponnesian war. On the other hand, the circulation of this money within the Persian empire seems to have been less than universal, and the silver sigloi were mostly confined to western Asia Minor, roughly the area of the old Lydian kingdom.

GREECE AND THE ISLANDS

The earliest phases of coinage in silver, less in evidence in Ionia, become clear on the Greek side of the Aegean, and it is generally agreed that the oldest mint was that of the island of Aigina, not far from Athens. Modern research shows that it is very unlikely that the Aiginetan coins can have started before about 600 B.C. and thus that it is difficult to adhere to the tradition that this mint was founded by King Pheidon of Argos, whose date is thought to be early in the previous century. That the coins replaced an older currency of iron cooking-spits may in principle still be accepted, along with the derivation of 'obol' from obelos (= a spit) and 'drachma' from drax (= a handful of spits), though the older currency may not have been displaced universally or all at once.

The Aigina coins were fashioned by a technique similar to that of the primitive Ionian coins, with a design on the front side and a rough punched 'incuse' on the reverse, and it seems clear that Aigina was following Ionian example. At Aigina the coin bears as its civic emblem, unchanged over a long period, the type of the sea- 32 turtle rendered in a high relief with a considerable stylization of details, such as the row of bosses along the ridge of the carapace and the head turned as if in profile view. The underlying reason for the use of this type is not clear, appropriate as it may seem as the emblem of a seafaring people who were enterprising traders. It is possible the turtle may have some connection with a lost local myth, and we may recall the occurrence in early Greek art of a turtle-riding hero. At all events the Aiginetan coins attained a very wide circulation. Their weight standard, with a didrachm-stater of about 12 grammes, was used widely by other cities of Greece, Crete and Asia Minor; and specimens remained long in circulation, sometimes turning up in hoards as late as the third century B.C. Both turtle and incuse show some signs of development in the later sixth and early fifth century.

We cannot know for certain whence the Aiginetans obtained their supplies of silver, though Herodotus says that there were mines on the island of Siphnos. The Aegean islands formed a natural sphere of Aiginetan influence, and it is significant that many of them during the sixth century produced coinages of their own on the Aiginetan model, with such devices as the amphora of Andros (once wrongly ascribed to Athens), the frog of Seriphos, the dolphins of Thera, a bunch of grapes at Tenos, a wine-kan- tharos at Naxos. Some sixth century island coins whose attribution is less certain are the satyr's head which might be Naxian, and the Gorgon which may be of Melos. The type of the Apolline lyre is appropriate to Delos where it continued into the fol- lowing century; and the attractive head of Apollo with the reverse of an eagle, minted at Siphnos, belongs to the latter end of the archaic period, perhaps just after the Persian wars.

Close in form to the Aiginetan coins were those of some mainland cities, notably those of Boeotia, where Thebes and the other cities of the Boeotian federation minted coins with the type of a Boeotian shield; this shield served to evoke older tradition recalling the ox-hide shields of the Bronze Age, and possibly affording at the same time one of those punning types which seem to have appealed to the Greeks—*bous* for Boeotia. As with the Aiginetan coins, there was soon a develop- ment of the reverse incuse into a neater form, which in Boeotia was distinguished by the initial letter of each city's name, ⊕ for Thebes, ⊟ for Haliartos and so on.

Among the most important archaic coinages of the Greek mainland, historically and artistically, was that of Athens. Already pre-eminent in the arts, she had the great advantage of having the raw material for coinage to hand in the famous silver mines of Laurion. A good deal of controversy still surrounds the earlier phases of her coinage, though it is at least now agreed that a whole series known as the 'Wappen- münzen', heraldic coins consisting of a number of different types without any identifying inscriptions, is indeed the earliest coinage of Athens. The coins are mainly didrachms of 'Euboic' weight, about 8.5 grammes, with incuse reverses, and the types include an amphora, an owl, a triskelis, a horse protome, a horse hindquarters, a wheel, an astragalos, a beetle, a bull's head and a Gorgon. It used to be thought that the types should be regarded as purely civic emblems of various cities and some of them were accordingly attributed to other places, notably to several cities of Euboia. It now seems certain however that they all form a single series, which is proved in some cases by the use of reverse dies which link different types. There remains some argu- ment as to the date of these coins—before or after Solon (*c.* 594 B.C.) or later ?, and the nature of the types, the variety of which recalls the manner of the Ionian electrum coinage. (There are in fact a few small electrum coins which belong with this silver.) The idea that the various types are in some sense emblems of prominent Athenian families is now less in favour, and it is possible that all the types can after all be regarded as civic devices related to the cult of Athena. The Gorgon didrachms show signs of an evolution towards a double-sided coin; one of the divisions of the reverse gives room to a small panther's 68 head; this is followed by a larger piece, a tetradrachm also with the Gorgon type and with a full reverse type consisting either of 72 a panther or bull's head.

The foregoing series was, at some date in the sixth century, superseded by a new type of tetradrachm showing the head of Athena 69, 70 and on the reverse the owl and the city's name, *Athe*. This was to become one of the most important coinages of the ancient world, and one of the most familiar to collectors today. There are still widely divergent theories about its origins. Archaeologically, from the evidence of hoards, these coins have been thought to begin only fairly late in the sixth century and after the death of the tyrant Peisistratos (527 B.C.). Yet from earlier attempts to estimate the date, based largely on the comparison of the Athena heads with other works of art, it has been held that the coins were in fact introduced by Peisistratos himself or even by Solon. It is still difficult to resolve this question satisfactorily, or even to be sure whether some of the coins claimed as more

63 Haliartos: *Reverse with initial, 550-500 B.C. (stater, 12.28 gm.; diam. 19 mm., PCG 4.23)*

64 Athens: *Wheel, (?) 575-525 B.C. (didrachm, 8.16 gm.; diam. 19 mm., BMC Chalkis 8; Seltman 35)*

65 Athens: *Astragalos, (?) 575-525 B.C. (didrachm, 8.42 gm.; diam. 19 mm., PCG 4.27; Seltman 21)*

66 Athens: *Bull's head, (?) 575-525 B.C. (didrachm, 8.65 gm.; diam. 18 mm., PCG 4.30, RPK; Seltman 81)*

67, 68 Athens: *Gorgon/Reverse with panther head inset, (?) 575-525 B.C. (didrachm 8.53 gm., diam. 19 mm., PCG 4.26; Seltman 89)*

69, 70 Athens: *Athena head/Owl with olive sprig, 525-500 B.C. (tetradrachm, 17.24 gm.; diam. 25 mm., BMC 23, RPK; Seltman 303)*

71 Athens: *Athena head, 525-500 B.C. (tetradrachm, 16.94 gm.; diam. 25 mm., PCG 5.35, RPK; Seltman 290)*

72 Athens: *Panther head reverse, (?) 575-525 B.C. (tetradrachm, 16.82 gm.; diam. 22 mm., BMC 17)*

73, 74 Corinth: *Pegasos with letter Koppa below/ Schematized reverse pattern, 570-550 B.C. (stater, 8.50 gm.; diam. 23 mm., PCG 5.39, RPK; Ravel 22)*

63

64

65

66

67

68

69   70

71   72

73   74

75

77

76

78

79

80

81

82

83

84

85

86

87

88

75 Corinth: *Pegasos, 525-500 B.C. (stater, 8.61 gm.; diam. 19 mm., BMC 61; Ravel 184)*

76 Corinth: *Head of Athena Chalinitis, 525-500 B.C. (stater, 8.66 gm.; diam. 17 mm., BM 1912; Ravel 97; from the Taranto hoard, 1911)*

77 Chalkis: *Four-horse chariot seen frontally, 550-525 B.C. (tridrachm stater, 16.78 gm.; diam. 25 mm., PCG 4.24)*

78, 79 Eretria: *Cow scratching nose/Octopus, 500-480 B.C. (didrachm, 8.67 gm.; diam. 24 mm., BM 1884)*

80, 81 Elis: *Flying eagle entwined with snake/Thunderbolt, 510-500 B.C. (stater, 11.79 gm.; diam. 20 mm., PCG 12.39; Seltman 2)*

82 Elis: *Nike advancing holding out wreath, 480-470 B.C. (stater, 12.00 gm.; diam. 20 mm., PCG 12.40; Seltman 34)*

83 Arkadia: *Zeus enthroned (Mantinea mint), 477-465 B.C. (hemidrachm, 2.75 gm.; diam. 13 x 16 mm., Williams 118)*

84 Arkadia: *Head of goddess (Kleitor mint), 490-477 B.C. (hemidrachm, 2.92 gm.; diam. 15 mm., BMC 7; Williams 2)*

85 Kyrene: *Lion's head with silphium plant and seed below, 525-480 B.C. (tetradrachm 17.20 gm.; diam. 21 mm., BMC 13)*

86 Kyrene: *Figure of Kyrene seated, 525-480 B.C. (tetradrachm, 15.44 gm.; diam. 23 mm., BMC 11; from the Naukratis hoard, 1885)*

87 Kyrene: *Head of Zeus-Ammon (reverse), 525-480 B.C. (tetradrachm, 17.20 gm.; diam. 19 mm., formerly Jameson collection 1346)*

88 Kyrene: *Head of Zeus-Ammon (obverse), c. 480 B.C. (tetradrachm, 17.08 gm.; diam. 24 mm., PCG addenda 13)*

primitive may not merely be inferior and imitative in style.

At all events, the new double-sided coins surely mark an important stage in the evolution of coinage as such. The head of Athena, in the first place, is often of the finest sculptural quality and rendered in very high relief; the best examples can stand worthily beside the Korai of the Akropolis as specimens of Attic art in the sixth century. The reverse provides a thematic counterpart in the shape of the owl, the goddess's sacred bird, and at the same time an artistic contrast, in a composition which, unlike the head, does not fill the space but which forms a looser grouping with the other elements of the design, the olive branch and the lettering. The scheme of this unity of contrasts became the normal and classic basis for most Greek coinage; indeed the pattern of all subsequent coinage in the European tradition may be said to be present already in essence in these early coins of Athens. The dominant position which the Athenian 'owls' soon attained among the currencies of the Greek world is demonstrated by the number of specimens which have come from archaic hoards found as widely apart as in Egypt and Sicily.

Corinth, on the Isthmus, was, like Aigina, a great trading rival of Athens, and her coinage perhaps began as early, though once again we are faced with one of the great uncertainties about the chronology of archaic coins. While some have suggested that the first Corinthian coins were minted by the tyrant Kypselos as a means of redistribution of wealth around 620 B.C., firm evidence for so early a date seems conspicuously lacking, and it is hardly safe to assume that minting had started much before 575 B.C. The Corinthian stater, equivalent in weight to the Attic didrachm of about 8.5 grammes, had in fact a subdivision into three, making it a tridrachm. The coins took a somewhat different form from those of the other mints and, unlike the globular pieces of Aigina and Athens, the Corinthian staters consist of flat spread discs; on one side is engraved a lively archaic Pegasos with the initial letter of the city's name given below (the archaic *koppa*). The winged horse of mythology, which was tamed by Bellerophon with the aid of Athena, has special connections with Corinth, for by stamping his hoof on the rock of Akrokorinthos he opened up the spring Peirene. The reverse side is marked by an incuse punch of a neat style, soon to develop into a swastika-like pattern.

These rather elegant pieces were eventually transformed, in the later sixth century, into double-sided coins: the head of Athena Chalinitis on the reverse shows the goddess wearing a Corinthian helmet without crest but complete with nose- and cheek-pieces. The face is carefully modelled but in comparatively low relief, and the head set in its square frame and on the reverse of the coin makes a somewhat modest and self-effacing impression by comparison with the Athenian coins. Yet this way of placing the head forms a fairly persistent tradition in the style of Dorian mints such as Knidos, Phokis, Kyrene, and even Syracuse.

The two greatest cities of the island of Euboia, Chalkis and Eretria, were long-standing rivals both in colonization and trade. Their coinages in the sixth century, though not plentiful, show an evolution similar to that of Athens. The earliest coins of Chalkis seem to be those which display the remarkable design of a four-horse chariot seen in frontal view—a motif not so uncommon in archaic Greek art and rather characteristic of the so-called Chalkidian vases (probably made in the West). The chariot is that of Hera and she is the charioteer, her head just visible in profile. The general aspect of this coin, with its incuse reverse, is close to that of the Athenian 'Wappenmünzen' and its date is probably about 550 B.C. In weight, it is the equivalent of an Attic tetradrachm, but it is in fact a Chalkidian tridrachm, with a drachm of about 5.8 grammes which is used in the western Chalkidian colonies. The smaller pieces, the drachm and its half, are aptly distinguished by variations of the type, a horseman leading a second horse in facing view, or a rider on a single horse. The facing chariot forms the reverse of a more developed type, and before 500 B.C. there are pieces with an obverse showing an eagle with a captive snake, similar to the Olympian coins of Elis, and on the reverse a wheel.

Eretria, on the other hand, gives prominence to the type of a cow, caught in a charming and instantaneous pose, turning to scratch her nose with a hoof. Euboia was a 'land of cattle' and the type of the cow, with a calf, recurs at Karystos. The first

Eretrian coin was minted with an incuse reverse; but there soon appeared a full reverse type of a stylized but lively cuttle-fish—possibly a specific city emblem, as there was a saying ascribed to Themistokles to the effect that Eretrians have a cuttlefish where their heart should be. Eretria's Macedonian colony Dikaia produced coins of identical design to those of her mother city.

In the Peloponnese, the spread of coinage in the archaic period is hardly significant enough to match the numerous schools of art which have been identified for several cities, possibly due to the wide circulation of the Aiginetan 'turtles'. An important exception to this, however, is the city of Elis, which from the late sixth century onwards began to produce an impressive array of coins minted in connection with the Panhellenic festival at Olympia. The Olympic games were held under the au-spices of Zeus, and as his temple dominates the sacred Altis so his symbols adorn the coins. First there is the eagle shown in a stiff archaic pose as if seen from below; it is the great bird of prey and, as it flies, grapples with a captive snake which writhes around it. A later coin shows the same type with greater clarity and dramatic expressiveness, with the wings of the eagle seen at full stretch and the snake, hanging in loops from the eagle's body, coils its head above for an attack on its captor. The reverse of the first coin shows the winged and flaming thunderbolt of Zeus in a rather heraldic form, but on the second coin the reverse is the goddess Nike, the peaceful winged messenger of Zeus person-ifying victory, coming to bestow the victor's crown. Treading lightly through the air in filmy garments whose folds blossom delicately about her legs, she lifts the hem with one hand and offers the wreath with the other. The figure has a fine organic and sculptural feeling. The name of the people of Elis is expressed on the coins by the letters F A—the *digamma* of *Faleion* being an archaism preserved on the coins until the third century.

Fine engravers also worked for the Arkadian league whose attractive coins were formerly thought, on the analogy of Olympia, to be an agonistic issue for the Lykaian games; but more weight is now given to the political significance of the league which came into being in opposition to Sparta about 490 B.C. Zeus is represented on the obverse, seated on a backless throne, his eagle flying from his hand, a thickset figure with affinities in Arkadian bronze sculpture, whereas the extremely stylish goddess' head—Despoina or Artemis—on the reverse with her hair done in a krobylos may be the work of an engraver brought in from some greater centre of art such as Corinth. This was minted at Kleitor, though the Arkadians also minted at Tegea and Mantinea, and a slightly later Man-tinean coin shows Zeus with a palmette-tipped sceptre. These small coins, of which the half-drachm is the largest, show a con-tinuous artistic evolution down to the end of the fifth century.

A peculiarly Dorian style of art appears again on the coins of the important city of

51

Kyrene on the north coast of Africa, originally colonized from Thera. By the later sixth century, Kyrene had become rich and flourishing agriculturally, not least by specializing in the export of the now extinct silphium plant. The silphium and its seeds forms a natural heraldic device on most of the earliest Kyrene coins, which are of very primitive aspect. By about 500 B.C., one engraver was able to combine the

85 silphium plant in a composition with a fine lion's head and a silphium seed below. Or there may be a goddess in a tight-fitting

86 robe, perhaps Kyrene herself, seated in front of a silphium plant. The head on the

87 reverse is of Zeus-Ammon, whose oracle in the Libyan desert was revered by the Greeks along with those of Delphi and Dodona, and Ammon's rams' horns are seen on the brows. Both the goddess and the head are of a severely Dorian style which recalls the art of Lakonia. But about 480 B.C. there is a strong Attic-Sicilian

88 influence in a splendid Zeus-Ammon head, a recently discovered coin of the highest quality.

THE NORTH

Northern Greece, the seaboard of Macedonia and Thrace, was profuse in coinage during the archaic period, as is readily intelligible since in addition to its agricultural wealth—notably in vines—the region possessed some of the most prolific silver mines in the ancient world. These resources

89 Akanthos: *Lion fighting with bull, 530-500 B.C. (tetradrachm, 17.17 gm., diam. 25 mm., BM 1939 ; Desneux 7)*

90 Potidaia: *Poseidon Hippios on horseback, holding trident, star below, 520-500 B.C. (tetradrachm, 17.57 gm., diam. 25 mm., PCG 3.9 ; RPK)*

91 Potidaia: *Head of Amazon, 500-480 B.C. (tetrobol, 2.70 gm., diam. 12 x 18 mm., BMC 2)*

92, 93 Skione: *Head of Protesilas/Stern of ship, 500-480 B.C. (tetradrachm, 16.47 gm., diam. 25 mm., PCG 11.20)*

94 Abdera: *Griffin seated, with raised forepaw, 520-492 B.C. (octadrachm, 29.51 gm., diam. 28 x 30 mm., BMC 1a ; May 50)*

95 Abdera: *Griffin, dancing satyr below, 492-470 B.C. (tetradrachm, 14.94 gm., diam. 26 mm., PCG 10.1 ; May 110)*

96 Samothrake: *Sphinx seated, 500-480 B.C. (hemidrachm, 1.94 gm., diam. 13 mm., BM 1937 ; from the Kiourpet hoard, 1930)*

97 Dikaia: *Head of Herakles wearing lion-skin, 520-500 B.C. (double-stater, 18.36 gm., diam. 22 mm., BM 1919)*

98 Thasos: *Satyr abducting a girl, 520-480 B.C. (stater, 9.75 gm., diam. 21 mm., BMC 5)*

99 Lete ?: *Satyr and girl, 520-480 B.C. (stater, 9.61 gm., diam. 23 mm., BMC 22 ; RPK)*

89

90

91

92

93

94

95

96

97

98

99

100

101

102

103

104

105

106

107

108

109

100 Macedonia, uncertain mint: *Two girls lifting amphora,* 500-480 B.C. *(tetradrachm, 16.93 gm., diam. 20 mm., BMC p. 135, 1 ; RPK)*

101 Neapolis: *Gorgon,* c. 500 B.C. *(stater, 9.52 gm., diam. 19 mm., BMC 6 ; RPK)*

102 Macedonia, uncertain mint: *Winged daimon,* c. 500 B.C. *(stater, 7.44 gm., diam. 19 mm, BMC p. 136, 2)*

103 Macedonia, uncertain mint: *Flower pattern with small head,* c. 500 B.C. *(didrachm, 8.18 gm., diam. 17 mm., BM 1915)*

104 Orreskioi: *Herdsman with oxen,* 500-480 B.C. *(octadrachm, 28.13 gm., diam. 30 mm., BMC 2 ; RPK)*

105 Derrones: *King riding in ox-cart, helmet in field above, flower below,* 520-500 B.C. *(dodecadrachm, 40.45 gm., diam. 37 x 31 mm., PCG 4.16 ; found at Istib, Serbia, 1859)*

106 Aigai: *Goat in kneeling posture,* c. 500 B.C. *(stater, 9.48 gm., diam. 25 mm., BMC 1)*

107 Macedonia, Alexander I: *Armed man leading horse,* 495-454 B.C. *(octodrachm, 29.00 gm., diam. 33 mm., PCG 11.18)*

108, 109 Peparethos: *Grapes/Naked winged figure running with wreath in each hand,* 500-480 B.C. *(tetradrachm, 16.91 gm., diam. 25 mm., PCG 4.18 ; found in the island of Kos, 1891)*

which were important for the kings of Macedonia and their neighbours were already in full exploitation during the archaic period. The numerous coins of this area were in many cases minted largely as a convenient way of exporting the precious metal, and we have many tangible traces of this export in the discovery of the coins far afield in the Levant and Egypt; the Macedonian and Thracian specimens are specially prominent in the hoards. The wealth of numismatic evidence from this region is a compensation for its comparative lack of products in other forms of art.

The region is not at all homogeneous. First there is the Chalkidike peninsula dotted with Greek colonies, mostly from Euboia. Then there are the Greek cities of Thrace, mainly of Ionian and east Greek origin. Finally there is the inland region inhabited by numerous indigenous tribes —of whom the Macedonians themselves were one—whose adoption of at least a veneer of Hellenic culture led to the production of some striking and original results in the field of coinage.

In the Chalkidic area, the city which minted the most impressive coins was surely Akanthos. Beginning about 530 B.C., her tetradrachms of Attic weight regularly depict the type of a lion attacking a bull. It 89 is a powerful expression of great beasts locked in mortal combat, albeit the type may also stem from older astrological symbolism. The strongly sculptural treatment displayed in the Akanthos coins is a splendid example of the archaic style at its best, avoiding both extremes of the merely decorative and the merely naturalistic; by contrast, versions which appear on coins of a century later, as well as on a marble relief of the same theme, found at Akanthos and now in the Louvre, seem feeble echoes. Alongside the Akanthos coins, there are those of other neighbouring cities each with a distinctive device—Terone with the wine amphora flanked by grape bunches, Sermyle the horseman, Mende the donkey of Dionysos with a suggestion of the vine, Dikaia the cow and the cuttlefish of Eretria, Olynthos a four-horse chariot like the early Syracusan type. Potidaia was a colony of Corinth and on her tetradrachms we see a rare type of Poseidon Hippios, her patron

90 deity, mounted on horseback and wielding his trident. Typical of the smaller coins in this region is the tetrobol, one-sixth of the tetradrachm and in fact equivalent to a drachm of Corinth; one of these, at Potidaia, bears a head which in style resembles the little Corinthian Athenas, but is in fact

91 an Amazon wearing the typical pointed skin cap, though the precise reason for the appearance of an Amazon at this city is obscure.

In the developed archaic period, around 500 B.C., one of the most remarkable coins from the Chalkidike is that of Skione; on the obverse we have the head of the hero Protesilaos, whose name is written along

92, 93 the helmet-crest, while the reverse shows the stern of a ship. This is one of the earliest examples in which a legendary hero is depicted quite explicitly on a coin, though we could not identify him without the thoughtfully provided inscription. In a

similar vein, an early coin of Larissa in Thessaly shows a head of Jason, identified by his sandal on the reverse; and in Macedonia itself, some rare specimens from Aineia have a remarkable type showing Aeneas rescuing Anchises from Troy. Protesilaos was also a hero of the Trojan war, and according to one account founded Skione on his return; alternatively he is supposed to have been the first of the Greeks to land on the shore of Troy, and the ship's stern shown on the coin must surely allude to this. In any case the head is undeniably impressive and recalls the finest archaic art of Athens in its strong and essentially sculptural treatment, especially the rendering of the cheeks and mouth and the subtle distinction between the upper and lower eyelids.

Among the Greek cities of Thrace, the first which must be mentioned is Abdera. Founded by colonists who came from Teos in Ionia in 544 B.C. to escape Persian domination, Abdera adopted for her coins the type of a griffin which was also the type of 94 Teos itself. Access to the local sources of silver made it possible for Abdera to mint her first coinage in the form of heavy octodrachms weighing about 29–30 grammes— the heaviest coins so far produced in the Greek world, the issue of which set the pattern that was soon followed by many of the semi-Hellenized tribes in this region. The griffin is seen crouching with the wings rendered in a curious manner as a sickle-shaped outline without feathers, a style copied for the sphinx which appears on some smaller coins of the island of Samo- 96

thrake. Somewhat later there is a splendid
95 griffin with fanlike wings, with the addition
of a small symbol, a naked satyr, and the
name of a magistrate, *Smor*. Related to the
early coinage of Abdera is the more modest
issue from Maroneia, showing a half-horse;
but most attractive of all the early Thracian
97 coins is the double-stater of Thracian
Dikaia on which the head of Herakles appears, wearing the lionskin cap which is his
distinctive garb in early Greek art. This
fine plastic conception has been justly compared with a masterpiece of Attic art, the
head of the Rampin rider in the Louvre, and
like the Skione Protesilaos, is an eloquent
testimony to the influence of Attic art on
the coinage of the north.

Quite another style is displayed by the
early coins of the important island of
Thasos; yet these too proved extremely influential both for their form and their subject matter among coinage of this region.
98 The type is of a naked satyr excitedly carrying off a girl who is making some gestures
of protest. The rendering of the stocky,
thickset figures with bulging muscles is
something which is quite hard to parallel
outside the coinage of this area, or indeed
elsewhere in archaic Greek art; its direct
and characteristic vitality recalls the Akanthos lion and bull. It seems likely that
Thasos was the origin of this style of coin,
which was taken up in the mintages of
others with variations such as, for instance,
the coins of the Zaielioi where the earthy
satyr and girl is replaced by a group of a
girl carried off by a centaur. In the coin
attributed to Lete the style is carried to its

extreme, and the scene of the wooing of a
muscular girl by an even more muscular 99
satyr comes close to the absurd. However,
such jolly rustic orgies are appropriate
enough in a region where Dionysos was the
important deity and the vine one of the
outstanding products; this god figures
again on later coins of Thasos and of Mende.
An intriguing coin, whose attribution remains uncertain, displays a scene which is 100
related to some of the above—a pair of
powerful, albeit shapely girls who are lifting a wine amphora. It is a perfectly balanced composition and the amphora which
is its focal point recalls the tetradrachms of
Terone, though it is unlikely that the coin
belongs to that mint. A flower-like ornament seen in the field on the right is rather
typical of this region.

On the mainland opposite Thasos was
Neapolis whose Gorgon, compared with 101
the jolly smiling Athenian Gorgon, seems
a more startling and horrific treatment, but
the design is assured and organic and has
nothing primitive about it. But another
coin of this region which has no secure
attribution is one showing a winged figure 102
of the same heavy build as the Thasian
satyrs; he is a divine messenger wearing
winged boots, depicted in the typical archaic kneeling posture which denotes running. Note also the abrupt transition between the torso shown in frontal view, and
the legs which are purely profile, an archaic rendering which is well seen again in
some of the south Italian coins. In front
as a filling ornament is a lotus flower, a
prominent feature of many Macedonian

coins; there are some types which are composed of several flowers grouped around a central ring, with one of the flowers replaced by a small figure of a boar (sometimes attributed to Stageira) or an eagle, or
103 a human head. Typically enough of the tendency for Macedonian coins to travel to the Near East, such coins with the winged figure type were very prominent in an important hoard found at Ras Shamra on the Syrian coast.

But in many ways the most characteristic of all the coins of this region, and certainly of those which were intended primarily for the export market, were a whole series of really large coins weighing 29–30 grammes or even more, evidently inspired to some extent by the octodrachms of Abdera. The large coins were typically those of some of the tribes in the Macedonian area, the Bisaltai, the Edones, the Orreskioi. Fortunately many of them have inscriptions so that we can be sure of their origins. Most of the types are compositions of men and animals. The Bisaltai for instance show a warrior or hero armed with spears and leading a horse—possibly Ares. Other coins,
104 of the Edones and the Orreskioi, show a bulky herdsman leading a pair of oxen; he too is armed with spears, though from the petasos which he wears on his head he might be Hermes. It is impossible to be sure whether these figures are gods or humans. The style of these compositions has much in common with the Thasian satyr style and the attractively powerful designs have a minimum of subtlety; the relief planes of the oxen stand out sharply from

110 ▶

111 ▶

112 ▶

110 Lydia, *Kroisos: Confronting heads of lion and bull, 560–546 B.C. (gold stater, 8.05 gm., diam. 16 mm., BMC 31)*

111 Persia: *Archer with spear, 490–400 B.C. (gold daric, 8.37 gm., diam. 14 mm., PCG 8.1)*

112 Babylon: *Archer with spear, Greek letters in field, c. 330 B.C. (gold double-daric, 16.67 gm., diam. 20 mm., BMC 4)*

113   114   115

116   117

118   119   120

121   122

the background with little transition. The inscriptions are placed either around the type, as here, or else in a frame on the reverse, as in the case of pieces which proclaim 'Getas king of the Edoni', some of whose coins have, typically enough, been found in Syria and even at Babylon. Largest and most impressive of all the large northern coins is that of the Derrones; it weighs 40 grammes and depicts a local 105 dynast or king riding in a primitive cart or wheeled throne drawn by massive oxen. Above and below, in true archaic fashion, every empty space has been filled, with a huge helmet above the oxen and a lotus flower—recalling the flower pattern on a previous coin—underneath. The reverse, not so well preserved, also has a type consisting of a triskelis with more lotus flowers around.

The large 'tribal' coins, with their combination of the monetary influence of Abdera and the strong animal style of Akanthos, came to an end as soon as the kings of Macedonia began to take a firmer grip on the whole region in the time of Alexander I (495–454 B.C.). Hitherto their chief city, Aigai-Edessa, had itself produced coins which are a fine example of the animal 106 style, with the type of a kneeling goat as the punning symbol of the city name. It is an impressive animal, admirably adapted to the circular frame by the turn of the head and the long horns drooping behind and by the bent-up front legs, and though it has no more plastic subtlety than the oxen of the Orreskioi, it is sharply and vividly drawn. The goat emblem was preserved on many

113-115 Persia: *Heads of lion and bull, Lydian type, 546-515 B.C. (silver siglos, 113: 5.29 gm., diam. 16 mm., BM 1914; 114-115: 5.40 gm., diam. 19 mm., BM 1948; from the Tchai hoard)*

116 Persia: *Archer, 515-490 B.C. (silver siglos, 5.40 gm., diam. 15 mm., BMC 185)*

117 Persia: *Half-length archer, 515-490 B.C. (silver siglos, 5.39 gm., diam. 14 mm., BM 1948; from the Tchai hoard)*

118 Persia: *Archer with spear, 490-400 B.C. gold daric, 8.28 gm., diam. 15 mm., BMC 43)*

119, 120 Persia: *Beardless archer/Reverse with small Pan head intaglio, c. 400 B.C. (gold daric, 8.20 gm., diam. 13 mm., PCG 18.1)*

121 Persia: *Archer with spear, fourth century style, c. 400-333 B.C. (gold daric, 8.32 gm., diam. 15 mm., PCG 18.4)*

122 Persia: *Archer with dagger, c. 400-333 B.C. (gold daric, 8.29 gm., diam. 17 mm., PCG 18.2)*

of the later coins of Macedonia after the reign of Alexander I. But the direct successor of the large octodrachms of the Bisaltai and other tribes is to be seen in 107 coins of similar format issued by Alexander himself; on them, a more spruce and civilized figure—perhaps representing the king —armed with spears is to be seen either leading or riding a horse, while on the reverse is a neat square incuse with the king's name framed around the square.

Peparethos, an obscure island off the coast of Thessaly, emitted a coinage only for a very short period just after 500 B.C. and in the process produced some masterpieces of archaic art which seem to come from another world from the Macedonian and Thracian coins. Here again, however, we have evidence of an important vine culture, and the obverse of the coins bears 108 the clear stamp of this in the shape of a large grape bunch. The island (modern Skopelos) was indeed said by tradition to have been colonized by Staphylos, the son of Dionysos. As a contrast to this rather heraldic device, there is a variety of reverse designs, a seated Dionysos, a boy riding a dolphin, a head of Herakles similar to that of the coin of Thracian Dikaia and, finest of 109 all, a miraculous winged figure wearing winged boots and carrying in each hand a wreath. The posture of kneeling or running is similar to what has been observed on a 102 Macedonian coin, and the wings curve gracefully upwards; there is no longer any abrupt transition between the attitude of the torso and of the legs. It is an exquisite and dream-like figure; we cannot certainly

identify him, though he might be Eros, or Agon, the god of contest.

THE WEST

In two other regions of the Greek world, southern Italy and Sicily, an extremely successful colonization by Dorians, Chalkidians and others had been going on since the eight century B.C. The earliest colony in Italy was Kymai near Naples, in Sicily Naxos under Mount Aetna. The natural riches of both countries had ensured a rapid growth and expansion of numerous cities, placed mainly on the west and southern shores of Italy and on the eastern and southern shores of Sicily, and in this new region of Greek civilization, distinctive local schools of archaic coinage came into being.

In Italy, coinage began in the latter part of the sixth century, when the Achaean cities of the Ionian shore devised a peculiar and original form of coin nowhere else seen in the Greek world. This form consisted of a fairly thin metal flan on which the main type was impressed in relief on one side while on the other side the same type is repeated as a sort of echo in concave form. The dies must have been carefully positioned in order to correspond. The precise technique of producing these pieces has been a subject of some controversy. It is still uncertain why this strange form of coin—which was evidently not easy to produce and which was abandoned in favour of a more normal form after a generation or so—was invented. The undeniable fascination of the concept of duality embodied in this form of coin has led to the suggestion that it must have required a great genius to invent it, and that this great genius was none other than Pythagoras, the Samian philosopher and mathematician who migrated to Italy about 530 B.C. and who is reputed to have had experience as a metalworker. Be that as it may, the 'incuse' technique, as it is usually called, was used at a number of cities simultaneously and spread to Sicily where it was briefly used at Zankle.

It is not certain which city started this form of coinage, though likely possibilities are Sybaris, Kroton or Metapontion. Sybaris, whose remains lie still undiscovered in the coastal plain of the Krathis river, was a city whose riches and luxury were a byword with the Greeks until its destruction by Kroton in 510 B.C. The early coins of
123 Sybaris depict a gracefully stylized bull with its head turned back as if to lick its flank. The precise significance of the type is, as so often, somewhat elusive, though one can easily guess that a bull may have a similar meaning here as in Euboia, for a country well stocked with cattle. On the other hand there is also the possibility of regarding the bull as a river-god. In any
25, 126 case it has a counterpart in the type of Metapontion, a corn ear equally expressive of agricultural wealth, and at the same time of the important cult of Demeter. As a civic emblem, an offering in the shape of corn ears made of gold was dedicated by the

Metapontines to Apollo at Delphi. The ear shown on the archaic coins has a fan-like arrangement of the hairs which gives it an irresistible appeal as a decorative motif.

The cult of Apollo was prominent in the coin types of two other cities, Kroton and Kaulonia; appropriately so in view of the role played by this god and the Delphic oracle in fostering Greek colonization. At Kroton we see the Delphic tripod elegantly 124 proportioned with the legs terminating in lions' feet; between the legs are decorative snakes and S-shaped ornaments. It is noticeable that the 'echo' type on the reverse is considerably simplified and lacks the extra ornamentation.

Kaulonia has coins showing Apollo him-127 self, and it is a figure of exceptional interest. It is the typical archaic drawing, with legs and head in profile but the torso more frontal, and the transitional areas of the stomach negotiated by stylized patterns. The hair is long, and in his right hand the god carries a lustral branch of laurel, while on the left arm is a minute running figure carrying a further branch. In the field is a stag. The type has been interpreted according to the myth in which the god, after his victory over the Python, had to cut laurel branches in the Vale of Tempe with which to purify himself before returning to Delphi to claim possession of the oracle. The little figure on his arm is the god's messenger being despatched to announce his arrival. This coinage of Kaulonia is unexpectedly prolific for a comparatively obscure city and, though the type is of great interest, its rendering cannot really

128, 129 compare with the finest coins of the west coast city of Poseidonia. The latter were of the same fabric but a slightly different weight standard. Here we have the figure of Poseidon; the attitude as he advances brandishing the trident is similar to that of the Kaulonian Apollo but is rendered with a lighter and more supple touch. There is the same transitional stylization of the stomach. The god wears long hair like so many elegant males in archaic art, but exceptionally this Poseidon has no beard. The decroated trident appears to pass behind the head. He wears a long tasselled cloak across the shoulders. It is interesting that in the 'shadow' version of the type on the reverse which shows the back view of the figure the cloak is indeed shown passing over the back.

The fall of Sybaris in 510 B.C. forms an important landmark for the development of the incuse coinage, and after this date there is some change of technique, the coins becoming smaller and thicker and the strict parallelism of the two sides being gradually abandoned. Sometimes the reverse is even given a different type, and some Kroton coins show an incuse eagle instead of the tripod. A city which started to coin about this time was Tarentum, a Spartan colony and later the most important of all the south Italian cities. Here the incuse technique was employed only for a short issue. The first

130 type is a Spartan god, Hyakinthos; he kneels holding a flower in his right hand and a lyre in his left, and we see that the rendering of the bodily forms is now more expert than in the previous examples. Next

123 Sybaris: *Bull with turned head, 530-510 B.C. (stater, 8.05 gm., diam. 28 mm., BM 1919)*

124 Kroton: *Delphic tripod with lions' feet, snakes between the legs, 530-510 B.C. (stater, 8.00 gm., diam. 29 mm., Lloyd 592)*

125, 126 Metapontion: *Corn-ear in relief/Corn-ear incuse, 530-510 B.C. (stater, 8.05 gm., diam. 30-29 mm., PCG 6.8; Noe 92)*

127 Kaulonia: *Apollo holding lustral branch, and small figure on his left arm, stag below in field, 530-510 B.C. (stater, 8.22 gm., diam. 30mm., Lloyd 571; Noe 2)*

128, 129 Poseidonia: *Poseidon brandishing trident/ The same incuse, 530-510 B.C. (stater, 7.48 gm., diam. 28 mm., PCG 6.9)*

130 Tarentum: *Hyakinthos kneeling, with lyre in his left hand and flower in his right, c. 500 B.C. (stater, 7.23 gm., diam. 24 mm., PCG 6.2; RPK)*

131 Tarentum: *Taras riding on dolphin, holding octopus in his hand, 490-480 B.C. (stater, 8.16 gm., diam. 17 mm., BMC 47)*

132 Tarentum: *Hippocamp, with shell below, 500-480 B.C. (stater, 8.07 gm., diam. 20 mm., PCG 13.6)*

133 Tarentum: *Head of goddess, 490-480 B.C. (stater, 8.09 gm., diam. 17 mm., BMC 52)*

134 Velia: *Forepart of lion attacking prey, 520-500 B.C. (drachm, 3.86 gm., diam. 14 mm., Lloyd 506; from the Taranto hoard, 1911)*

66

123

124

125

126

127

128

129

130

131

132

133

134

135

136

137

138

139

140

141

142

143

145

144

146

147

148

149

135 Zankle: *Dolphin leaping within sickle-shaped harbour, 520-500 B.C. (drachm, 4.87 gm., diam. 22 mm., Lloyd 1075)*

136 Himera : *Cock, 550-500 B.C. (drachm, 5.80 gm., diam. 21 mm., PCG 7.22 ; RPK)*

137 Selinus: *Leaf of wild parsely (selinon), 550-520 B.C. (didrachm, 7.97 gm., diam. 19 mm., Lloyd 1203)*

138, 139 Naxos: *Head of Dionysos with ivy-leaf crown/Bunch of grapes and vine-leaves, 530-490 B.C. (drachm, obverse: 5.64 gm., diam. 21 mm., Lloyd 1147 ; Cahn 42 ; reverse: 5.50 gm., diam. 20 mm., BMC 2 ; RPK ; Cahn 40)*

140, 141 Akragas: *Eagle/Crab, 520-500 B.C. (didrachm, obverse: 8.58 gm., diam. 24 mm., Lloyd 786 ; reverse: 8.63 gm., diam. 24 mm., BMC 4 ; RPK)*

142, 143 Syracuse: *Four-horse chariot/Plain quartered incuse square with small head in centre, 510-490 B.C. (tetradrachm, 17.48 gm., diam. 25 mm., Lloyd 1276 ; Boehringer 10)*

144, 145 Gela: *Horseman brandishing spear/Forepart of man-faced full (the river-god Gelas), 495-485 B.C. (didrachms, obverse: 8.13 gm., diam. 20 mm., BM 1958 ; Jenkins 6 ; reverse: 8.69 gm., diam. 18 mm., Lloyd 953 ; Jenkins 1)*

146, 147 Zankle: *Lion's scalp/Prow of galley, 493-489 B.C. (tetradrachm, obverse: 16.86 gm., diam. 24 mm., Lloyd 1081 ; reverse: 17.31 gm., diam. 22 mm., PCG 7.17 ; from the Messina hoard, 1875)*

148, 149 Messana: *Lion's head/Calf's head, 489-484? B.C. (tetradrachm, 17.31 gm., diam. 21-23 mm., PCG 7.25 ; RPK)*

comes the type of the dolphin-rider which 131 was to be the Tarentine emblem par excellence; at first in the incuse technique, then as the regular obverse of a two-sided coin with a hippocamp on the reverse in relief. 132 The dolphin-rider, sometimes shown brandishing an octopus, is either Phalanthos the Spartan founder of Tarentum, who is supposed to have been rescued from the sea on a dolphin's back like the poet Arion in Herodotus' story; or else the eponymous Taras, son of Poseidon, whose dolphin he is riding, according to the tradition preserved by Aristotle. Towards 480 B.C. there are sometimes on the reverse little heads which it is 133 hard to identify as male or female, but whose style has been recognized as typically Spartan from its close relationship to other works of art of that school. Equally Spartan are some of the early coins with the seated figure of Taras as the founder, recalling heroic reliefs from Lakonia; we shall see another such seated founder on later coins 456 of Rhegion.

By contrast the archaic coins of the Phokaian colony Velia were of a purely Ionian type showing a lion devouring his prey; 134 close links with another Phokaian centre, Massalia, are underlined by the circulation of these coins, specimens of which were present in the Auriol hoard.

The Italian 'incuse' style was however adopted for a short time at Zankle (modern Messina) on the Sicilian side of the Straits for its coins showing a dolphin leaping in the sickle-shaped harbour; the name of the 135 city preserved the indigenous word for 'sickle.' The normal style of Zanklean coin has, however, not an incuse version of the dolphin but a schematized pattern with a shell in the centre, possibly inspired by some of the earlier Corinth reverses. The standard is the Chalkidian drachm, as at the other Chalkidian colonies, Himera and Naxos; the latter was traditionally the first Greek colony on the island, being founded in 733 B.C. But the first Sicilian coins were those of the two most westerly cities on the north coast, Himera, and on the south coast, Selinus. Sicily has no silver, and it has been plausibly conjectured that since the position of Himera and Selinus would favour trading connections with Carthage, that silver may have been obtained from 137 Spain via Carthage. The coins of Selinus have the comparatively primitive aspect of mid-sixth century coins in Greece with an incuse punch reverse; this didrachm, of Attic-Euboic weight, shows the typical local plant, a selinon leaf (wild parsley) which was used as the civic emblem and sometimes dedicated like the corn ear of Metapontion. Himera, however, coining on the standard of the other Chalkidian cities, produced drachms with the type of a 136 cock, rendered with great vigour and life. The sixth century coinage of Naxos already adopts the two-type form with full reverse; these are splendid works of art depicting 138 the head of Dionysos whose fluid modelling is well up to the quality of the best Attic art, while the reverse of a grape bunch 139 shows the leaves in an outline drawing. The adoption of the classic two-sided concept must be roughly contemporary with its appearance at Athens. It was towards

the end of the sixth century when the other Dorian cities of Sicily began to mint coins, and of these Akragas and Syracuse are the most important. The long series of Attic weight didrachms of Akragas introduced the types of eagle and crab which persisted for almost a century. The eagle is the bird 140 of Zeus and lord of the air, the crab, iden- tified as a freshwater variety, expresses the watery element of river and seashore; one 141 can almost imagine from the coins the splendid position of the city which seems to hang between sky and sea.

Roughly at the same time must come the first coins of Syracuse which are tetra- drachms of Attic weight, minted by the landowning aristocracy of Gamoroi. The obverse shows a chariot with ponderous 142 horses in a severe style emphasized by the sharp relief planes (which recalls some of the early Macedonian coins). Only the nearer horse is depicted in full while the others are merely suggested by extra out- lines; the charioteer holding the reins is a dominating figure. Combined with this chariot type, which was to become even- tually the hallmark of all Sicilian coins, is a reverse of a transitional form and fabric such as we have seen already at Athens; superimposed on a plain quartered incuse square is a circular depression containing 143 a small female head whose strong and log- ical form is characteristic of Dorian style. Early in the fifth century, the city of Gela on the south coast became, under her tyrant Hippokrates (498–491 B.C.), for a brief period the leading power in Sicily, and for the payment of her mercenary soldiers emitted a profuse coinage of didrachms, bearing the type of an armed naked rider on horseback, brandishing a spear, and sometimes wearing a helmet—probably to represent the famous Geloan cavalry which was the instrument of Hippokrates' conquests. The reverse shows the forepart of the river-god Gelas as a man-faced bull, the form in which Achelous and other river-gods appear in Greek art and which is particularly frequent in Sicily.

Special circumstances intruded into Sicily a quite new element, the Samian emigrés who, fleeing from the Persians, in 493 B.C. seized Zankle and proceeded to mint there a coinage of purely Ionian type. The lion's scalp is taken over directly from the coins of Samos, and the prow of the Samaina appears on the reverse, where we also see a series of letters denoting the years of the Samian regime at Zankle, from 493 to 489 B.C. The Samians were expelled finally by Anaxilas the tyrant of Rhegion, who then took over Zankle and renamed it Messana; as master of the Straits he minted a new coin at both cities displaying the head of a lion and the head of a calf. The significance of these types has provoked some discussion, for the lion's head—quite distinct from the Samian lion scalp—seems to stand for the sacred animal of Apollo, while the calf may refer to 'Italia' (by a pun on the word *italos* — vitulus = calf), or alternatively both types may pertain to the cult of Hera of Chalkis.

The beginnings of Sicilian coinage seem, even at Syracuse, unpretentious by comparison with the brilliance of its later flowering; but the full sweep of its development which gathered momentum in the period of the great tyrants—Gelon and Hieron at Syracuse, Theron at Akragas—must be left to form a separate chapter in Greek numismatics.

III. THE FIFTH CENTURY

The archaic period of Greek coinage, covering a little more than the first century of its history, terminates conveniently at the time of the Persian wars. Coins had already become the vehicle for a great variety and flexibility of artistic expression. Some techniques, such as that of the Italian 'incusi', were not continued; others, such as the single-sided Ionian electrum, were conservatively pursued. Already the classic form of coin as a double-sided object with the head of a god and a contrasting reverse thematically related to the obverse had become established, and ensured the main line of creative development in the following periods. During the classical period, from the Persian wars to Alexander, we can observe in coinage, as in other forms of Greek art, that specifically local styles gradually give place to a more homogeneous development throughout the central Greek world: whereas, as we shall see, on the fringe of that world from Lykia eastwards the full-blown fifth century style takes longer to become established, while the west (Italy and Sicily) gives us evidence of an advanced development on the artistic side which has to be viewed in isolation from the Aegean.

Within the central area of the Aegean, the leading role of Athens both politically and culturally during the fifth century B.C. makes it logical to consider first the coinage of Athens herself. Copious, and having a wide distribution all over the Greek world and beyond, it was certainly the most important currency historically and economically. The 'owls' were familiar everywhere where Greek traders penetrated, ever since the sixth century when Athenian tetradrachms were already prominent in several big hoards unearthed in Egypt and in Sicily—nearly 200 of them in the hoard found at Gela in 1956. The development of the Laurion silver mines had made great strides in the late sixth and early fifth century, and the discovery of a new and rich vein of ore had led, in 483 B.C., to the proposal that the profits of the mines be shared out among the citizens (as had been done at Siphnos in earlier times). But the far-sighted Themistokles, we are told, persuaded them instead to invest in the building of a navy, whose existence stood Athens in good stead during the years of the Persian invasion. At all events it is clear that Athens was in an extremely fortunate position in having a virtually

77

inexhaustible supply of precious metal within her own borders, which could be used for export in exchange for essential commodities. The fact that Attica is poor in agricultural produce and that Egypt and Sicily were among the richest granaries of the ancient world soon makes it clear how and why Athenian coins found their way there in such large numbers. Indeed, Athenian coins are one of the foremost exports of the Greek world to an even wider range of places within the Persian empire, and the spread of these coins can be studied from discoveries made at Al Mina in Syria, at Babylon, at Malayer in Iran and even in Afghanistan at Chaman-i-Hazouri; other Greek coins have an equally wide distribution, but those of Athens are predominant. Such export of money was as bullion and not for use as currency. The coins were often, especially in Egypt, defaced by chisel cuts to test the purity of the metal, which alone was of interest to foreign recipients.

Athenian coins, apart from their role for export, were also designed for use as currency at home and in Greece, and show an articulated range of denominations which seem to indicate the extensive use of money for daily payments and transactions. 151*, 152* The standard large coin, the tetradrachm, is naturally the one which is most prominent in the export field. Its value would represent something like an average wage for a week, at least on the basis that the daily pay for jury service at the end of the fifth century was three obols (half a drachm). The drachm itself was subdivided into six

150

151

152

150 Athens: *Owl, with olive and crescent above, Bacchos-ring below, 296 B.C. (gold stater, 8.59 gm., diam. 16 mm., PCG 23.38), reverse of 157*

151, 152 Athens: *Head of Athena with olive leaves on helmet/Owl, olive-sprig, crescent, c. 460-450 B.C. (silver tetradrachm, 17.14 gm., diam. 25 mm., BM 1948; Starr 204)*

153

154

155

156

157

158

159

obols; and coins were minted for the values of 3-obols, 1½-obols (trihemiobol), obol and hemiobol; the tetartemorion or quater-obol may also perhaps have existed in the fifth century and certainly in the fourth. The types of some of the smaller coins are varied 160 to enable them to be easily distinguished—thus the triobol has an owl in frontal view with folded wings, the trihemiobol an owl with open wings, though the other pieces, at least in the fifth century, follow the type of the tetradrachm and are distinguished only by size. The obol and hemiobol are indeed very minute, and we learn from an incident in the *Wasps* of Aristophanes that it was quite often the custom to go shopping carrying such small change in one's mouth. With such minute coins, it is easy to see how loss and confusion might occur but it was not before the end of the fifth or even the fourth century that the smallest denominations had any counterpart in the more convenient form of bronze coins.

Apart from the small pieces, there were also occasional larger denominations, the dekadrachm and the didrachm; the deka-drachm was a momentary special issue of some kind, which has often been associated with the victories of 480–479 B.C. but more recently dated down to 467. At all events it was around 480 B.C. that the main change in the design took place, the addition of olive leaves to the helmet of Athena, perhaps in recognition of the victory over Persia. At the same time a small waning moon was added on the reverse beside the owl, the significance of which has been

153, 154 Athens: *Head of Athena/Owl, as on tetradrachms but reverse has olive-sprig above and below, 406 B.C. (gold stater, 8.53 gm., diam. 15 mm., private possession; photo from electrotype)*

155, 156 Athens: *Athena/Facing owl within wreath, 406 B.C. (gold quarter-stater, 2.16 gm., diam. 10 mm., PCG 11.36*

157 Athens: *Athena head, 296 B.C. (gold stater, 8.59 gm., diam. 16 mm., PCG 23.38), obverse of 150*

158, 159 Athens: *Athena/Owl; countermarks on obverse, 393–300 B.C. (silver tetradrachm, 158: 17.19 gm., diam. 20 mm., BM 1913; 159: 17.15 gm., diam. 20 mm., BMC 138)*

much disputed; it has been held to be an allusion to the battle of Salamis, fought in the moon's last quarter, but more intelligibly it is simply the symbol of the nocturnal owl. The main point about these new tetradrachms, however, is that they are indeed only archaic coins modernized a little, and the type continues without the least change right through the fifth century, showing no development of style at the very time of the greatest creative phase of Greek art. We look in vain here for reflections of the Parthenon, although such reflections were very apparent in the coins of other Greek cities; but not at Athens, where the Athena head remains frozen in an archaic formula with the eye still rendered in the typically archaic frontal view on a profile head, and the hair very stylized. The stereotyped nature of the fifth century coins of Athens has never really found any convincing explanation, although no doubt a great commercial currency tends to continue without alteration in order to maintain faith in its reliability (and the Maria Theresia thaler of modern times is often quoted in this connection). This may not be the whole truth, and the necessity to step up production to a vast extent during the second half of the fifth century may also have tended to inhibit artistic enterprise. In any case we may well regret the results, especially when we contrast the case of Corinth, for example, whose coins had an equally commercial motivation but which managed to find scope for artistic freshness, at the same time providing not only an attractive

post-archaic style but also a more advanced one which in fact seems to recall such contemporary Athenian art as that of Myron.

The patriotic Aristophanes, who in the *Frogs* laments the degeneracy of the debased coinage of 405 B.C., could describe the normal fifth century Athenian coins as the 'finest in the world'—and they were certainly of the highest quality metal, but usually quite carelessly minted, so that even allowing for the archaism of the design we hardly ever see on any specimen the design of Athena complete with her helmet-crest.

This artistically paradoxical coinage moreover was what Athens produced not merely for her own use and for export to remote parts, but which she wished by deliberate policy to establish as the sole standard currency for the whole of the Aegean area which was under her control. One of the most remarkable enactments of imperialistic Athens under Perikles was the decree, probably passed in 449 B.C., forbidding the 'allies' of Athens to strike silver coins of their own—an enactment of the greatest interest and importance in the history of coinage and apparently the earliest attempt to regulate by law the currency of a large and complex political region; a measure of astonishing audacity. The scope of the decree took no account of gold coins, and as we shall see the exception was an important one. However, the very heterogeneous nature of the existing currency circulating on many different standards must have created many difficulties—not least for the Athenian treasurers. In any case the suppression of the mints of other cities was a nakedly imperialistic act, for a city's coin was its sign manual of independence. The actual provision of currency by Athens for all the allies was a task which probably far outran her resources and there is little sign that it was ever fully accomplished.

One particular result of the Athenian policy, which was probably precisely calculated and also successful, was that the coins of Aigina were no longer left as a serious rival currency. Most of the other islands who had coined in the archaic period had done so only briefly, and Aigina was left with a monopoly which it became especially important to the Athenians to smash. Aigina's coins had maintained the type of **164** the stylized sea-turtle with little change though there was a certain morphological development of the reverses away from the primitive punch mark towards neater and more explicit shapes, such as the neatly **165** executed square divided by skew lines, in the early fifth century. Coins like these undoubtedly continued to be issued down to the time of the first conquest of Aigina by Athens in 457 B.C., though about this time the old sea-turtle type was replaced by that of the land-tortoise—the precise significance of the change still awaits a convincing explanation. The currency decree certainly prevented any further coinage at Aigina until, after the fall of Athens, the **166** tortoise type was resumed.

Aigina, which Perikles once called the 'eyesore of the Piraeus', was eliminated as a serious rival to Athens and even settled as an Athenian colony in 432 B.C. But the Aiginetic standard of coinage remained predominant in large areas of the Greek mainland, from Thessaly to the Peloponnese, which lay outside the Athenian sphere of influence; the only important exceptions being of course Corinth, whose coinage of staters became vastly extended during the Peloponnesian war, and Sparta, which does not enter the history of coinage until the Hellenistic period. Two of the most interesting major mints of the Greek mainland, both using the Aiginetic standard, were those of Thebes and Elis. Thebes, after her victory against Athens at Koronea in 446 B.C., was unquestioned head of the Boeotian league; and her mint during the next decades concentrated on types relating to Herakles who was claimed as the special local hero. The obverse of the coins continued with the old Boeotian shield, but **171** some of the reverses are masterpieces of relief and figure composition, sometimes calling to mind temple metopes and possibly related to lost works of sculpture. A small and muscular figure of Herakles wielding **167** his bow and club is a simple and straightforward type, like some little archaic bronze statuette; in another scene Herakles is shown in the act of stealing the Delphic **168** tripod—a theme which had been a favourite in archaic art and which has an agreeably light-hearted flavour, like the later Kroton coin of Apollo shooting the Pytho. Best of **472** all is the very fine composition of Herakles **169** kneeling to string his bow; here he is no muscular colossus but a slim lithe youth, and the interplay of lines in the composition well expresses the tension and concentration of his action. Yet another theme from the Herakles saga brings us back to the very birth of the hero—he was the child of a mortal woman Alkmene but fathered by Zeus, whose consort Hera in a jealous fury sent snakes to attack the infant Herakles; but he succeeded in strangling the snakes, as is to be seen on several coins of Thebes and of other cities. The other protagonist of Theban coinage is the god Dionysos, whose splendid head decked with ivy leaves appears on the coins at the end of the fifth century and who, as the god of wine, is also associated with the amphora which later became the regular Theban type.

In the Peloponnese the major mint, that of Elis, during the fifth century employed some notable artists to make dies for the Olympic festival coins. The eagle of Zeus on a coin of 450 B.C. is again shown as the bird of prey in flight grasping a snake, though sometimes its prey is shown as a hare (as on the coins of Akragas in Sicily) or a tortoise. The free and vigorous composition contrasts sharply with the tight archaic version of this type. The reverse of the same coin is a superb Nike who with rustling garments descends from the skies holding the victor's wreath. Numerous different versions of the divine winged thunderbolt abound, often forming extremely decorative compositions. About 430 B.C. there is a new version of the Nike figure, no longer in flight but reposing lightly on a step and holding a long palm branch across her shoulder; below is an olive twig. The grace of this figure is something quite new for the Elis mint and

160 Athens: *Small silver coins*. Upper row, *480-406 B.C., left to right: drachm (4.03 gm., and 4.23 gm., BM 1949); triobol (2.05 gm., BM 1949); trihemiobol (1.03 gm., BM 1920 and 0.90 gm., BM 1949); obol (0.68 gm., and 0.64 gm., BM 1949); hemiobol (0.35 gm., BMC 116 and 0.36 gm., BM 1920). Lower row, 393-300 B.C., left to right: drachm (4.06 gm., and 4.23 gm., BM 1949); triobol (2.11 gm., BM 1949); diobol (1.36 gm., BMC 176); obol, crescents reverse (0.54 gm., BM 1949); tritartemorion, crescents reverse (0.50 gm., BM 1949); hemiobol (0.34 gm., BMC 121); trihemitetartemorion, Bacchos-ring reverse (0.22 gm., BM 1949); tetartemorion, crescent reverse (0.16 gm., BMC 205). All actual size.*

161 Corinth: *Head of Athena, c. 460 B.C. (stater, 8.67 gm., diam. 18 mm., BMC 64; Ravel 222)*

162, 163 Corinth: *Pegasos/Athena head, c. 430 B.C. (stater, 8.59 gm., diam. 20 mm., PCG 51.18)*

164, 165 Aigina: *Turtle with T-shaped pattern/ 'Skew' reverse, 480-457 B.C. (stater, 12.34 gm., diam. 20 mm., PCG 12.37; RPK)*

166 Aigina: *Tortoise, c. 400 B.C. (stater, 11.83 gm., diam. 22 mm., BMC 189)*

167 Thebes: *Herakles with club and bow, 446-426 B.C. (stater, 11.99 gm., diam. 20 mm., PCG 11.28; RPK)*

168 Thebes: *Herakles stealing the Delphic tripod, 446-426 B.C. (stater, 11.92 gm., diam. 22 mm., PCG 11.29)*

169 Thebes: *Herakles kneeling, stringing bow, 446-426 B.C. (stater, 12.18 gm., diam. 23 mm., PCG 11.27)*

170 Thebes: *The infant Herakles strangling snakes, 400-390 B.C. (stater, 12.12 gm., diam. 24 mm., PCG 23.22)*

171, 172 Thebes: *Shield/Head of Dionysos, 420-400 B.C. (stater, 12.32 gm., diam. 22 mm., PCG 51.15; RPK)*

173, 174 Elis: *Flying eagle with snake/Nike alighting, c. 450-430 B.C. (stater, 11.99 gm., diam. 23-24 mm., PCG 12.41; Seltman 78)*

84

160

161

162

163

164

165

166

167

168

169

170

171

172

173

174

175

176

177

178

179

180

181

182

183

184

185

186

187

188

189

175 Elis: *Winged thunderbolt, 450-430 B.C.* (stater, 11.75 gm., diam. 23 mm., BM 1889; Seltman 113)

176 Elis: *Nike seated, olive-sprig below, 430-420 B.C.* (stater, 11.86 gm., diam. 27 mm., PCG 12.44; RPK; Seltman 133)

177 Elis: *Head of Zeus, c. 420 B.C.* (stater, 11.99 gm., diam. 20 mm., PCG 12.42; RPK; Seltman 147)

178 Elis: *Eagle's head, poplar leaf below, c. 420 B.C.* (stater, 12.13 gm., diam. 22 mm., BMC 38; Seltman 150)

179, 180 Elis: *Head of Hera wearing decorated stephane/Thunderbolt, wreath border, c. 420 B.C.* (stater, 12.14 gm., diam. 23 x 19 mm., BMC 61; RPK; Seltman 243)

181, 182 Euboian league: *Reclining cow/Head of nymph, c. 411 B.C.* (stater, 12.18 gm., diam. 20-22 mm., PCG 51.16; Wallace 4; from the Euboio-Boiotian hoard, 1951)

183 Melos: *Apple, c. 450 B.C.* (stater, 14.56 gm., diam. 22 mm., BM 1940; from the Malayer hoard)

184 Melos: *Circle of dolphins, 420-416 B.C.* (stater, 13.70 gm., diam. 25 x 20 mm., BM 1938; from the Melos hoard, 1907)

185 Melos: *Ram's head, 420-416 B.C.* (stater, 13.90 gm., diam. 24 mm., PCG 52.22; from Jameson collection 1303 and Melos hoard, 1907)

186 Kos: *Diskobolos, with tripod in the field, c. 460 B.C.* (triple-siglos, 16.73 gm., diam. 25 mm., BMC 8; RPK)

187 Chios: *Sphinx, with amphora and grapes in front (reverse has magistrate's name Basileides), c. 412 B.C.* (tetradrachm, 15.03 gm., diam. 22 mm., PCG 19.39)

188, 189 Samos: *Lion scalp facing/Forepart of cow wearing ornamental harness, with olive-sprig, 454 B.C.* (tetradrachm, 13.16 gm., diam. 24 x 18 mm., PCG 8.29; Barron p. 188, 67)

even in some ways recalls the seated Nike of Terina in Italy; it has been suggested that she may have some connection with the presence in Elis of Athenian artists at the time when Pheidias was working there on the great cult-statue of Zeus. However, it would be hard to say that we see even a distant reflection of that Pheidian work in the head of Zeus which makes its **177** appearance on the coins about 420 B.C. for the first time; and the affinities of this head have been discerned rather as being more with the style of the older sculptures of the temple of Zeus finished in 457 B.C. But unfortunately few extant specimens show the details at all well and hardly do justice to the noble character of this head. Almost more remarkable is the eagle's head which **178** adorns another coin; masterly in its conception and execution, this is one of the high points of the Olympic coinage. It was created by a man called *Da . . .* the initials of whose name are sometimes legible on the poplar leaf below the eagle's head. It has been surmised that this may stand for Daidalos of Sikyon, but this remains conjectural; probably the eagle was from the same hand as the Zeus head. A further addition to the range of types is the Hera **179** head, of about the same date; she is wearing a stephane decorated with palmettes, a serene and dignified counterpart to the Zeus, and well set off by the reverse showing a new type of thunderbolt, a pillar **180** of fire enclosed in a wreath. It has been suggested that the Hera coins may have been produced at a separate mint from the Zeus coins, each of the great Olympic temples having a separate minting establishment attached to it.

The Aiginetic standard of coinage, that of the enemies of Athens, was sometimes adopted almost as an anti-Athenian gesture in itself—as was the case in Euboia, after her breakaway from Athenian control in 412 B.C., along with many of the erstwhile 'allies'. The new staters of the Euboian league show a recumbent cow, the traditional symbol of the island, with a female head on the reverse who is probably the eponymous nymph Euboia. The coins have an importance as historical documents, as they are the only tangible evidence for the establishment of the Euboian league at this time. A number of them were found in a hoard together with Theban staters of the Dionysos head type.

A smaller island whose history, like that of Aigina, clashed tragically with the ambitions of Athens, was Melos, whose Dorian inhabitants had steadfastly refused to join the Athenian confederacy. Melos was commercially of little account, and it was only at a fairly late stage, in 426 B.C., that Athens attempted to dragoon her into becoming an ally. The attempt failed and ten years later Athens undertook the bloody conquest of the island which is described in some of the grimmest pages of Thucydides. Perhaps foreseeing the likely course of events, the Melians made preparations, including the minting of a varied but concentrated coinage, most of the extant examples of which came from a single hoard found on Melos in 1907. Using the punning type of an apple (*melon*) expressive

of the island's name, there is a large repertory of reverse types including such devices as star, flower, wheel, corn grains, circle of dolphins, head of Dioskouros, Gorgon, triskelis, ram's head and others. It is an attractive local art which supplements what we know of the island's artistic capacities from the fine Melian reliefs and the best specimens such as the ram's head, are of superb quality.

The eastern side of the Aegean, from the Hellespont to Karia, was fully part of the Athenian empire and subject to its regulations. However, since many of the coinages in this region were a direct continuation of the archaic electrum issues, the currency decree of 449 B.C.—which affected only silver—did not make too radical a change in the general picture of coinage. Minting of silver however was on the whole severely restricted during the period of Athenian power and only revived to any significant extent after the general revolt of the allies in 412 B.C.

In some cases the coins afford interesting sidelights on the relationships between Athens and other cities. In the island of Kos, for instance, in the period preceding the 449 B.C. decree, there were some fine silver coins whose type was a diskobolos, with a large tripod beside him in allusion to the prize at the games held in honour of Apollo at the Triopian Cape. The lean wiry form of the athlete's body just about to be released like a spring, is vividly conveyed in the taut style which belongs to the early classical period; the tripod completes and at the same time balances the composition. The reverse has a strangely transitional aspect, a crab superimposed on a plain incuse square, though the latest issues show the crab alone. A combination of the evidence from the coins and from epigraphy shows that Kos was a somewhat refractory ally to Athens, and actually in revolt during the 440's, continuing her coinage for a time after the general prohibition had come in. The weight of these coins was in fact the Persian standard, triple sigloi making a coin of about 16.60 grammes, somewhat lighter than an Athenian tetradrachm, as at Ainos. The Persian standard was also used for a spasmodic issue at Kolophon which seems to have continued until that city was occupied by the Persians in 429 B.C.

The greater islands, Lesbos, Chios and Samos, were Athenian allies who provided ships instead of money contributions to the alliance, and their precise status under Athenian control is not always clear. Chios, for instance, may not seriously have interrupted her issue of silver coins with the type of the sphinx which she had issued since archaic times, and which, at a date towards the end of the fifth century, 187 adopts a more sophisticated form with a fine curled wing and the wine amphora surmounted by grapes in front; this tetradrachm, with a magistrate's name on the reverse, dates to the period after the revolt of the allies. At Samos, the coinage affords us a closer view of historical developments in relation to Athens; the fine tetradrachm on the local standard of 13 grammes displays types which were already introduced in the archaic period— the lion scalp and the ox, emblems of 188, 189 Samian Hera. On a Samian coin datable to 454 B.C. the reverse shows the ox wearing an ornamental collar of a chariot harness in allusion to the festival of Hera in which her priestesses were drawn by white oxen in a chariot. On this occasion, it has been deduced, the festival was the moment of an oligarchic coup which left Samos for the next fifteen years hostile to Athens; the immediately succeeding coins are marked with a letter series denoting the years in question—an instance of Samian custom which had its parallel in the coins of the Samian emigré regime at Zankle. This 146 phase culminated in 440 B.C. with a full-scale revolt against Athens, which was duly crushed, bringing to an end both the oligarchic regime and the coins.

The regular Athenian policy can be seen at work in the coinage of Knidos whose issue of Aiginetic drachms with the head of Aphrodite continued unabated until 449, after which the issue hardly revives until towards the end of the century. We then see new versions of the Aphrodite head 207 reflecting the same rich development that we find everywhere at the end of the century, as the full and mature style of the Parthenon filters through to every region of the Greek world. About the same time an important new coinage came into being in the eastern Aegean, that of Rhodes; in 408 B.C. the cities of the island were amalgamated into one, and one of the first signs of the existence of the new Rhodes is to be seen in the issue of remarkable tetradrachms displaying the head of Helios. The first of these heads is extraordinarily vivid and the flame-like hair suggests the radiating power of the god. The reverse is the punning symbol of a rose (for which compare coin 301).

Elsewhere in Asia Minor the important coinages are those of electrum, which were permitted to continue throughout the period of Athenian dominance. Thus it was on the island of Lesbos; as we have seen in the archaic period, there was also silver coinage at Methymna and Mytilene, beside an electrum issue minted on the same pattern as that of Phokaia on the mainland. The Mytilenean and Phokaian issues of electrum hektai (sixths of the stater) continued to run closely parallel during the fifth and fourth centuries and were in fact the subject of a treaty between the two cities which is preserved from the early years of the fourth century. In it they undertook to mint coins by joint agreement in alternate years and made various regulations for the issue. It is important to notice that the treaty clearly implies that the electrum used was an artificial alloy and not, as had been the case during the earliest phases of coinage in Asia Minor, a natural alloy. At Phokaia, the coins continued with the archaic form of incuse reverse down to the fourth century but there is nothing anachronistic about the fine series of obverse types many of which still have the subsidiary symbol of a *phoka* as the mint-mark, for instance beside an Aphrodite head of 470 B.C. or accompanying the forepart of a griffin. The types are mostly heads, notably an Athena

190 Lampsakos: *Pegasos forepart, within vine-wreath, 450-430 B.C. (stater, 15.23 gm., diam. 20 mm., PCG 8.17)*

191 Kyzikos: *Poseidon with fish, 440-420 B.C. (stater, 16.02 gm., diam. 16 mm., BMC 62; Fritze 146)*

192 Kyzikos: *Satyr with amphora, 440-420 B.C. (stater, 16.06 gm., diam. 16 mm., BMC 67; Fritze 172)*

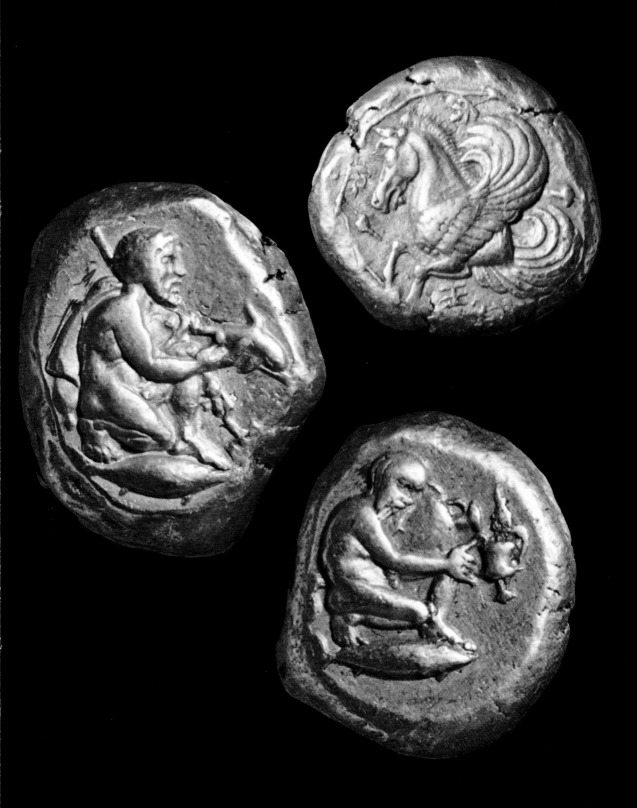

193 194 195 196 197

198 199 200

201 202 203

204 205

193 Phokaia: *Female head, with seal symbol,* c. *460 B.C. (sixth, 2.55 gm., diam. 10 mm., BMC 2)*

194 Phokaia: *Pan head,* c. *450-420 B.C. (sixth, 2.54 gm., diam. 10 mm., BMC 38)*

195 Phokaia: *Griffin forepart,* c. *480-450 B.C. (sixth, 2.53 gm., diam. 10 mm., BMC 12)*

196 Phokaia: *Athena head, griffin on helmet, 450-425 B.C. (sixth) 2.54 gm., diam. 10 mm., BMC 45)*

197 Lesbos: *Dionysos head,* c. *460 B.C. (sixth, 2.53 gm., diam. 10 mm., BMC 59)*

198 Lesbos: *Owl with open wings, 440-420 B.C. (sixth 2.51 gm., diam. 10 mm., BMC 29; RPK)*

199 Lesbos: *Confronting calves' head, 440-420 B.C. (sixth, 2.52 gm., diam. 10 mm., BMC 37)*

200 Mytilene: *Head of Apollo Maloeis, 428 B.C. (stater, 15.45 gm., diam. 18 mm., PCG 8.23)*

201 Kyzikos: *Zeus-Ammon head, 440-420 B.C. (stater, 16.01 gm., diam. 16 mm., BMC 55; Fritze 130)*

202 Kyzikos: *Tyrannicides statue, 460-440 B.C. (stater, 15.94 gm., diam. 17 mm., BMC 75; RPK; Fritze 120)*

203 Kyzikos: *Kekrops, 460-440 B.C. (stater, 16.10 gm., diam. 16 mm., PCG 8.9; Fritze 158)*

204 Kyzikos: *Gaia and Erichthonios, 460-440 B.C. (stater, 16.02 gm., diam. 14 mm., PCG 8.8; Fritze 157)*

205 Kyzikos: *Eagles on omphalos, 430-400 B.C. (stater, 16.07 gm., diam. 17 mm., PCG 8.7; Fritze 220)*

with a griffin adorning the helmet, in a developed fifth century style. The outward form of the Mytilenean pieces was to some extent distinct from those of Phokaia, as the earlier phase of intaglio reverses was succeeded by the adoption of normal reverse types in relief, among which we 198, 199 may note an owl with outspread wings like some Athenian coins, and again the pair of calves' heads which harks back to a traditional archaic type of the Lesbian billon coins. As at Phokaia, however, the obverses yield a large variety of head types, 197 among which is an interesting Dionysos from the middle of the fifth century and, a little later, an early example of a female head in the three-quarter view which was widely exploited by Greek engravers in the later fifth and fourth centuries, most notably in Sicily and in northern Greece.

The Phokaian and Lesbian electrum as it has survived consists almost solely of the small hektai, though staters of Phokaia must have existed as they are mentioned in inscriptions, while of Mytilene a single example does survive—it is an extremely beautiful head of Apollo Maloeis, of the 200 purest Parthenon style; contrasting with this head is a reverse of a quartered incuse unlike the other coins of Mytilene. It is a special issue for a special occasion and this has been identified as the revolt against Athens in 428 B.C. which, like the previous revolt at Samos, was forcibly suppressed. Electrum staters were evidently minted over a longer period at Lampsakos on the Propontis, where the type is a forepart of 190·

Pegasos sometimes encircled in a vine wreath with a letter below.

The most important of all the electrum coins were still, as in previous times, those of Kyzikos, Lampsakos' neighbour and rival. Her prolific output of electrum staters and smaller coins, with a new type at least once a year, made Kyzikos a key centre of the commerce of Greece. Strategically placed at the entrance to the Black Sea, her prosperity must have depended largely on her predominance in trade with the rich agricultural lands of the Crimea and beyond. The great commercial currency of the Black Sea was not, as in Egypt, the Athenian tetradrachm but rather the Kyzikene stater, as is proved by the incidence of such coins found in the area, as well as by the fourth century law of the city of Olbia regulating the tariff of local currency in terms of the all-important Kyzikenes. There is no need to doubt that the interests of Kyzikos and those of Athens were closely linked; it has been said that Kyzikos was 'the mint of Athens on the Propontis' and indeed it is possible to find, among the almost inexhaustible variety of Kyzikene staters, plenty of signs of the Athenian connection. All the types still have the local emblem of the tunny fish as a subsidiary detail, and among the main designs many seem to be borrowed or suggested by those of other cities, sometimes quite remote, such as Syracuse, Gela and Tarentum. It is, nevertheless, most interesting to find types which are based purely on Athenian myth or history and which never occur elsewhere as coin types. Such are the stater showing the infant Erichthonios held up by his mother Gaia, the earth-goddess; or again the mythical ancestor of the Athenians, Kekrops, whose human form terminates in a scaly serpent's tail and who, springing from the earth, symbolized, like Erichthonios, the Attic claim of autochthony. There is also Triptolemos in his serpent-car and, going from myth to history, the so-called tyrannicides copied from the Attic statues of Harmodios and Aristogeiton set up early in the fifth century to commemorate the assassination of Hipparchos. Beside these Athenian types are many others of gods, heroes, animals and figure compositions, including the two eagles perched on the Delphic omphalos, the centre of the earth; this must relate to the myth in Plutarch of the two eagles sent from each extremity of the earth and the spot where they met was Delphi. Then there is a fine kneeling Poseidon holding up a dolphin as his special emblem, or a satyr, also kneeling, as he fills a wine cup from a huge amphora. Figure compositions remained a strong element in the Kyzikene coinage down to its end in the time of Alexander, though there are also some excellent heads such as that of Zeus-Ammon, recalling Kyrene, and in the fourth century some very interesting portraits. In the general fabric and mintage these staters were virtually unchanged in two hundred years, the reverse still a plain incuse divided into segments but with no second type. They are strongly attractive as objects in their own right, appealing not only to the sense of sight but also to that of touch, and

191*, 192*, 201-5

204

203

202

205

191*

192*

201

96

preserving in their thick and knobbly form much of the irregularity of shape so characteristic of archaic coins. We do not know how the choice of the various annual types was arrived at, but we may guess that most probably it was determined by the mint-master of the year as his individual device, in much the same way as at Abdera in Thrace, another city of Ionian origin, where it was the reverse type of the coin which was varied and each new type accompanied by the name of the magistrate in office. In the case of Kyzikos, we may further guess that the choice of types which have a special reference to Athens or to another city may be due to the fact that certain mint-masters may have had close ties, personal or other, with those cities.

Another important segment of the Athenian empire was the northern Aegean seaboard. Here already in the archaic period as we have seen, the presence of great mineral wealth had stimulated coinage production, and the fifth century sees its continuation. Moreover it is interesting to see what happened during the period of maximum Athenian power, for while the ban on local coinages certainly must have operated here as elsewhere, there were also many exceptions and some relaxations must have been permitted in this area.

209, 210 The fine tetradrachms of Ainos, showing the head of Hermes wearing a felt cap, were one of the important coinages of this area going back before the Athenian decree, and whose restrained and rather solemn character remind us of the style of the Olympia sculptures. The reverse shows a goat, with a mint-master's symbol beside. These pieces, like those of Kos, were slightly lighter than the Attic tetradrachm. The issue was interrupted at 449 B.C. but Ainos seems to have been allowed to continue coining again after only a few years, perhaps, as has been suggested, to help to pay Athenian troops in the area. Some such reason may account for the comparatively rapid resumption of coinage at other mints too, most of whose remarkable productions belong to the second half of the fifth century. Thus at Mende an older type showing merely the donkey of Dionysos was replaced by a splendid group with the god himself 211, 212 seated on the donkey's back and holding a wine cup. The vivid and brilliant execution of this piece with the careful delineation of the contrasting texture of the robe and the body, the balance and serenity of the composition and the turn of the god's head, give the coin an irresistible charm, and we feel the full influence of the Parthenon style. The reverse has a rigid square frame with the city's name and inside, a vine with several clusters.

The contrast provided by the rigidly 'geometrical' reverse is very much a feature of these northern mints, and is seen again on the brilliant coins of Amphipolis. This important city was an Athenian colony on the river Strymon which was lost to Sparta in 424 B.C., and only after this date did the coinage begin. The head of Apollo on the obverse is one of the first and best examples 213, 214 of the semi-frontal pose, rendered in high relief and with the hair blowing in the wind. It is difficult to think that the creator of this type with its splendidly three-dimensional

97

and sculptural quality could be anything but an Athenian. The severely rectangular reverse containing a race-torch makes an effective foil to the head. The issue of these coins, with many later nuances of style, continued into the fourth century as did those of the Chalkidian league of Olynthos; here again we have a head of Apollo, but in profile view, a type which would not be at all out of place among the best Attic art of the later fifth century for the controlled subtlety of its modelling. The Olynthian Apollo has a kithara on the reverse, which in later phases of the coinage is accompanied by the name of the mint-master (as on the gold coins).

A final example from the northern Aegean deserves special attention for it foreshadows a whole new development of the art of Greek coinage. It is a coin of Abdera, whose series through the fifth century maintained on the obverse the traditional griffin but each reverse type differed at the choice of the mint-master. About 425 B.C. there occurs a reverse which displays, within the square form customary in this region, the head of a bearded man complete with an indication of the neck, shoulders and clothing, and it seems an undoubted portrait. The name which frames this head is that of one Pythagoras, the Abderite mint-master. But whose is the portrait? The interesting suggestion has been made that it is intended to represent the famous Samian philosopher-mathematician of the sixth century, and namesake of the unknown Abderite. If so, this would be the first example in the realm of Greek coinage of a portrait purporting to show the features

216, 217

233

215

206, 207 Knidos: *Lion's head and forepaw/Head of Aphrodite, 411-394 B.C. (drachms, obverse: 6.20 gm., diam. 18 mm., PCG 9.33; Cahn 115; reverse: 6.10 gm., diam. 16 mm., BM 1928; Cahn 114)*

208 Rhodes: *Facing head of Helios, 408 B.C. (tetradrachm, 16.77 gm., diam. 25 mm., BMC 1)*

209, 210 Ainos: *Head of Hermes wearing close-fitting petasos/Goat, with crescent and star symbol, c. 458 B.C. (tetradrachm, 16.52 gm., diam. 22 x 25 mm., BM 1890; May 47)*

211, 212 Mende: *Dionysos reclining on the back of a donkey, holding wine-cup/Vine with grape-bunches in a square frame, c. 430 B.C. (tetradrachm, 17.28 gm., diam. 26 mm., PCG 10.12; Noe 93; from the Kaliandra hoard, 1913)*

213, 214 Amphipolis: *Facing head of Apollo/Race-torch in square frame, c. 400 B.C. (tetradrachm, 14.19 gm., diam. 23 mm., BM 1896)*

215 Abdera: *Portrait of a bearded man, set in a frame with the name of the mint-magistrate Pythagores, c. 430-425 B.C. (tetradrachm, 13.98 gm., diam. 24 mm., formerly in the Jameson collection 1999; May 218)*

216, 217 Chalkidian league: *Apollo head/Seven-stringed lyre, c. 410-400 B.C. (tetradrachm, 14.40 gm., diam. 24 mm., PCG 22.13; Robinson-Clement 22)*

206   207   208

209   210

211   212

213

214

215

216

217

218

219

220

221

222

223

224   225   226

227   228

229   230

218, 219 Miletos: *Portrait of the Persian satrap Tissaphernes/Owl and olive-sprig as on coins of Athens, 411 B.C. (tetradrachm, 16.96 gm., diam. 27 x 22 mm., PCG 51.4 ; found at Karaman, ancient Laranda, 1947)*

220 Lykia: *Head of Persian satrap (reverse of coin of Khäräi?), 425-410 B.C. (stater, 8.35 gm., diam. 20 mm., PCG 9.42)*

221 Lykia: *Head of Aphrodite (obverse of coin of Täthiväibi), c. 450-425 B.C. (stater, 9.64 gm., diam. 18 x 21 mm., BM 1934)*

222 Lykia: *Head of Hermes (reverse of coin of Väkssärä), c. 420-410 B.C. (stater, 8.35 gm., diam. 24 mm., PCG 9.40)*

223 Lykia: *Head of Herakles (reverse of coin of Täläbähihä = Telmessos?), c. 420-410 B.C. (stater, 8.47 gm., diam. 20 mm., PCG 9.41)*

224 Karia: *Winged Nike holding caduceus and wreath, c. 430-420 B.C. (stater, 11.47 gm., diam. 22 mm., PCG 9.45)*

225, 226 Aspendos: *Armed warrior/Triskelis superimposed on lion, 440-400 B.C. (stater, 10.56 gm., diam. 21-24 mm., PCG 9.44 ; RPK)*

227, 228 Cyprus: *God or hero felling trees with axe/Bull crushed by falling tree, c. 450 B.C. (stater, 10.44 gm., diam. 22 mm., PCG 51.5)*

229 Cyprus, Salamis: *Head of ram (reverse of coin of Euanthes) ; Cypriote letter* ba *below, c. 460-450 B.C. (stater, 9.41 gm., diam. 21 mm., BMC 38 ; RPK)*

230 Cyprus, Kition: *Seated lion snarling (reverse of coin of Baalmelek), 479-449 B.C. (stater, 10.76 gm., diam. 25 mm., PCG 9.48)*

of a famous man of an earlier age when portraits did not exist; and there is a kind of parallel for this, a 'portrait' of Homer on a fourth century coin of the island of Ios. But another theory is that Pythagoras of Abdera simply placed his own portrait on the coin. There seems no way of deciding the matter. What is important, however, is the quite definite portrait character of the head and the veracity and force with which it is realized.

Abdera was an Ionian foundation, and the Pythagoras portrait can thus be ascribed to an Ionian artist; at about the same date, another great Ionian artist, Dexamenos of Chios, cut on a gem a portrait head of equal calibre and in a similar style. This new interest which Greek artists were taking in the depiction of individual features is exemplified by another outstanding coin of a few years later, again by an Ionian artist, and here it is quite beyond doubt that we have before us the head of a living man. 218, 219 The fact that he is a Persian and not a Greek is, if anything, an advantage for it has been possible to isolate the occasion and place; it was a coin minted for the satrap Tissaphernes at Miletos in 411 B.C., in order to pay a subvention to his Spartan allies. The magnificent head shows the satrap wearing a soft tiara with loose flaps at the sides and tied in front—distinct from the upright tiara of the Persian king (as worn by Darius in the Issus mosaic, for instance). The dignified and majestic face seems in some ways hardly distinguishable from that of a Greek god yet the features are also strongly individualized. It is recognizable as the same man whose portrait was made by another

Greek artist at Iasos in the early fourth century. It is interesting to see that the reverse of the coin is adapted from the coins of Athens, the name of the city here being replaced by the word *Bas* (for Basileos, a coin 'of the Great King'). On the owl is stamped an Aramaic countermark. This unique coin was found together with a number of ordinary Athenian tetradrachms at Karaman in southern Turkey as recently as 1947 and ranks as one of the most important coin discoveries of our time, alike for its artistic and historical interest. As we shall

289*, 297, 315 — see portraits were very rare on coins before the Hellenistic period, but there are further examples from fourth century Asia Minor.

This new Ionian portraiture is thrown into even greater relief as a new phenomenon when we compare a contemporary

220 — head from a coin of Lykia showing the head of a satrap which is of a purely traditional and Persian type and has little in the way of individual characterization. The influence of the latest Greek styles was slow to reach Lykia, and about contemporary with the Parthenon at Athens a Lykian dynast called Täthiväibi had minted coins with a

221 — head of Aphrodite which is full of charm but still of an archaic aspect. Local style is still in evidence later when coins were mint-

222 — ed bearing heads of Athena, and of Hermes

223 — or of Herakles; each of these is accompanied by a legend in the Lykian script usually giving the name of the ruler but in the case of the Herakles that of the city Telmessos (= Täläbähiha). Much still remains to be learned from the historical evidence of the Lykian coins which have a

remarkable subsequent development, even though at this time they seem less receptive

224 — to the latest Greek styles than the neighbouring district of Karia.

Even the cities of the southern shore of Asia Minor nominally belonged to the Athenian alliance, though there is little sign of any direct interference with their coinage:

225, 22— and the issues of Aspendos, for instance, seem to have continued uninterrupted and in a rather archaic style; the reverse type is of special interest displaying a triskelis in association with a lion, both solar symbols. Beyond even the nominal reach of Athens and the politics of the Aegean lay the island of Cyprus, with its mixed culture of Greeks and Phoenicians. Here, too, we find coins datable to the middle of the fifth century which look earlier, and which preserve older styles. An intriguing and unique spec-

227, 22— imen, from an unknown mint, depicts some mythological scene—a bull being crushed by a falling tree, while on the reverse, in the act of felling the tree is a figure who may be a primitive sky-god. Two other striking

229 — images are the head of a ram, the animal which regularly appears on coins of Salamis, the earliest of which have a smooth blank reverse that can only be paralleled on coins of Etruria; this coin is of King Euanthes, and a Cypriote letter appears in the field. A magnificent lion forms the

230 — reverse of a coin of Kition which bears the inscription, in Phoenician letters, 'of King Baalmelek'. The coinage of Cyprus, like that of Lykia, is a rich and varied source of historical information which is still in the process of being fully elucidated.

IV. THE FOURTH CENTURY

The fall of Athens at the end of the long war against Sparta marked an epoch in her history which is clearly reflected in the coinage. Reduced to her last gasp in 406 B.C., she was forced to melt down golden treasures from the Akropolis from which to 153-6 mint gold coins in the effort to fit out a new fleet, and then temporarily after the final defeat in 404 B.C. to mint copper coins with a mere coating of silver. Silver coinage was revived only in 393 B.C., and the traditional type saw little change except the one concession that the eye of Athena was 158, 159 now correctly drawn in profile. This new type—with fresh variants for some of the smaller coins—was in turn frozen until the third century, as we can see from the ex-156°, 157 ample of another emergency gold issue made as late as 296 B.C. under the tyrant Lachares, which swallowed up all the remaining gold dedications from the Akropolis, including the gold plates from the Athena Parthenos. The coinage of Athens, then, originally so creative and always of the greatest historical importance, gives no more sign of artistic enterprise in the fourth century than in the fifth.

Yet, in almost every other part of the Greek world, it is clear that on the contrary the fourth century down to the time of Alexander was richer than ever in interesting and creative developments, in coinage as in the other arts. The style of the new period is especially well exemplified by the splendid head of Zeus minted at Elis 246 in 364 B.C. In place of the somewhat distant and withdrawn Zeus of earlier times, we now see a comparatively youthful god of fresh and debonair aspect, unquestionably more human in form and expressive of human feeling. The style of this head, with its delicate modelling, has aptly been associated with the influence of Praxiteles. Elsewhere in the Peloponnese, the shift in political gravity caused by the upsurge of Thebes had a liberating effect after the Spartan hegemony. The Arkadian league, which through the fifth century produced its small drachm coinage at three mints, now blossomed out into a splendid stater 244, 245 coinage at the new federal capital Megalopolis. The masterly head of Zeus, which by contrast with Elis emphasizes the majesty of the god, has yet a new freedom and elaboration of treatment, and although a similar type does later appear at Elis it never has the overwhelming impact it has here. For the reverse, we see a figure of Pan superbly modelled and relaxed, reclining on a rocky seat, holding his lagobolon (throwing stick) and his syrinx below as a detail. On the rock is engraved the name *Olu...* (sometimes *Olum...*) undoubtedly the artist's signature, presumably a name such as Olympios, but anyhow one of the masters of fourth century die engraving, whether or not he has anything to do with the gem-engraver of the same name. Independently of Megalopolis, other mints in Arkadia also became active at this time, such as Stymphalos, where the coins celebrate the labours of Herakles, and Pheneos where, on the reverse of a stater we see

247, 248 Hermes rescuing the infant Arkas, child of Zeus and Kallisto, in order to entrust it to his own mother Maia—whose head it may be that occurs on the obverse of the coin. Stylistically the 'Maia' head clearly owes much to the inspiration of the Syracusan dekadrachms by Euainetos, which were imitated widely in the Greek world. Behind her neck appear the letters *ΠΟ*, perhaps the signature of another engraver who is also known from certain coins of Elis. The attractive Hermes figure once again seems to recall the work of Praxiteles.

249, 250 A contemporary drachm of Argos has a reverse which is of a similar kind to that of Pheneos, this time however showing a group of the hero Diomedes carrying off the palladion from Troy; his cloak swells out behind and he carries a dagger in his right hand. The splendid Hera on the obverse seems a counterpart of the Arkadian Zeus. Further mythological scenes in-

251, 252 clude the fine fierce Chimaera from Sikyon,

balanced by a peaceful dove set in a wreath on the reverse. Finally there is an intriguing and unique scene on the reverse of a stater 253 of the island of Zakynthos; long interpreted as yet another version of the infant Herakles strangling snakes, as at Thebes, it has been rightly pointed out that this infant is certainly not strangling the snakes but caressing them, and the fact that the child seems to be receiving food from the mouth of one of them confirms the identification as Iamos, a son of Apollo who was worshipped at Zakynthos and who was nourished by snakes at his birth.

The mint of Corinth continued to be one of the most important on the Greek mainland, though it contrasts with the rest of the Peloponnese, for the Corinthian sphere of influence and interest lay in western Greece and the Adriatic; in that region a number of cities issued a coinage of purely Corinthian type—among them Leukas, Anaktorion and Ambrakia. The coins of those cities were distinguished by the appearance of their own initial or name instead of that of Corinth and further by a whole series of attractive symbols or secondary designs placed beside the Athena head, such as the Eros on dolphin on a 255 stater of Ambrakia. Symbols of this kind were also widely used at Corinth, where during the later fourth century production of coins was vastly extended and re-organized, with a new system involving the use of both letters and symbols to mark the various issues. Sometimes the helmet is 254 wreathed. This new phase at Corinth seems to coincide with Timoleon's refoundation of Syracuse (344 B.C.), a city which also became an important producer of Corinthian-style coins at this period.

Intimately connected with the Peloponnese, however, was the island of Crete, which in itself constitutes something of a separate sphere of coinage. A few of the Cretan artists can equal the Peloponnesians, though Cretan work is apt to be very uneven in quality. There is however a similar marked preference for mythological types, and the same use of the Aiginetic weight standard for the coins. Indeed for long the Cretans used only imported Aiginetan coins which they sometimes imitated, and only in the later fifth century when the supply of 'turtles' began to run out did they begin to strike their own types, often re-using Aigina coins in the process. Thus it was only towards the end of the fifth century that Knossos minted staters with the figure of 256, 257 the Minotaur, shown in the old archaic kneeling-running position; the deceptively archaic aspect of this coin is also evident on the reverse, a square divided into rectangular segments worked into a design supposed to represent the Cretan labyrinth. Another attractively primitive-looking coin shows the sea-god of Itanos with his huge head and fishy tail raising a thunderbolt, 258 and in front a rather incongruous cicada symbol. In the south of Crete, the neighbouring cities of Gortyna and Phaistos show a close parallelism in their coins and 259 both have the type of Europa riding on a bull who was, of course, Zeus in disguise carrying her off. Later coins of Gortyna show the scene of a girl seated in a tree,

who is probably still Europa or else some more shadowy figure of lost Cretan myth— sometimes she is partly stripped and in the 260 embrace of a giant eagle, another manifestation of Zeus, who seems to be alluded to also in the bull's head below. The scene at once recalls Leda and the swan. The bull alone remains a constant type for the coins of both Gortyna and of Phaistos and is often seen in a charging attitude. Phaistos 262 has another mythical figure, Talos the wing- 263 ed giant made by Hephaistos for King Minos as a protector for the island of Crete. More central to the Greek saga is the type of another Phaistian coin, this time of super- 261 lative quality, showing Herakles battling with the hydra of Lerna; his lionskin over his shoulder, he grasps one of the hydra's manifold heads and swings his club to crush it. Beneath his right foot is shown the crab sent by the ever-jealous Hera to help the hydra. All this is superbly executed and the whole composition has an enormous vigour.

One peculiarity of Cretan coins towards the end of the fourth century is that they are often restruck on coins of Kyrene; this fact has proved a valuable clue for the true chronology of Cretan coins, many of which are to be dated much later than was formerly thought, since the great influx of Kyrenaic money to Crete has now been convincingly connected with the presence of Cretan mercenaries in Africa and their return thence in 322 B.C. The gold coinage of Kyrene is to be seen later, but it is appropriate to mention at this point an exceptionally fine silver issue of the earlier 264, 265 fourth century on which we see an impressive head of Zeus Ammon in almost facing view with a fine rendering of the ram's horns, while above the brow he wears a uraeus-like ornament; the reverse gives a typical fourth century version of the silphium plant.

Turning from the far south to the northern part of the Greek mainland, we find among new coinages of the fourth century that the influence of Syracuse which has left traces in the Peloponnese (and even in Crete) is again perceptible—for instance in the important and stylish issue of the
266 Opuntians of Lokris, around 350 B.C. though the precise historical motivation for this issue still awaits discovery. The local hero was the lesser Ajax, son of Oileus, leader of the Lokrian contingent in the Trojan war; he is duly shown on the
267 reverse of the coins in a warlike attitude, a stocky aggressive figure wielding a short sword and a shield decorated with a snake design. The figure may well contain some
421 reminiscence of the Syracusan Leukaspis. In any case the head is quite certainly modelled closely on the Euainetos heads
266, 441 from Syracuse, with an elaborate rich hair treatment set with a wreath. A more original coinage is that of Delphi, whose precise occasion is known from epigraphic records; it was in the year 336 B.C. that the Amphiktyonic council decided to remint into new coins the mass of older miscellaneous money in the Delphic treasury, in order to pay for the work on the new
268, 269 temple. The head on these coins, that of Demeter wearing a veil and a crown of

231 Pantikapaion: *Griffin biting spear, above corn ear, c. 320 B.C. (stater, 8.54 gm., diam. 22 mm., BM 1921), reverse of 243*

232 Philip II of Macedonia: *Chariot, kantharos symbol, 359-336 B.C. (stater, 8.58 gm., diam. 18 mm., BM 1866), reverse of 235*

233   234   235

236   237   238

239   240   241

242   243

233 Chalkidian league: *Apollo head, 352-350 B.C. (stater, 8.59 gm., diam. 16 mm., PCG 22.12 ; Robinson-Clement p. 83 No. IV)*

234 Philippi: *Head of Herakles, 358-350 B.C. (stater, 8.62 gm., diam. 17 mm., PCG 22.16)*

235 Philip II of Macedonia: *Apollo head, 359-336 B.C. (stater, 8.58 gm., diam. 19 mm., BM 1866), obverse of 232*

236 Philip II of Macedonia: *Apollo with long hair, later fourth century B.C. (stater, obverse, 8.61 gm., diam. 17 mm., BM 1878)*

237, 238 Philip II of Macedonia: *Herakles head/ Lion, kantharos symbol, 359-336 B.C. (half-stater, 4.25 gm., diam. 14 mm., BM 1877)*

239 Philip II of Macedonia: *Bow and club, trident symbol, 359-336 B.C. (quarter-stater, reverse, 2.13 gm., diam. 11 mm., BM 1949)*

240 Philip II of Macedonia: *Thunderbolt, 359-336 B.C. (eight-stater, reverse, 1.06 gm., diam. 9 mm., BM 1949)*

241 Pantikapaion: *Pan head semi-facing, c. 350 B.C. (stater, obverse, 9.10 gm., diam. 18 mm., PCG 21.1)*

242 Pantikapaion: *Pan head in profile, c. 340 B.C. (stater, obverse, 9.08 gm., diam. 19 mm., BMC 2 ; from the Saida hoard)*

243 Pantikapaion: *Pan head of 'Scythian' style, c. 320 B.C. stater, 8.54 gm., diam. 21 mm., BM 1921), obverse of 231*

corn, is a lovely and sensitive creation; while the reverse shows Apollo seated on the omphalos, with a great lyre in the background on which he leans his elbow, and a small tripod in the field.

Farther to the north, in the semi-feudal land of Thessaly, the coinage of various mints had been fairly abundant since the early fifth century, and there was certainly no lack of local talent as can be seen from the very competent and spirited coins of 270, 271 Larissa. The horse is important in this country, and the obverse of the coin shows a special Thessalian sport of bull-wrestling, evidently akin to the bull sports of Minoan Crete. One may without detriment compare this with another bull wrestling scene from 379 Sicily. In the fourth century, Thessalian engravers were, as elsewhere, receptive to Sicilian influences, as can be seen on many coins of Pherai, Pharsalos and other mints. A highly unusual and intriguing drachm of 272, 273 Larissa shows the head of Aleuas, the legendary *tagos* or leader of Thessaly, with the double-axe, the symbol of his power, while on the reverse is an eagle perched on a thunderbolt and the cryptic legend *hella* beside it. The interpretation of this coin has occasioned some controversy, and it has recently been proposed that it was minted as late as the time of Alexander the Great, in allusion to his claim to be regarded as the leader of the Thessalian nation.

In Macedonia and Thrace, there is complete continuity between the coins of the later fifth century and those of the fourth, and each mint gives an interesting view of the development of style step by step. It is rather typical of this region to find on the coins either the name or symbol of successive mint-masters making the successive issues, as had always been the practice at Abdera, for instance. At the Chalkidic mint of Olynthos, magistratal names began to be introduced; a certain Eudoridas is named on the reverse of one

233 of the gold staters of fourth century style on which Apollo is shown with long hair. Gold coins gradually became more frequent and, beside occasional issues at Abdera and Maroneia, there were more regular issues at Thasos, to whom belonged some rich gold mines on the mainland opposite. These gold staters follow exactly the same pattern

274, 275 as the Thasian tetradrachms in silver, a series of which had started as early as 410 B.C. with the head of Dionysos on the obverse, bearded and with ivy leaves in his hair, very minutely executed. The reverse shows Herakles as an archer, his lionskin drawn up over his head, and his somewhat archaic aspect is explained by fact that this is indeed a copy of an earlier sculptured relief found on Thasos—one of the very few instances in classical times when we can be quite sure that a coin design is taken from large-scale art. The splendid tetradrachms of Amphipolis continued to develop in unrivalled quality through the earlier fourth century, and when for instance the mint of Ainos tried a facing head the difference was all too apparent. Not so

276, 277 however on some smaller coins of Ainos, which have a charming Hermes head well placed within the curve of his flat hat, and for the reverse an interesting type showing

244, 245 Arkadian league: *Head of Zeus/Pan seated on rock, syrinx below ; signature olu, c. 371 B.C. (stater, 12.31 gm., diam. 23 mm., PCG 24.48)*

246 Elis: *Head of Zeus*, c. *364 B.C. (stater, 12.31 gm., diam. 26 mm., PCG 23.43 ; RPK ; Seltman 176)*

247, 248 Pheneos: *Head of Maia/Hermes carrying the infant Kallisto, 370-360 B.C. (stater, 12.03 gm., diam. 23 mm., PCG 24.49)*

249, 250 Argos: *Head of Hera/Diomedes carrying off the Palladion, 370-360 B.C. (drachm, 5.35 gm., diam. 20 mm., BMC 44)*

251, 252 Sikyon: *Chimaera/Dove within wreath, c. 400-370 B.C. (stater, 12.28 gm., diam. 23 mm., BMC 48)*

253 Zakynthos: *The child Iamos being fed by snakes, c. 370-360 B.C. (stater, 11.62 gm., diam. 24 mm., PCG 23.44)*

254 Corinth: *Head of Athena with wreathed helmet, letters* ar *and Medusa symbol, c. 320 B.C. (stater, 8.61 gm., diam. 22 mm., BMC 253)*

255 Ambrakia: *Head of Athena, with symbol, Eros on dolphin, c. 360-350 B.C. (stater, 8.22 gm., diam. 24 mm., BMC 30 ; Ravel 150)*

244

245

246

247

248

249

250

251

252

253

254

255

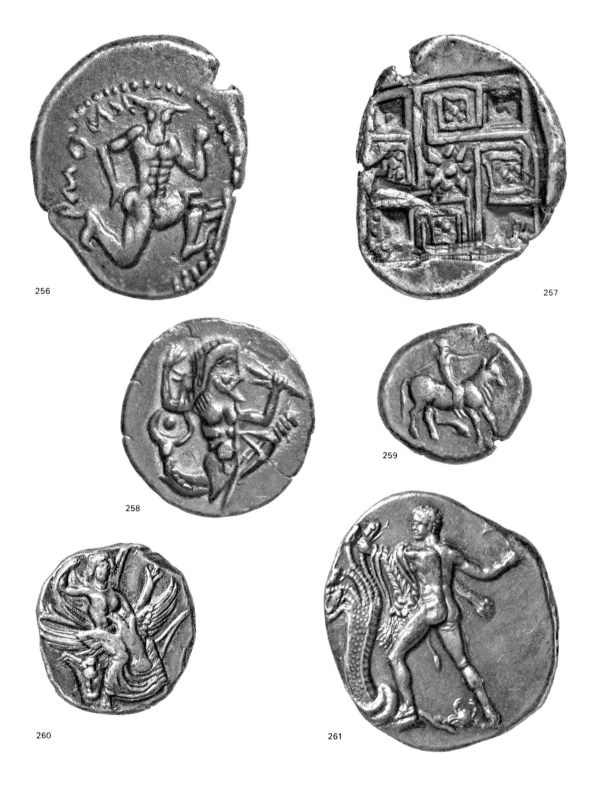

256

257

258

259

260

261

262

263

264

265

266

267

the primitive *xoanon* (cult image) of the god
placed on a throne.

The independent cities of Macedonia and
Thrace all eventually fell to Philip II and
their coinages then ceased. Within a few
years he had taken possession of the mainland mines belonging to the Thasians near
the Pangaean mountain, where they had at
first minted some gold coins with the head
of Herakles and the tripod, inscribed
Thasion epeiro. This city was renamed after
Philip himself as Philippi and for some time
during his reign the gold coins continued 234
to be minted under the new name. This,
however, was not before Philip had inaugurated a new and impressive coinage of
his own both in gold and silver, whose
abundance was based on a yearly revenue of
1,000 talents from his mines. His gold
staters were, like those of the former 232*, 235
Chalkidian league, of Attic weight and
showed the head of Apollo possibly
inspired by Olynthian types (one rare
Philip stater even has a long-haired Apollo), 236
but there are many variations of style and
much originality. The reverse shows a two-
horse chariot below which is simply the
name of Philip, with no royal title. There
were also fractional pieces, the half-stater, 237
the quarter and eighth, each with the head 239, 240
of Herakles on the obverse and respectively
a half-lion, a bow and club, and a thunderbolt for reverse. Beside this array of gold,
from several mints, Philip also minted
silver tetradrachms with didrachms and
smaller pieces. On the tetradrachm the head 278, 279
was that of Zeus, and at least on the first
issues it is of outstanding quality and equal

to the best Peloponnesian work. The reverse shows a massive racehorse mounted by a boy-jockey, to commemorate the king's victory at the Olympic games in 356 B.C. Other tetradrachms show, instead of the boy-jockey, a military man, possibly representing the king. The enormous quantity of the coinage of Philip was something of a new phenomenon in the Greek world, rivalling that of Athens, and the output of the various mints has not yet been fully studied and arranged. At all events it is clear that the impression his coins made on the Greeks of his own day led to the types being repeated even after his death; they had a wide circulation in the Balkans where they formed the prototype for a whole new development of coinage in Celtic Europe.

The Black Sea had been an important area of Greek colonization by Milesians and others, and numerous Greek cities were ranged around its shores. The importance of the agriculture of this region to the Greeks of the Aegean has been mentioned above; but there was also gold—so prominent in the rich burial-treasures of the local Scythian rulers—and this was extracted perhaps from as far away as the Urals, anyway from a region remote enough for Herodotus to repeat that the Black Sea gold was purloined from the griffins by the one-eyed Arimaspeans. On the gold coins of the city of Pantikapaion in the Crimea we see the griffin itself with its horned lion's head, and it stands on a great ear of corn, as if to allude to both the great sources of wealth of this region. But it is

268, 269 Amphiktyonic council: *Head of Demeter/Apollo seated on the omphalos, 336 B.C. (stater, 12.14 gm., diam. 22 mm., PCG 23.30)*

270, 271 Larissa: *Bull wrestler/Horse, c. 400-360 B.C. (drachm, 6.01 gm., diam. 20 mm., BMC 31)*

272, 273 Larissa: *Head of Aleuas wearing helmet with cheek-piece and double-axe in right field/Eagle on thunderbolt, c. 336 B.C. (drachm, 5.99 gm., diam. 18 mm., BMC 53)*

274, 275 Thasos: *Head of Dionysos/Herakles as archer, c. 370 B.C. (tetradrachm, 15.39 gm., diam. 22 mm., BM 1934; from the Thasos hoard)*

276, 277 Ainos: *Head of Hermes facing/Cult-image of Hermes Perpheraios on throne, c. 357-342 B.C. (drachm, 3.78 gm., diam. 16 mm., BMC 23 ; May 438)*

268

269

270

271

272

273

274

275

276

277

278

279

280

281

282

283

284

285

286

the obverses of the coins which are the truly impressive feature; the head of Pan, used as the punning device for the city's name, as it appears on staters of about 350 B.C., is of the purest Greek style, with 241, 242 pointed ears, snub nose and unkempt hair. One of these heads is in profile, the other in a semi-facing view excellently conceived. These staters were first minted on a standard somewhat heavier than the Attic but later the normal Attic weight came in. We must note too the remarkable way in which a Scythian artist takes over the Greek design, 243 even adding to the head a wreath of vine leaves, but adapting the facial forms to the stylization characteristic of the splendid gold objects of Scythian art—a fruitful mixture of styles which is brilliant in a semi-barbaric way. The earlier staters of Pantikapaion were conspicuous in the hoard found at Prinkipo on the Sea of Marmara, along with gold coins of Philip and of Lampsakos and the ubiquitous electrum of Kyzikos, an eloquent testimony to the great trade routes of the Black Sea area.

There were few other coinages in this region to equal those of Pantikapaion. At Sinope, on the southern shore, and equally at Istros near the Danube mouth, silver coins were minted showing a sea-eagle and 280, 281 a dolphin, a motif derived from earlier bronze coins of Olbia. The Istros coins have an intriguing obverse, consisting of two young facing heads placed in contrary directions; recently it has been suggested that this strange type should be related to the geographical myth, current in antiquity,

278, 279 Macedonia, Philip II: *Head of Zeus/ Young rider on horse, thunderbolt symbol below, 359-336 B.C. (tetradrachm, 14.52 gm., diam. 25-24 mm., PCG 22.20)*

280, 281 Istros: *Two young heads, one upright, one inverted/Sea-eagle attacking dolphin, 400-350 B.C. (stater, 5.87 gm., diam. 17 mm., BM 1905)*

282, 283 Kyzikos: *The infant Herakles struggling with snakes/Lion's head with tunny symbol below, 394 B.C. (double-siglos, 11.39 gm., diam. 20 mm., PCG 18.15)*

284 Samos: *Facing lion's scalp (reverse of the same issue as 282, 283), 394 B.C. (double-siglos, 11.53 gm., diam. 23 mm., PCG 19.37; RPK)*

285, 286 Ephesos: *Bee/Forepart of stag with palm-tree, 370-340 B.C. (tetradrachm, 15.31 gm., diam. 23-24 mm., BM 1929; from the Makri hoard)*

of the two branches of the Danube river, one of which emerges in the Black Sea but the other was supposed to come out in the Adriatic. However that may be, the type remains a challenging one that is unique in the repertory of Greek coins.

IONIA AND THE EAST

On the eastern side of the Aegean, the first important numismatic event of the fourth century directly reflects the revival of Athenian naval power which, under the leadership of Konon, inflicted a notable defeat on the Spartans at the battle of Knidos in 394 B.C. At this time there came into being a maritime alliance of whose existence we know solely from the evidence of the coins minted by the cities concerned: Rhodes, Knidos, Iasos, Kyzikos, Ephesos, Samos and Byzantion. The members of the alliance all in common used the type of the 282 infant Herakles strangling snakes, undoubt-170 edly derived from similar types which had previously appeared at Thebes, although the appeal of the type must in the circumstances be considered to be anti-Spartan rather than specifically pro-Theban. The type is accompanied by the legend *syn* (= *synmachikon*, alliance coinage) and each city used its own distinctive reverse. That of Kyzikos, for instance was a lion's head 283 with the Kyzikene tunny below; that of 284 Samos was the lion's scalp precisely like that of her own tetradrachms. The coins of this alliance were all minted on a common

standard, that of Persia, though the normal coins of the Ionian cities continued mostly, as before, to be struck on local standards. A very prolific new coinage began at this 285, 28 time at Ephesos where the obverse was a bee and the reverse the forepart of a stag with a palm tree, all alike emblems of Ephesian Artemis, whose priestesses were known as 'bees' (*melissai*). The magistrate's name appears beside the stag, and there is a very large series of these coins in the fourth century, comprising some two hundred names in all. The minute rendering of the detail of the bee is remarkable and recalls the intense study accorded to these valuable insects in antiquity, which has been thought even to anticipate modern discoveries. Such a coinage is however typical of the Ionian cities in its comparatively unchanging and emblematic character—as opposed, for instance, to the more elaborate mythological compositions of the Peloponnese.

A great variety of artistic expression was afforded by the issue of gold coins, which now became quite widespread, and of these the most important and brilliant was that of Lampsakos. The old winged horse type, 291 as seen on the fifth century electrum coins, is now relegated to the reverse of the new stater issues, which perhaps significantly were made on the standard of the Persian daric. The obverse now became the vehicle for a long series of types, both figure compositions and heads, which are of unsurpassed quality and variety. One of the first was in fact a Herakles with snakes like the type of the maritime league, to which perhaps Lampsakos also belonged. Other compositions of extremely brilliant execution include two showing Nike, and displaying a considerable mastery in the rendering of the female body. In the first of 287• these Nike is slaying a ram, with the knife poised at its throat and her drapery falling to her knees. The second, somewhat later, 288• shows again a partially naked Nike, kneeling to hammer a nail into a trophy of arms, an interesting type to compare with 590, 552 the later versions of this motif on coins of Agathokles of Syracuse and of Seleukos I. Then there is the rich and fascinating series of heads, gods and heroes. An early 295 example is the Dionysos which may be 274 compared with the Thasos tetradrachm; 290 after this, a maenad with wild flowing hair 293 blowing out behind; and a Zeus which is 244 the equal in majesty to that of the Megalopolis coin and surpassing it in serenity of 296 expression. Nike is represented again by a head with a symbolic wing springing from 294 the neck; then there is an Aktaion with the stag's horns placed on his head by Artemis 292 clearly seen, and a bearded Kabeiros wearing a pointed cap wreathed with olive leaves. Finally there is, on only one issue, a portrait, and clearly a Persian satrap as we see 218 from the comparison with Tissaphernes; 297 here however it is Orontas who headed the great revolt against the Persian king in 360 B.C.

The great series of Lampsakos staters lasted from about 390 to 330 B.C., and many were found in the treasure of Prinkipo which we have mentioned in connection with the Pantikapaion coins. But the Lampsakos staters were probably also hoarded by mercenaries as well as by merchants, which would account for the presence of a number of them together with Persian darics, even in a hoard found at Avola in Sicily.

The Orontas portrait from Lampsakos is one of several Persian satrap portraits which survive from the earlier fourth century. It is interesting to see that portraiture, heralded by the Abdera and Miletos examples in the fifth century, was beginning to become established at least intermittently in the idiom of coinage in fourth century Asia Minor. Other examples are to be found among the electrum staters of Kyzikos; some of these show extremely lifelike heads of elderly bearded men wear- 289•, 298 ing laurel crowns, and so characteristic and personalized are their features that it seems possible to distinguish two or perhaps more individuals. The first has a much thicker neck and seems younger, with hair on the top of the head; the second has a more puckered face and a bald crown. It is scarcely possible to surmise who these individuals can be, to be celebrated in such a fashion; but it is idle to guess more than that these must be distinguished men honoured by the city of Kyzikos for outstanding merits. In any case they are the first Greeks whose features are preserved to us by the medium of coinage, unless we accept the Pythagoras of Abdera as a 215 forerunner.

We find a further instance of early coin portraits, however, among the local, semi-Hellenized dynasts of Lykia. Here there had been in the fifth century a certain tradition of depicting the head of a satrap

220 but in a more or less stylized and impersonal form. In the fourth century, under the influence of the new Ionian portraiture, Lykian engravers produced some remarkable works in a purely Greek style, some of which are known to us only from quite recent discoveries. First and foremost

315 there is the fine profile head of Mithrapata, vividly realized in sculptural form; he wears no insignia of rank, but the well-characterized features leave no doubt whatever that this is a living individual. His name, in Lykian script is written around the head and the traditional Lykian triskelis symbol is also included; while on the ob-

316 verse is a splendid lion forepart full of fire. Another Lykian head is even more remarkable; this time not profile but in nearly facing view, again bearded, and with

317 wildly tossed hair and in some of the variant versions also wearing a wreath. It seems to be agreed that this is not a god but the portrait of a man, and if so then it is the dynast Päriklä, whose name appears on the reverse with a design of a warrior like the

267 Ajax of Opuntian Lokris. Here then is an almost isolated occurrence of the facing portrait, a form which does not recur in Greek coinage and only in late antiquity in the Roman. As such it may be ranked as a Lykian invention, especially as again in Lykia there had been an earlier 'satrapal' head shown in this attitude. But again here as elsewhere it must be admitted that the facing head as such was something which owed not a little to outside inspiration,

287 Lampsakos: *Nike slaying ram*, c. *390-380 B.C. (gold stater, 8.42 gm., diam. 17 mm., PCG 18.18 ; Baldwin 7)*   287 ▶

288 Lampsakos: *Nike erecting trophy*, c. *360-350 B.C. (gold stater, 8.44 gm., diam. 17 mm., PCG 18.27 ; Baldwin 26), obverse of 272*

289 Kyzikos: *Portrait of elderly man with wreath*, c. *370-350 B.C. (electrum stater, 16.04 gm., diam. 16 mm., PCG 18.8 ; Fritze 199)*

290 Lampsakos: *Maenad head*, c. *370-360 B.C. (gold stater, 8.47 gm., diam. 17 mm., PCG 18.22 ; Baldwin 17)*

291 Lampsakos: *Winged horse (reverse of 288)*

292 Lampsakos: *Head of Kabeiros*, c. *340-330 B.C. (gold stater, 8.37 gm., diam. 17 mm., PCG 18.19 ; Baldwin 39)*   288 ▶

293 Lampsakos: *Head of Zeus*, c. *350-340 B.C. (gold stater, 8.46 gm., diam. 17 mm., PCG 18.28 ; Baldwin 29)*

294 Lampsakos: *Head of Aktaion*, c. *340-330 B.C. (gold stater, 8.46 gm., diam. 16 mm., PCG 18.26 ; Baldwin 33)*

295 Lampsakos: *Head of Dionysos*, c. *380-370 B.C. (gold stater, 8.41 gm., diam. 14 mm., PCG 18.21 ; Baldwin 10)*

296 Lampsakos: *Head of Nike*, c. *350-340 B.C. (gold stater, 8.46 gm., diam. 17 mm., PCG 18.24 ; Baldwin 30)*

297 Lampsakos: *Portrait of the satrap Orontas*, c. *363 B.C. (gold stater, 8.43 gm., diam. 16 mm., Glasgow, Hunter ; Baldwin 21 ; photo from electrotype)*   289 ▶

298 Kyzikos: *Portrait of old man with wreath*, c. *370-350 B.C. (electrum stater, 16.02 gm., diam. 15 mm., PCG 18.9 ; Fritze 197)*

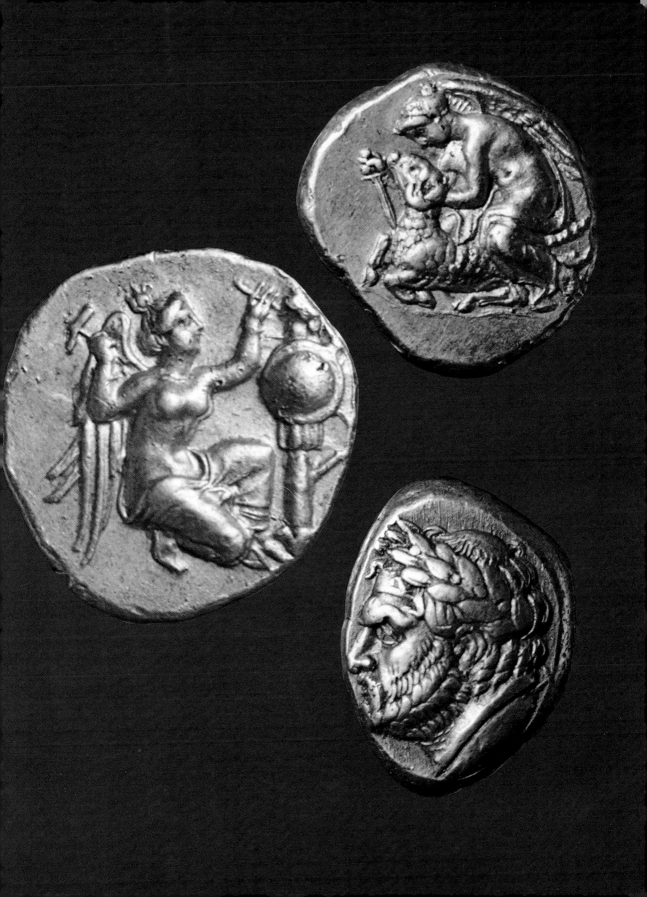

290   291   292   29

293   294   295   30

296   297   298   30

302   303   304

305   306   307   308

309   310   311

312   313   314

299 Klazomenai: *Swan, with name of Athenagoras and symbol winged boar, c. 370-360 B.C. (stater, 5.70 gm., diam. 16 mm., PCG 19.32 ; RPK), reverse of 304*

300, 301 Rhodes: *Head of Helios/Rose, c. 350-340 B.C. (stater, 8.59 gm., diam. 16 mm., PCG 19.45 ; from the Saida hoard)*

302, 303 Pergamon: *Head of Herakles/Athena statue, symbol helmet, c. 350-340 B.C. (stater, 8.21 gm., diam. 17 mm., PCG 28.25 ; from the Saida hoard)*

304 Klazomenai: *Apollo head, c. 370-360 B.C. (stater, 5.70 gm., diam. 16 mm., PCG 19.32 ; RPK), obverse of 299*

305, 306 Pixodaros of Karia: *Head of Apollo/ Zeus Labraundos, 340-335 B.C. (half-stater, 4.15 gm., diam. 14 mm., PCG 19.43)*

307, 308 Euagoras I of Salamis: *Facing Herakles head/Goat, c. 411-374 B.C. (quarter-stater, 2.04 gm., diam. 11 mm., PCG 20.52)*

309 Kyrene: *Zeus-Ammon with ram, holding Nike, c. 331-332 B.C. (gold stater, 8.61 gm., diam. 18 mm., BMC 107 ; Naville 69)*

310 Kyrene: *Galloping chariot, c. 331-322 B.C. (gold stater, 8.50 gm., diam. 18 mm., BMC 112 ; Naville 19)*

311 Kyrene: *Zeus enthroned, with the name of Kydios, c. 331-322 B.C. (gold stater, 8.58 gm., diam. 20 mm., BMC 114 ; Naville 30)*

312 Kyrene: *Facing chariot with Nike as charioteer, c. 331-322 B.C. (gold stater, 8.55 gm., diam. 19 mm., BMC 108 ; Naville 22-4)*

313 Kyrene: *Zeus-Ammon before altar, c. 322-313 B.C. (gold stater, 8.61 gm., diam. 20 mm., BMC 117 ; Naville 85)*

314 Kyrene: *Walking chariot, with sun above, c. 322-313 B.C. (gold stater, 8.62 gm., diam. 20 mm., BMC 116 ; Naville 83)*

133

especially that of Syracuse, as we can see 318 from another Lykian coin, that of Zagabaha, reproducing faithfully the appearance 400 and spirit of a facing Athena by Eukleidas.

The fourth century predilection for facing heads was however not confined to any single region and there are other fine examples from the Greek mints of Asia 304 Minor. Firstly, there is the Apollo of Klazomenai; the visionary look and the delicate modelling of the head on this gold stater are fully equal to those of a more famous tetradrachm where a similar head is signed by Theodotos; to judge by the many similarities of treatment, the head of the gold coin could well be by the same hand. The reverse of a swan flapping its wings is one of the most vivid of bird pictures; and around is the abbreviated city name, with that of the magistrate Athenagoras, while 299 below is the small forepart of a winged boar, the minute relic of the original civic emblem of archaic times.

Another Apollo head, of vastly different character, is to be seen on a gold stater of 300•, 301• Rhodes, with the rose as punning type on the reverse. After the sensitive, withdrawn look of the Klazomenaian Apollo, the keynote here is the strength and living force of the sun-god which, at Rhodes, Apollo supremely was. The modelling is bold, simple, and completely convincing. This coin is a generation before the famous colossus was set up, but perhaps we may imagine that his face was something like this. This stater represents the culmination of the first phases of the Rhodian coinage 208 which began in 408 B.C., and may well be

about contemporary with Alexander as specimens were present in the great hoard discovered at Saida (ancient Sidon) in Syria during the last century, and buried about 324 B.C. Of about the same date, and also represented in the Saida hoard, is a rare gold stater of Pergamon showing a 302, 30 head of Herakles and on the reverse a cult statue of Athena; this piece bears no name, but the identification is supplied by other smaller coins of the same type. Although the history of Pergamon before Alexander is obscure, the issue suggests that it was already a place of some consequence.

Close to Lykia, where such remarkably original coins had been minted, lay Karia, the home of the dynasty of Maussollos, whose capital, and famous tomb, was at Halikarnassos. His coins, however, in no way rival those of Lykia, and their obverses are simply a somewhat overblown version of the Rhodian Apollo head; but the reverses are interesting as they represent the 319 cult statue of Zeus Labraundos equipped with spear and double-axe. This statuesque type is also seen on a small gold coin of 305, 30 Maussollos' successor Pixodaros, with an obverse of Apollo in profile.

In Pamphylia, the important mint of Aspendos began in the fourth century B.C. to produce a new type of coin depicting a 320 pair of wrestlers, preserving as part of the reverse the solar triskelis from the older coinage. The other city of this region was Side, which notably enough possessed its own special language written in a semi-Semitic script that has not yet been fully deciphered; this appears on the fourth century coins beside a fine Apollo standing before an altar—a good example of the many statuesque figures that appear on coins of southern Asia Minor. Further along the coast, in Cilicia, the city of Aphrodisias seems to be the mint of a fine stater showing a standing Athena and a seated Aphrodite. The latter, who is also figured on coins of Nagidos, is shown here reclining in diaphanous robes rather sumptuously on a throne flanked by two sphinxes, and raising a flower in her hand. She makes the impression of an oriental goddess. Whether or not she reproduces a large-scale prototype, it is clear that the Athena on the other side of the coin does so, quite clearly recalling the Athena Parthenos of Pheidias at Athens; she has the triple crested helmet, the typical attitude and dress, the shield at her side and Nike on her extended right hand. The only element which may be an addition by the die-engraver would be the olive tree placed below her hand as a support, for the existence of a support on the original has been a matter of much dispute.

Yet another Athenian statue seems to underlie the figure who appears on a Cypriote coin of the early fourth century, but this time it is the earlier Pheidian work, the colossal Promachos who stood out-of-doors on the Athenian Akropolis. The reverse of this coin has a Herakles wielding bow and club with the lionskin draped across his back, and on the right a legend in Phoenician script denoting the coin as of Demonikos, king of Lapethos, while below is an Egyptian *ankh* sign frequently met

with in Cyprus. The coin has a historical importance for the history of Demonikos, who had formerly been confidently (and wrongly) placed at Kition on account of the coin type of Herakles, also used there. The coins bear many signs of the admixture of cultures which is found in Cyprus, and even those which are purely Greek in style still bear inscriptions in the old and rather clumsy syllabic notation which had survived from the Bronze Age. Thus on a small and attractive gold coin of Euagoras I of Sal- amis, with a charming youthful Herakles in facing view, and a recumbent goat on the reverse, there is a legend reading *E u va go ro Pa si le vo se,* as the equivalent of the normal Greek *Euagorou Basileos.*

The spread of Greek-style coinage into regions which were beyond the normal scope of Greek culture or institutions shows many interesting features of cultural admixture. At Tarsos, for instance, several Persian satraps during the fourth century minted copiously for their own military expenses, and such are the coins of Tiribazos, Datames, Pharnabazos, Mazaios. A splendid example is the coin of Datames (378–372 B.C.) on which we see a seated figure of the satrap in full Persian dress, testing an arrow for his bow. His name in Aramaic letters *tdnmu* appears behind and in front of the small winged sun-disk familiar in Persian art. Yet the satrap figure in itself remains predominantly Greek in treatment, as does the god (Baal Tars) on the obverse who with his attributes of vine and corn seems to be a vegetation deity, surrounded by a border representing the fortifications of the city. Tarsos has close connexions with Phoenicia, and some coin types are shared with, for instance, Tyre; notably the figure of Melqart, the

328 Phoenician Herakles, riding over the sea on a hippocamp; here, however, the reverse of

329 a hieratic owl with the Egyptian crook and flail evokes a further blend of cultures. A more obviously Greek style is found in an attractive coin of Byblos; the galley with armed men and a hippocamp and shell

330, 331 below, together with the reverse of the older lion and bull, make the impression of something that, in Greece, would be of the archaic period, but this is a coin of fourth century Phoenicia and is inscribed with the name of Adramelek, king of Gebal (Byblos). A more distinctively 'Persian' character seems to attach to certain coins of Sidon. A shekel of the early fourth century, with an obverse of a fortified town by the sea, has a most interesting reverse which, with small alterations, might come from Perse-

332 polis—a king or hero slaying a lion. The king is very like the comparable figure on the Achaemenid coinage, but here holds a dagger against his heraldic foe. The letters *bd* give an elusive clue to the name of a

333 local dynast. A double-shekel of Sidon ascribed to the reign of Bod'ashtart (384–370 B.C.) shows a chariot conveying a kingly figure while another figure, at first sight an Egyptian, follows on foot; the latter has recently been explained as the king of Sidon following the procession of Sidonian Baal who rides in the car. The whole design has an unmistakeably Achaemenid flavour.

315, 316 Lykia, Mithrapata: *Portrait head of Mithrapata/Forepart of lion, c. 380-370 B.C. (stater, 10.02 gm., diam. 22 mm., BM 1958; from the Podalia hoard, 1957)*

317 Lykia, Päriklä: *Facing head of Päriklä, c. 370-360 B.C. (stater, 9.53 gm., diam. 23 mm., BM 1964; from the Podalia hoard, 1957)*

318 Lykia, Zagabaha: *Facing head of Athena, copied from Syracusan type, c. 390-380 B.C. (third-stater, 3.03 gm., diam. 15 mm., BM 1959; from the Podalia hoard, 1957)*

319 Karia, Maussollis: *Standing figure of Zeus Labraundos with spear and double-axe, 377-353 B.C. (tetradrachm, 15.07 gm., diam. 25 mm., BMC 7; RPK)*

320 Aspendos: *Wrestlers, c. 373-350 B.C. (stater, 10.88 gm., diam. 21 mm., BM 1948)*

321 Side: *Apollo standing (inscription in local language), c. 360-333 B.C. (stater, 10.69 gm., diam. 20 mm., BMC 18; Atlan 153)*

322, 323 Aphrodisias: *Aphrodite, holding a flower, seated on throne flanked by sphinxes/Athena Parthenos, c. 350 B.C. (stater, 9.88 gm., diam. 22-24 mm., PCG 19.48)*

315

316

317

318

319

320

321

322

323

324

325

326

327

328

329

330

331

332

333

334

324, 325 Cyprus, Lapethos: *Athena standing with shield and spear/Herakles brandishing club and bow, with inscription in the name of King Demonikos*, c. *380-360 B.C. (stater, 9.28 gm., diam. 17 x 21 mm., PCG 51.6)*

326, 327 Tarsos: *Seated figure of Baal Tars holding grapes and corn ear, within a border of battlements/Persian satrap Datames seated, holding arrow, with the bow on the right ; above, small Ahuramazda symbol*, *378-372 B.C. (stater, 10.34 gm., diam. 23-24 mm., BMC 32 ; from the Oxus Treasure, 1877)*

328, 329 Tyre: *Melqart, with bow, riding on hippocamp ; waves and fishes below, cable border/Owl with crook and flail, cable border*, c. *400 B.C. (double-shekel, 13.37 gm., diam. 24 mm., from the Babylon hoard, see* Iraq, *1950)*

330, 331 Byblos: *Galley with armed men ; below hippocamp and shell/Lion attacking bull, with inscription of King Adramelek above*, c. *350 B.C. (double-shekel, 13.19 gm., diam. 26-25 mm., PCG 51.7)*

332 Sidon: *'Persian King' confronting standing lion*, c. *400 B.C. (reverse of shekel, 6.28 gm., diam. 18 mm., formerly Naville sale, XII, Geneva, 1926, 2006)*

333 Sidon: *Horse-drawn chariot containing king or god, attendant following on foot*, *384-370 B.C. (reverse of triple-shekel, 28.04 gm., diam. 28 mm., BMC 20)*

334 Egypt: *Owl and olive spray as on Athenian coins, with Egyptian demotic inscription mentioning 'Tachos.....pharaoh'*, c. *380-360 B.C. (reverse of tetradrachm, 15.41 gm., diam. 23 mm., PCG 51.11)*

Other coinages in the pre-Hellenistic Near East tended to follow to some extent models culled from the coins of Athens, which played such an important role as a sort of universal currency in the Persian empire, and as such recognizable derivatives are met with in Palestine and Philistia. As has been remarked above, Athenian coins had also long been reaching Egypt, though only in isolated cases do there seem to be authentic local adaptations of them. One such is a unique silver tetradrachm of 334 the early fourth century of unquestionably Egyptian origin. The typical owl of the reverse appears somewhat transformed but the important feature is the legend which is here written in Egyptian demotic characters; it is not quite complete on the coin but has been read as signifying 'Tachos, officer of the Pharaoh'. It is not certain if this Tachos can be identified with the Pharaoh of that name who joined the satraps' revolt in 360 B.C. and who minted a Greek-inscribed gold coin of Athenian type. At all events the demotic tetradrachm remains an isolated example of a truly Egyptian coinage, the only other being the gold 559, 560 pieces minted later by Nektanebo II with hieroglyphic designs.

The growth of gold coinage in the Greek world is one of the significant phenomena of the fourth century B.C., especially in northern Greece and Asia Minor, and it is a development that also has a certain importance at Kyrene—whose silver coinage, as we have seen, played a special role in the currency of Crete. The bulk of the gold coinage of Kyrene is of fairly late date, 309-14 during the time of Alexander, yet is in form and style wholly of the classical period. Minted on the Attic standard, this gold shows signs of the influence of Sicilian coinage in the prevalence of chariot designs which, however, are not mere imitations, save perhaps one where the chariot is run- 310, 389 ning in a manner first invented at Syracuse about 425 B.C. In another the horses are 314 walking, and the sun is indicated shining above; again there is a version of the chariot seen stationary but head-on in the archaic 77 manner of Euboian Chalkis, the charioteer 312 being Nike as we can see from her outspread wings. The other sides of these gold coins are devoted to Zeus Ammon, but as a figure type and not, as on the silver, his head. Sometimes he holds a small Nike on his hand, and has the sacred ram standing be- 309 side him; or he stands at an altar with a 313 patera for sacrifice. In both these he wears the ram's horns on his head. In another version, in which the god relaxes on an elaborate throne, he wears no horns and, with the eagle on his right hand, seems to be the Greek Zeus rather than the Egyptian Ammon, recalling the Zeus on the coins of 311, 49 Alexander.

V. SICILY — FIFTH AND FOURTH CENTURIES

The coins of fifth century Sicily form so characteristic a contribution to Greek art that they deserve to be considered separately and as a homogeneous series, impressive for the brilliance and originality of its scope and development. As we have seen, the influence of Sicilian coins was widely felt in other parts of the Greek world, and it is clear that their appeal must have been on aesthetic grounds. Imitations of Sicilian coins, produced at mints in Greece and Asia Minor, were not made because these were coins familiar in ordinary currency, since coins of Sicily had virtually no circulation in the eastern Mediterranean; though no doubt specimens may have been brought to Greece by individuals, such as diplomats or returning mercenaries.

A considerable impetus was given to the development of coinage by the brilliant court of the tyrants, of whom Gelon made Syracuse his capital in 485 B.C. At about 355 this time we see the four-horse chariot given a new look, rendered in subtler planes, with Nike in diaphanous archaic draperies hovering above. Even more fraught with artistic promise is the way in which the tiny head of Artemis now bursts from the confinement of the incuse square to become a self-subsistent type framed by circling dolphins, symbolically expressing the dwell- 356 ing place of the goddess. For she is not only Artemis but, by assimilation, also Arethusa, who in the mythology was pursued by the river-god Alpheios in the Peloponnese but passing under the sea re-emerged as the nymph of the freshwater spring on the island of Ortygia, the original site of Syracuse. The subsequent variations of this theme which appear on the Syracusan coins are almost infinite. During the time when Gelon ruled (485–478 B.C.) and defeated the great Carthaginian invasion in 480 at Himera, this coinage was minted in vast quantities, mostly tetradrachms.

In one instance, however, a larger piece, the dekadrachm, was struck as a special issue. It is a coin of extraordinary quality. 357, 358 The horses on the obverse are walking with a decided forward lunge of their lean bodies, as the charioteer crouches tensely above as if to inspire them to real action, while Nike descends from the skies to place her wreath on their heads. Below, in the exergue, is a running lion once thought to symbolize the defeat of Carthage but whose true explanation is more difficult to find. It is, however, the Arethusa head which makes the coin the masterpiece it is; encircled by dolphins which move in one direction, against the inscription moving in the opposite direction. At once firm and delicate in modelling, the head has a subtlety and inner life which pervades every detail; the eye preserves still the archaic frontal form, the hair—crowned with an olive wreath as for victory—moves in precise undulations with a loose lock trailing behind the ear, while the waves above the forehead are echoed on the far side in such a way as to hint that we can almost see round to that side too, giving a depth to the composition.

The precise place of this wonderful creation in the series of Syracusan coins, its exact date and significance, are today less easy to define than used to be thought. The coin has long been regarded as the 'Demareteion' mentioned by the sources, a coin weighing fifty silver litrai minted at the behest of Demarete, Gelon's queen, who is supposed to have intervened on behalf of the vanquished Carthaginians after their defeat in 480 B.C. Recently this tradition has been under attack and somewhat later dates proposed for the coin, though the question can hardly be said to be settled. But whether minted in 480 B.C. or later, the intrinsic beauty of the coin itself is unaffected. We cannot make any plausible guesses about the artist responsible for it, who seems to be distinct from those who regularly worked on the Syracusan coinage; but it seems likely that we have another work from his hand, in the shape of a fine tetradrachm, no doubt minted at the same time, of Leontinoi a city which during the tyranny was closely connected with Syracuse. Here we have the head of Apollo showing much of the same quality even down to details of treatment—for instance the loose lock of hair behind the ear and the delicate suggestion of the hair on the far side of the brow. The Apollo is framed by a group of bay leaves, corresponding to the dolphins of Arethusa, and below is a lion which also recalls that below the Syracusan chariot. Here, at Leontinoi, the lion has a clear explanation both as a verbal allusion to the city's name and as the sacred animal of Apollo the sun-god, and as such, on a slightly later series of Leontinoi coins, we see a lion's head on one side forming the counterpart to the Apollo head. This lion head is a splendid sculptural creation vividly recalling the waterspouts which are a feature of Greek temple architecture; and again there is the device of the frame, here composed of corn grains. The later Apollo head dating to 466 B.C. after the end of the tyranny retains some archaic features and in general stems from the style of the Demareteion and its Leontinoi counterpart though it is of a fresh and very unusual style, some details being given a more modern treatment, such as the eye in true profile with the pupil modelled and the upper lashes clearly indicated.

The continuation of the regular mint tradition at Syracuse, however, seems to owe little to the Demareteion, as can be seen from a tetradrachm which does not quite break out from archaic conventions, with its gravely formal head and the chariot horses still rather stolid and heavy. Below them is a ketos or sea-monster which has been thought to be an allusion to the great sea victory won by Gelon's brother and successor Hieron over the Etruscans at Kymai in 474 B.C. and the creature retains its place on the coins for a generation, so that it is likely to have had some special significance.

Two other masterpieces stand out from the early classical period in Sicily, the tetra-drachms of Aitna and of Naxos. Aitna was the name of Hieron's Dorian colony at Katane which he founded after expelling its original inhabitants in 476 B.C.; the colony was short-lived and did not long survive the fall of the tyranny at Syracuse, but one coin produced during that time is among the most splendid of all the achievements of Greek coinage. A single specimen survives. The obverse is an astonishingly vigorous and strong head of Silenus full of animal ruggedness yet expressed with precision and restraint, the snub nose and horse ears, an immense bushy beard and smooth bald cranium, on which a wreath of ivy leaves is lightly etched as if to contrast with the powerful sculptural forms of the head. Below, a scarabaeus beetle stands for the typical local fauna of Mount Aetna. On the reverse we see Zeus enthroned on a carved seat covered with a leopard skin, his robe neatly stacked in semi-archaic folds, holding a winged thunderbolt in his left hand and a jagged staff in the right. One leg is withdrawn below the seat and the solid forms of the body are well revealed through the robe. In front the picture is completed by a lofty fir tree on which perches the sacred eagle. It seems likely that this outstanding coin was minted towards the end of the period of Hieron's Aitna. Its overwhelming quality may be due to a sculptor from Greece, as its affinities are with Attic art rather than with anything in Sicily.

It is likely enough that the same artist, or someone very close to him, was responsible a few years later for the almost equally magnificent design of a coin of Naxos, a city which recovered from the devastations of the Syracusan tyrants only towards 461 B.C. The head of Dionysos, god of the vine, which flourished locally, had adorned the earlier Naxian coins. Here it achieves a new and impressive brilliance; like the Aitna Silenus, encircled by an ivy wreath, there is throughout a slightly freer rendering, in the forms of the long hair, bound up at the back of the head, in the beard jutting across the border in a way that gives an added depth, and in the expressiveness of the mouth with its hint of a smile. Even surpassing the head, however, is the squatting Silenus of the reverse, a figure in whose pose and modelling there is a complete sculptural mastery, with a skilful foreshortening of the right foot. The whole composition has an intense vitality and expressiveness which is interesting to compare with the Aitna coin and which certainly has no other equal, making it one of the assured masterpieces of Greek art of this time.

The city of Katane, which had been drastically converted into Hieron's Aitna, was restored to its own inhabitants at about the same time as Naxos, and for a few years produced some remarkable and unusual

369 coins; on one side Nike is seen alighting with a wreath in her hand, and there is still a touch of the archaic in this exquisite figure which has led some scholars to place the issue at an earlier date, before the tyranny. But it is now clear that these coins date to the time of Katane's restoration. On the other side, the local river-god, the

368 Amenanos, is depicted, as at Gela, in the form of a man-faced bull, whose attitude suggests swimming and whose watery surroundings are indicated by the fish placed below or, as here, by a sea-monster. An intriguing fancy is the Silenus figure who is seen leaping over the bull like a Minoan bull-jumper. This coinage was deliberately replaced towards 450 B.C. by a new type, more on the Syracusan model with an obverse of a horse-drawn chariot, but without the Nike flying above. The head at Katane,

370 like that at Leontinoi, was of Apollo and we can observe a considerable interweaving of artistic traditions through the fifth century at the two Chalkidian cities. The early Katane Apollo combines a high degree of formalization with a new sense of freedom and vitality, that characteristic tension which makes the early classical period so attractive. The very regular form of the head with the incised lines of the hair conforming almost exactly to its shape, save the more elaborately curled ends; and the expressiveness of the mouth and the eyes, which are most minutely drawn with every eyelash in place.

A contemporary Syracusan head has

371 many similar features but yet a recognizably

335 ▶
336▶▶

337 ▶

335 Gela: *River-god Gelas, with corn-grain, 405 B.C. (dilitron, 1.75 gm., diam. 11 mm., PCG 15.26; RPK; Jenkins 490), reverse of 344*

336, 337 Syracuse: *Arethusa head by Euainetos/ Herakles fighting lion, c. 390-380 B.C. (100-litra, 5.78 gm., diam. 15 mm., Lloyd 1422)*

338   339   340   341

342   343   344

345   346   347   348

349   350

351   352   353   354

338, 339 Akragas: *Eagle and hare/Crab and fish, 406 B.C. (dilitron, 1.74 gm., diam. 13 mm., BM 1956)*

340, 341 Akragas: *Eagle with snake/Crab, with name Silanos, 406 B.C. (diobol?, 340: 1.32 gm., diam. 11 mm., BM 1907; 341: 1.34 gm., diam. 11 mm., Lloyd 815)*

342, 343 Kamarina: *Athena head with hippocamp on helmet/Olive-sprig, 405 B.C. (1 ¹/₃-litra, 1.17 gm., diam. 11 mm., PCG 14.27; from the Catania hoard, 1875)*

344 Gela: *Horseman, 405 B.C. (dilitron, 1.75 gm., diam. 11 mm., PCG 15.26; RPK; Jenkins 490), obverse of 335*

345, 346 Syracuse: *Herakles head/Small female head in quartered square, c. 405 B.C. (1 ¹/₃-litra, 345: 1.16 gm., diam. 10 mm., BMC 135; RPK; 346: 1.14 gm., diam. 10 mm., PCG 17.61; RPK)*

347, 348 Syracuse: *Athena head/Gorgon on aegis, c. 405 B.C. (obol?, 347: 0.69 gm., diam. 9 mm., Lloyd 1418; 348: 0.64 gm., diam. 9 mm., Lloyd 1417)*

349 Syracuse: *Arethusa head, star, c. 390-380 B.C. (100-litra, obverse, 5.79 gm., diam. 14 mm., Lloyd 1421)*

350 Syracuse: *Herakles and lion, c. 390-380 B.C. (100-litra, reverse, 5.79 gm., diam. 14 mm., BM 1891; from the Avola hoard)*

351, 352 Syracuse: *Head of Anapos/Horse, c. 390-380 B.C. (50-litra, 2.88 gm., diam. 11 mm., PCG 17.63; RPK)*

353, 354 Syracuse: *Zeus Eleutherios/Pegasos, with three pellets below, 344-317 B.C. (hemidrachm, 2.13 gm., diam. 12 mm., PCG 26.36; RPK)*

different character, for which analogies have been sought in the art of Corinth. To the same artistic milieu belong the coins of Gela, whose tetradrachms of *c.* 450 B.C. have close analogies with both Syracuse and Katane. The river-god bull at Gela even shows many stylistic affinities to some of the contemporary Arethusa heads at Syracuse, suggesting that some of the same artists may have worked at both cities. A rather exceptional piece, also from Gela, **372, 373** shows a powerfully modelled river-god accompanied by a goddess placing a wreath on his head; she is Sosipolis, a local deity also depicted at a later date on some gold coins, and whose presence seems to mark some special occasion—perhaps the victory over Duketios in 440 B.C. alluded to again on a Syracusan coin. The Sosipolis coin, however, may have been the work of an engraver from Himera, and stands apart from the usual style of eastern Sicily.

The Syracusan chariot type was gradually becoming the characteristic mark of most Sicilian coins, and Himera and Selinus, which had been the earliest mints in the island, were no exception. Both cities inaugurated new coinages after the period of the tyranny and in other respects their style is rather different from that of eastern Sicily. Himera, released from the grip of the Akragantine tyrants in 472 B.C., proceeded to mint coins showing the chariot **374** of Pelops—whose name, after the fashion of the vase-painters, is inscribed above; this may simply be evidence of a local cult of this hero, or more recondite may serve as an allusion to Olympia, where in the mythology Pelops had by a trick killed Oinomaos in a chariot race. If so, there may be some connection with the fact that Ergoteles, a Himerean, had about this time won a victory in the Olympic games. The reverse is also interesting, as here we see Himera personified standing in her array of elaborate and rather archaic pleated garments, holding out her cloak, though her gesture, apparently of welcome, may conceal some lost mythological allusion. Another Himerean figure, of a slightly later date, forms part of a more complex scene; here again she has a rather archaic-looking dress, a light chiton covered by one or two other garments. She is sacrificing before an altar and seems to be caught in an attractive momentary gesture as she swings round with a patera in her hand. Above, a corn grain seems to be a mere filling ornament. But on the right we see a most interesting group consisting of a satyr standing in a basin washing below a fountain which pours from a lion-head spout; the engraver's acute observation is strikingly apparent in the fact that we can see the legs of the satyr diffracted in the water. This bathing satyr must stand as a reference to the hot springs at Thermai in the vicinity of Himera, with the local nymph as the presiding genius.

Of a somewhat similar aspect is the figure which we see on the contemporary coins of Selinus. Here it is a naked male figure who is seen sacrificing in a sacred precinct. The altar is bound with a fillet and a sacrificial cock stands ready. On the other side is a monument of a bull on a plinth. The naked youth, who holds a lus-

tral branch in his left hand, is the river-god Selinus, here portrayed in fully human form but with the small bull's horns sprouting from his forehead. A similar humanized version of the river-god, formerly always depicted as a man-faced bull, is met with again at Gela and elsewhere. The exceptionally fine rendering of the spare muscular forms of the body is a remarkable piece of work dating to about 460 B.C. strongly recalling the famous bronze *kouros* (itself probably a Selinuntine work) preserved at Castelvetrano. It is however only a matter of conjecture whether these coins were in fact derived from sculptural prototypes. The composition is completed by the appearance of the *selinon* leaf—the old civic emblem of Selinus—now reduced to a small appendage in the field. The whole scene has obvious analogies to the water-nymph of Himera. It used to be thought that the scene with the river-god Selinus should be interpreted as an allusion to the legend of Empedokles and his purification of the Selinuntine marshes, but this idea is now generally discounted. The reverse of the didrachm gives us a companion piece showing the god of the other Selinuntine river, the Hypsas, in a similar vein.

The obverse of the Selinus tetradrachm presents an interesting variant of the chariot type for the charioteer is no mere mortal; instead we see that the chariot is driven by Artemis with her brother Apollo standing beside her aiming with his bow. Again in some later coins at Syracuse, Kamarina and elsewhere we find a chariot

375

376

377

378

driven by a god. The obverse of the didrachm, however, is very different, a group 379 of Herakles performing one of his canonical labours, the vanquishing of the Cretan bull. The composition is one which strongly suggests relief sculpture and would be highly suitable, for instance, to a temple metope; a rather freer version of the same basic 270 theme is also to be seen on a Thessalian coin of the early fourth century. This Herakles group, not only highly appropriate to a Dorian colony, has a special relevance at Selinus, whose public seal apparently bore a similar device of Herakles grasping a bull by the horn and raising his club to subdue the animal.

If the Pelops chariot at Himera was conceivably be related to an Olympic victory, the main design of the coins of Messana, a chariot drawn by mules, certainly does so. We have it on the authority of Aristotle that the coins showing the mule-team commemorate the victory with the mule-team gained by Anaxilas, tyrant of the two cities Rhegion and Messana, about 480 B.C. (and whose earlier coin types we have seen above). The identical coinage was for a time minted at both cities, but after the end of the tyranny (in 461 B.C.) this type was abandoned at Rhegion; Messana however maintained it, except for a brief interval also about 460 B.C., until the end of the 0, 381 fifth century. The mule-car is here shown in a comparatively late version from the 420's B.C., in which some rudiments of a perspective treatment have been worked in, especially as regards the chariot wheels. The lively hare on the reverse probably

owes his presence to being the animal of Pan, whose head appears below, and who on one occasion makes an appearance as a complete seated figure, anticipating that of the fourth century Arkadian league coins.

An exceptional issue of Gela dating to about 425 B.C. is a didrachm on which a mounted cavalryman is shown in the act of 383 riding down a hoplite—a warlike scene probably connected with the war of 427–424 B.C., in which Gela was involved as an ally of Syracuse against an attempted Athenian intervention. The composition is somewhat strange and the hoplite rather curiously placed in relation to the horse, whose hindquarters do not appear at all; the problem of the juxtaposition has been perceived but not entirely solved. By contrast there is on the reverse a head which is that of the 384 river-god Gelas in a rare appearance in human form, such as we have seen in the river-gods of Selinus; the head—which might be an Apollo but for the bull's horn above the brow and the bull's ears—has a grave and rather formal aspect allied to a considerable degree of sensitivity. Some have suspected that the engraver may be following some prototype from sculpture of an earlier date. In any case the head is startlingly dissimilar from an almost contemporary Apollo from Katane which with its restless hair and expressive alert face conveys an impression of the utmost vi- 385 vacity. An obverse of Katane of the same period shows an interesting though ten- 382 tative attempt at giving some sense of movement to the horses by means of the upward rearing attitude; this particular scheme clearly owes something to the horses of the Parthenon frieze, though it had already been tried out briefly on coins of Syracuse about 440 B.C.

As for the Syracusan coinage, its prolific series of delightful and varied Arethusa heads—a veritable procession of *korai*—had continued to pour from the mint without interruption, though the main scheme remained more or less unaltered until about 425 B.C. We are hardly aware of outside influences, so inexhaustible seems the invention of the Syracusan artists with the infinite variety of heads each differing from the next in coiffure and individuality. Just before 440 B.C. there is a girl with a wide band holding a tightly coiled hair-do which has a kind of 'early Victorian' charm. A near-contemporary of hers has her hair tied up in a topknot like Nike and for the first time has a more elaborate spiral ear-ring in place of the plain drop-type hitherto used. Another type has her hair almost entirely enclosed by a *sakkos*, a cap decorated with maeander patterns and with the hint of an olive wreath above the brow—a token of some victory, perhaps that which the Syracusans and their allies had won over the formidable Sikel leader Duketios in 440 B.C. In every case there is a meticulous care in the execution of details and full use is made of the decorative potentialities of the surrounding dolphins and the lettering. The numerous unknown artists who created this series of *korai* were to be followed by others who, in the more expansive and sophisticated atmosphere at the end of the fifth century, have attained a degree of

355, 356 Syracuse: *Four-horse chariot walking, with Nike above alighting with wreath/Head of Artemis-Arethusa with four dolphins, c. 490-485 B.C. (tetradrachm, 17.08 gm., diam. 27 mm., PCG 7.30 ; RPK ; Boehringer 46)*

357, 358 Syracuse: *Four-horse chariot walking, with Nike flying down above and, below, lion at bay/Head of Artemis-Arethusa wearing olive-wreath, with dolphins, c. 480 B.C. (deka-drachm, 44.43 gm., diam. 33×35 mm., PCG 16.54 ; Boehringer 376)*

359 Leontinoi: *Head of Apollo, with three laurel leaves around and lion at bay below, c. 480 B.C. (tetradrachm, reverse, 16.35 gm., diam. 27 mm., PCG 15.44 ; RPK)*

360, 361 Leontinoi: *Head of Apollo/Lion's head with four corn-grains, c. 460 B.C. (tetradrachm, obverse: 17.46 gm., diam. 25 mm., Lloyd 1055, from the Selinunte hoard, 1925 ; reverse: 17.28 gm., diam. 24 mm., BM 1949)*

362, 363 Syracuse: *Four-horse chariot with Nike, and Ketos below/Arethusa head with pearled hair-band, c. 470 B.C. (tetradrachm, 17.33 gm., diam. 27-26 mm., BMC 71 ; Boehringer 409)*

364, 365 Aitna: *Head of Silenos, with scarab-beetle below/Zeus enthroned, holding thunderbolt, with eagle on fir tree, c. 470-465 (tetradrachm, 17.23 gm., diam. 25 mm., Brussels ; de Hirsch 269)*

355

356

357

358

359

360

361

362

363

364

365

366

367

368

369

370

371

372

373

374

375

376

377

366, 367 Naxos: *Head of Dionysos/Squatting Sil-*
enos with wine-cup, c. *460 B.C. (tetradrachm,*
17.44 gm., diam. 27 mm., PCG 15.48 ; Cahn
54)

368 Katane: *River-god Amenanos with Silenos*
above and Ketos below, c. *460 B.C. (tetra-*
drachm, obverse, 17.19 gm., diam. 26 mm.,
Lloyd 887)

369 Katane: *Nike with wreath*, c. *460 B.C. (tetra-*
drachm, reverse, 17.29 gm., diam. 25 mm.,
PCG 7.20)

370 Katane: *Head of Apollo*, c. *460-450 B.C.*
(tetradrachm, reverse, 17.21 gm., diam. 26 mm.,
Lloyd 892)

371 Syracuse: *Arethusa head with dolphins*, c. *460*
B.C. (tetradrachm, reverse, 17.27 gm., diam.
26 mm., BMC 72 ; Boehringer 481)

372, 373 Gela: *Four-horse chariot with Nike/*
River-god Gelas with Sosipolis, c. *440 B.C.*
(tetradrachm, 17.15 gm., diam. 29 mm.,
Käppeli collection ; Jenkins 371)

374, 375 Himera: *Chariot of Pelops, with palm-*
branch below/The nymph Himera, c. *472 B.C.*
(tetradrachm, obverse: 17.12 gm., diam. 24
mm., PCG 15.40 ; reverse: 17.31 gm., diam.
24 mm., Lloyd 1016)

376 Himera: *Nymph sacrificing at altar, with satyr*
in fountain, c. *450 B.C. (tetradrachm, reverse,*
17.13 gm., diam. 27 mm., Lloyd 1019 ; Gut-
mann-Schwabacher 15 ; from the Selinunte
hoard, 1925)

377 Selinus: *River-god sacrificing at altar, with*
bull monument, 467-445 B.C. (tetradrachm,
reverse, 17.04 gm., diam. 27 mm., Lloyd 1221 ;
Schwabacher 3 ; from the Selinunte hoard, 1925)

personal immortality by signing their works with their own names.

The last quarter of the fifth century brings us to the climax of the art of coinage in Sicily. We can for a time follow the progress of individual artists and glimpse something of their personalities as they transform older themes into new forms. Syracuse retained a position of primacy though we can by no means neglect the achievements of other cities of Sicily and there is some interchange of artists between cities. The existing tradition of Sicilian coinage became enriched and extended by new and bold experiments, which have parallels in the other arts.

The first of the new developments at Syracuse seems to have been due to a pair of artists whose names were Sosion and Eumenes, and who began work about 425 B.C. They seem to be close associates and would be difficult to tell apart without the signatures. Their first innovation is to free the chariot type from its old static mould and to infuse it with a rapid movement; it is remarkable that although as far back as the sixth century Greek vase painters had made successful attempts at showing fast-moving chariots, this had scarcely been tried on coins, with a few isolated exceptions. On the first of the new dies, probably by Sosion, the row of horses is extended in a fan-like formation, all the legs very regular, and spaced out from the nearest to the farthest. It cannot be called a real perspective treatment, as each further horse is merely placed more forward; and the composition is built up basically by the

389

same means that had been employed for the chariot groups in the Parthenon frieze, each element seen in direct view yet giving a definite effect of depth to the whole. This first solution to the problem is found only on the coins of Syracuse and of Kamarina (possibly also the work of Sosion); exact parallels are not really found in sculpture though the same scheme does sometimes appear in vase-paintings towards the end of the century.

390 Both Sosion and Eumenes also signed dies with heads, of which an example by Eumenes is typical. Deriving ultimately from the head type used on Syracusan coins of earlier generations, we find here a quite new freshness of feeling—the girl has an expression of rather endearing solemnity, her hair elaborately bound and rolled, with some loose strands on the neck which are a sort of fingerprint of the style of this artist. His signature is to be found on the hair-band above the brow. The ear-ring is of the spiral form which had come in on some of the earlier heads. The way in which the dolphins are placed is an innovation, for almost always hitherto they had formed a continuous circle around the head, and here they are shown in pairs in front and behind, while the 'frame' is completed only by the lettering. A similar layout is adopted for another head perhaps also by Eumenes but without the signature. Here we have not only a different model but the treatment of the hair makes a quite 391 different effect—it is bound in place with cords and the loose ends are partly tied in a topknot but partly flutter loose, forming a

striking and restless pattern which anticipates a more famous later work by Eukleidas. Yet another head of this period and 392 perhaps by one of the same artists or a close associate has a form which in general is similar to that of the signed Eumenes head, even down to the loose locks on the neck, but the proportions and treatment are again very different and show how wide a range of expression could be derived from a single basic type.

Towards 415 B.C. when Eumenes was still active, other fresh personalities, Eukleidas and Euainetos, begin to make their appearance at the Syracusan mint. The former began very much in the style of Eumenes but soon broke away from this prototype and together with Euainetos began to revolutionize even more profoundly the whole aspect of the coinage. Mainly to Euainetos are due some radical innovations in the chariot scheme which bring us much closer to a real feeling of perspective and at the same time of a real and not merely apparent sense of speed and movement. His first chariot shows very 393 well the direction of this development. The horses are no longer arranged on a strict symmetrical row, and the far-side horse seems to be breaking away—literally so, as indicated by the broken trailing rein— while the hooves make a more jagged and irregular pattern, none of them in fact quite touching the ground line. Equally important, the charioteer and the chariot are shown in a definite three-quarter profile complete with the offside wheel, which was never the case with the first animated chariots of Sosion. The angle of the chariot is indeed sharper than that of the horses, which are still seen more or less straight, though the discrepancy hardly matters, so well are the elements blended together. By such empirical steps did the Greek artist feel his way towards the understanding of true perspective. Below, in the exergue, is shown a wheel which has evidently fallen from another chariot, presumably wrecked in the race—a touch which adds to the vivid picture of an exciting and dangerous moment. On this die the name of Euainetos is concealed in minuscule letters along the exergual line, scarcely legible except through a microscope; but on his next die the artist

394 leaves nothing to chance and proclaims his name on a tablet held aloft by the Nike flying above. Here Euainetos has perhaps achieved a greater harmonization of the elements in his composition and the effect, though smoother, has somewhat less of dramatic exuberance, although the far-side horse is again shown having broken its rein.

395 The head on this coin is an undoubted masterpiece of Euainetos' style and quite unequalled by a similar head which Eukleidas produced at about the same time; the elegant sophistication and rich treatment of detail combined with a minute delicacy and restraint, all set a new standard among the Sicilian coins. The sensitively modelled face is well set off by the free yet orderly arrangement of the hair, bound behind in a sphendone decorated with stars and in front with a tiny dolphin leaping over waves, with a few locks fluttering loose.

A *tour de force* of minute engraving is accomplished by the appearance, on the body of the dolphin in front of the mouth, of the signature *EVAI*.

Still further artists who at this point began to make their contribution to the rich and expressive new style of Syracusan coin include Phrygillos; who about 413 B.C.

396 gives us a head with the attributes and symbolism really belonging to Persephone the goddess of the underworld, whose cult was of such importance in Sicily. Here she wears a wreath of corn ears interwoven with an oak leaf and a poppy head; but the setting is still the frame of dolphins characteristic of Arethusa, and it is not easy to be sure how we should identify this goddess. The signature of Phrygillos, only partly visible, is here placed below the neck. The corresponding chariot was made by another

397 hand, identified only by his abbreviated name *Euth . . .*; here we see a firm grasp of the principles of the new perspective composition, in which the nearer horse partly obscures the chariot wheel while the spread of the four horses is well emphasized, helping to give the impression that they are advancing across the field of view. This remarkable die is closely paralleled by a very similar chariot at Selinus, which can be dated to 410 B.C. just before the Carthaginian invasion, and this in turn affords a valuable peg for the chronology of the Syracusan series. The charioteer on the *Euth . . .* die is a winged figure, seemingly a naked youth who may perhaps be Eros (or Agon) but in any case no mere mortal. Below is depicted Skylla with her dogs and

fishtail; above, Nike carries not only a wreath but also in her left hand an *aphlaston*, the stern-ornament of a warship and an invariable emblem of naval victory. This detail recurs on other dies at this period, and has been thought to refer to the final defeat of the Athenian armada in the great harbour of Syracuse in 413 B.C.

398 Phrygillos followed his 'Persephone' with another head of such different style that we would hardly know it to be by the hand if we had not the signature, here incorporated in the head-band. However, this is not the only instance which proves that the same artist could work in more than one manner, and which makes it hazardous to conjecture too much about the identity of artists. (In the case of Phrygillos it is specially difficult to be sure whether we have the right to assign to him also certain coins of Terina and Thourioi, as has been suggested.) The second Phrygillos head, it will be noticed, is placed on the obverse of the coin, a definite break with the previous technical procedure of the Syracuse mint, and the chariot accordingly becomes the reverse. The idea may well have been that as the obverse die is set in the anvil it is thus better protected against possible damage in the process of striking, especially if the die is engraved in high relief. This might well be a good reason for placing a head on the obverse, but in fact the degree of relief used at Syracuse is hardly ever so pronounced as for instance at Rhegion or Amphipolis. But no doubt individual engravers had their own preferences. It is noteworthy

399 that on the chariot side we now have

378 Selinus: *Chariot of Apollo and Artemis, 467-445 B.C. (tetradrachm, obverse, 17.31 gm., diam. 30 mm., Lloyd 1230; Schwabacher 11; from the Selinunte hoard, 1925)*

379 Selinus: *Herakles fighting the Cretan bull, c. 450 B.C. (didrachm, obverse, 8.11 gm., diam. 23 mm., Lloyd 1248; from the Selinunte hoard, 1925)*

380, 381 Messana: *Mule-drawn chariot with Nike above/Leaping hare with head of Pan below, c. 425-420 B.C. (tetradrachm, 17.24 gm., diam. 25 mm., Lloyd 1101)*

382 Katane: *Chariot with prancing horses, c. 420 B.C. (tetradrachm, 17.20 gm., diam. 26 mm., Lloyd 898)*

383, 384 Gela: *Armed horseman felling a hoplite/Head of river-god Gelas within wreath border, c. 425 B.C. (didrachm, 8.58 gm., diam. 21 mm., Berlin; Jenkins 463)*

385 Katane: *Head of Apollo, with laurel-sprig, c. 420 B.C. (tetradrachm, reverse, 17.20 gm., diam. 26 mm., PCG 14.31; RPK)*

386 Syracuse: *Arethusa head with bound hair, c. 445 B.C. (tetradrachm, reverse, 17.05 gm., diam. 28 mm., Lloyd 1336; Boehringer 594; from the Selinunte hoard, 1925)*

387 Syracuse: *Arethusa head with hair in topknot, c. 440 B.C. (tetradrachm, reverse, 17.45 gm., diam. 25 mm., Lloyd 1341; Boehringer 604; from the Selinunte hoard, 1925)*

388 Syracuse: *Arethusa head wearing sakkos, c. 435 B.C. (tetradrachm, reverse, 17.02 gm., diam. 27 mm., Lloyd 1351; Boehringer 646)*

389 Syracuse: *Chariot attributed to Sosion, c. 425 B.C. (tetradrachm, obverse, 17.04 gm., diam. 25 mm., Lloyd 1362; Tudeer 1)*

390 Syracuse: *Head by Eumenes, signed on hair-band, c. 425 B.C. (tetradrachm, reverse, 17.24 gm., diam. 28 mm., PCG 16.60; Tudeer 7)*

378

379

380

381

382

383

384

385

386

387

388

389

390

391

392

393

394

395

396

397

398   399

400   401

402   403

391 Syracuse: *Head without signature, c. 420 B.C. (tetradrachm, reverse, 17.30 gm., diam. 30 mm., BM 1896; Tudeer 20)*

392 Syracuse: *Head in the style of Eumenes, c. 420 B.C. (tetradrachm, reverse, 17.30 gm., diam. 25 mm., BMC 143; RPK; Tudeer 12)*

393 Syracuse: *Chariot by Euainetos, wheel below, c. 415 B.C. (tetradrachm, obverse, 17.38 gm., diam. 24 mm., BMC 190; RPK; Tudeer 37)*

394, 395 Syracuse: *Chariot by Euainetos with Nike holding signed tablet/Arethusa head signed on dolphin in front, c. 415 B.C. (tetradrachm, 17.29 gm., diam. 24-26 mm., PCG 17.64; RPK; Tudeer 42)*

396, 397 Syracuse: *Head with corn-wreath, by Phrygillos/Chariot with winged charioteer, and Skylla below, signed euth, c. 412 B.C. (tetradrachm, reverse: 16.74 gm., diam. 25 mm., Lloyd 1382; Tudeer 47; obverse: 17.10 gm., diam. 24 mm., BMC 153; RPK; Tudeer 46)*

398, 399 Syracuse: *Head by Phrygillos, second style/Chariot driven by Persephone, with corn below, c. 410 B.C. (tetradrachm, 17.13 gm., diam. 34-33 mm., BMC 160; Tudeer 51)*

400 Syracuse: *Head of Athena, facing, by Eukleidas, signed on helmet, c. 410 B.C. (tetradrachm, reverse, 17.21 gm., diam. 28 mm., PCG 17.69; Tudeer 58)*

401, 402 Syracuse: *Arethusa head with floating hair, by Eukleidas/Chariot obverse, with dolphin below, c. 400 B.C. (tetradrachm, obverse: 17.39 gm., diam. 25 mm., Lloyd 1403; reverse: 17.22 gm., diam. 25 mm., Lloyd 1407; Tudeer 104)*

403 Syracuse: *Head with hair in topknot, anonymous artist, 410-400 B.C. (tetradrachm, reverse, 17.30 gm., diam. 26 mm., PCG 17.70; Tudeer 62)*

Persephone as charioteer holding aloft the torch which is one of her regular attributes; the arrangement of the horses is even freer and more varied than hitherto, with the heads in diversified positions. However, it is not at all sure that this die was by Phrygillos; it is a type which became prominent among the later Syracusan coins and the only example of the style which is signed bears the name of an otherwise unknown Euarchidas.

Another new phase begins with an impressive work from the hand of Eukleidas, whose head of Athena seen in semifacing view seems to open up new possibilities of sculptural and three-dimensional effects in coinage. This masterpiece has an unparalleled force and animation in the contrast between the solid forms of the face, the masses of the hair and the turbulent design of the helmet with its waving crests and winged sidepieces. The sculptural effect is further enhanced by the way in which one of the dolphins appears from behind the head. The mastery of the whole concept is the more impressive in that the relief cutting is achieved in comparatively low planes. The bowl and visor of the helmet are richly decorated and the name of Eukleidas is seen written upon it. It is indeed remarkable to find the head of Athena on a Syracusan coin instead of the usual Arethusa, especially as the dolphins are included; but Athena was also a great goddess at Syracuse, and her temple survives, incorporated into the present-day cathedral. 400

Another original and imaginative work is Eukleidas' later version of the Arethusa 401 head, perhaps a decade later. Here the mass of the hair streams above, perhaps thought of not so much as blowing in the wind as floating in the water, which was the element appropriate to this local divinity. The accompanying chariot group conveys an extremely restless and excited movement accentuated by the way in which the charioteer's dress billows out behind.

402

In this miraculous creative decade of the Syracusan mint there are also several other important artists at work, some of whom are unknown to us by name, but who must not on that account be underestimated. One of the splendid heads from this group shows us Arethusa with her hair tied up into a tight topknot suggestive of Nike (as on a previous occasion). An effect of great richness is achieved by comparatively simple means; and the ear-ring is here of a triple-pendant form. Another head which has some affinity with the last on account of its ample proportions and modelling, gives once more a Persephone with a wreath of corn ears; the great mass of hair which cascades down the neck is an original feature. An ominous break has appeared in the die, cutting into the head.

403

416

417

A quieter type of head, deriving distantly from the first Euainetos type, is one where the hair is bound in a sphendone richly decorated and the pattern of the dolphins rather original. Below the neck truncation is a small head of Pan, whose significance is quite obscure, unless it is the signet of the artist or mint-official; no name appears on this die, though on others closely similar we have the signature of *Parme . . .* (e.g. Parmenides).

Arguably the greatest of the artists at the Syracusan mint at this period was Kimon, who some have argued may have been of Athenian origin, though there is no way of determining this. In any case he has a bold touch combined with an unequalled degree of delicate control and harmony of design. His best known work is certainly the facing Arethusa head with the goddess' name written above and that of the artist on the hair-band. We can hardly avoid a comparison with the Athena of Eukleidas, and in Kimon's work we find again the same sculptural solidity of the head conveyed without any great depth of relief cutting, but the infinitely authoritative and skilful rendering by Kimon has more fresh and natural charm. Amid the excited array of hair there are traces of four dolphins, partly concealed but moving about in a three-dimensional element which is a delightfully imaginative effect. Above all, the harmonious relationship of all the elements is very characteristic of Kimon's style and it can be followed in his other works. His chariots are no less admirable, and he made two variant versions to accompany the Arethusa. One of these displays a composition which proves at once Kimon's masterly imagination in the way that it transforms the group of horses into an irresistible surge of power as no one had conceived it before, while the charioteer crouches tensely above them. The signature is on the exergual line. On this die, Nike flies above in the usual manner, but on the second Kimon die she

418

419

420

seems to hover in an upright position as if about to alight. Here the horse group is perhaps less exciting but foreshadows the delicate and supremely harmonious treatment on Kimon's dekadrachms; below, on the ground line, there lies a small column overturned, evidently representing the turning-column of the racecourse, flattened by some collision—a reminder of dangerous moments, rather in the manner of the lost wheel and broken rein on some of Euainetos' dies.

Among the Syracusan coins of this period are some drachms with a facing Athena on the obverse and a reverse 421 showing a warrior who, as suggested by the altar and the head of a sacrificed ram beside him, may have been the object of a local cult. His name, written below, is Leukaspis, who was, it seems, a hero of the indigenous Sikans, (the pre-Greek inhabitants of Sicily), and was vanquished by Herakles. His precise significance at Syracuse has been much discussed and his appearance there has been interpreted as an oblique expression of the Dorian Greeks' claim to the heritage of Herakles and the possession of Sicily. Herakles himself was to appear slightly later on some of the Syracusan gold coins.

Syracuse was not alone in the production of splendid coins at this period, and some of the same artists are to be found working for other cities. Euainetos, for instance, 422 also made dies for Katane, such as a fine tetradrachm giving an extremely exciting view of the chariot group rounding the corner of the racecourse marked by the turning-column, shown as an integral part of the composition. He has again contrived to include his name in the picture, as he had at Syracuse, held aloft by Nike. Few of the Sicilian chariots make a more vivid impression than this one, which shows a splendid development of this artist's style. By contrast the head of Apollo seems to lack 423 something of his best and most sensitive touch. A sacred fillet with a bell hangs in front, and a crayfish, a local emblem of Katane is shown behind. But Euainetos' imagination is seen at its best in a didrachm 424 which he made for Kamarina. It is the head, in facing view, of the river-god Hipparis, with horns sprouting from his brows like the river-god of Gela; on each side is placed a fish, and around the edge is a border of waves, as if to suggest the god glimpsed fleetingly in the ripples of the water. Euainetos' signature is to be found on the neck. It is however impossible to be sure that he also made the reverse which is 425 a delightful group showing the local nymph reclining on the back of a swan and holding her veil above her head as the swan skims over the water—again indicated by a pattern of waves.

Kamarina also possessed an artist called Exakestidas who made another version of 426 Hipparis' head seen in the more normal profile; it is signed on the neck truncation. We are reminded of the Gela river-god of some years earlier and also of Euainetos, with whose style Exakestidas seems to have much in common. In any case it is virtually certain that he created the excellent head of Herakles seen on a tetradrachm of Kamarina 427 since another almost identical die has his signature. The youthful hero with his lionskin head-dress gives an ideal opportunity for the contrast of the smoothly modelled face, and a slight suggestion of side whiskers, with the shaggy lion's mane knotted round his throat. The corresponding chariot—whether or not by the same hand—is likewise remarkable; it has some affinity with the earlier chariots of Euainetos at Syracuse, but the way in which the horses are here shown surging up, with the heads forming a rising arc, is most impressive. The perspective effect is indicated by the chariot wheel. The charioteer is here Athena, herself the chief deity of Kamarina.

Another strong personality is the artist Herakleidas who made the facing head of Apollo at Katane. In many ways quite the equal of the Syracusan facing heads, this is the product of a rather different approach as it is rendered in much higher relief planes, and is on that account more reminiscent of the Amphipolis heads than other Sicilian work in this line. Its serenity and warmth of expression are deeply impressive.

A close echo of some of the Syracusan styles we have seen is to be found in Segesta, in western Sicily. This Elymian city, whose culture and remains are to all appearance entirely Greek, had long reflected Syracusan styles distantly, but in the late fifth century we suddenly encounter an unexpected splendour in some of its tetradrachms, such as the head of the local nymph with her exuberant hair bound in an elaborate sphendone and welling out from

404 Syracuse: *Athena wearing wreathed Corinthian helmet, c. 344 B.C. (litra?, 34.21 gm., diam. 28 mm., PCG 26.32), obverse of 413*

405 Himera: *Gorgon, c. 450 B.C. (hemilitron, 23.85 gm., diam. 26 mm., PCG 15.43), obverse of 406*

406

407 408

409 410

411 412

413

414 415

it. It is a masterly piece, many aspects of which would be exactly in place at Syracuse at the time of *Parme*... and his contemporaries—to whose circle, rather than that of Kimon as once was suggested, it could well belong. The obverse of the same coin 431 is of great interest showing a youthful huntsman with his dogs, his foot resting on a rock, and with a herm standing in front. He may have had some sculptural prototype, and has been variously identified either as Aigestos, legendary ancestor of the city, or Krimissos the river-god; recently, it has been argued that he is Pan.

Here in passing should be mentioned a coin of the other Elymian city, Eryx, famous for one of the most important shrines of Aphrodite in the ancient world. A late fifth century tetradrachm shows the 432 goddess enthroned holding a sacred dove in her hand, with her winged son Eros standing in front of her. The last coins of both Eryx and Segesta, dating to about 400 B.C., have a rather stereotyped version of the chariot type on the obverse.

If any other of the Sicilian cities could be said to rival the eminence of Syracuse, it would be Akragas, whose wealth and luxury were almost as proverbial as those of Sybaris had once been. Her archaic coinage of the eagle and crab didrachm set a style that remained almost unchanged until the later fifth century, when suddenly the artistic impulse began to quicken; on a tetradrachm of about 420 B.C. we still see 433 the crab, but it shares the space with a fierce-looking fish (identified as the giant sea-perch) or with a Skylla. On other coins

406 Himera: *Six pellets (mark of value)*, c. *450 B.C. (hemilitron, 23.85 gm., diam. 26 mm., PCG 15.43), reverse of 405*

407, 408 Messana: *Head of Pelorias/Trident with hare, c. 400 B.C. (trias, 4.37 gm., diam. 17 mm., Lloyd 118)*

409, 410 Piakos: *Head of river-god, with six pellets (mark of value) and inscription/Dog seizing fawn by the throat, c. 420 B.C. (hemilitron, 4.54 gm., diam. 17 mm., PCG 16.15)*

411, 412 Gela: *Head of river-god/Bull, with olive above, c. 410 B.C. (trias, 3.98 gm., diam. 17 mm., Lloyd 991 ; Jenkins 523)*

413 Syracuse: *Dolphins and starfish, c. 344 B.C. (litra ?, 34.21 gm., diam. 28 mm., PCG 26.32), reverse of 404*

414, 415 Rhegion: *Lion mask/Head of Apollo, c. 350-300 B.C. (uncertain denomination, 9.07 gm., diam. 21 mm., Lloyd 709)*

the quiet dignified eagle is replaced by a group of two eagles perching on a rock with their prey, a dead hare, in their talons. Other coins again introduce the type of the racing chariot, dating to the period of Euainetos' first experiments at Syracuse; one of these has the name *Myr* . . . below, evidently that of the artist (Myron?), and another name, *Polyk* . . . (perhaps Polykrates) is to be found on one of the eagle types. It has been suggested that these two artists were in fact the creators of the most impressive of all the coins of Akragas, the dekadrachms, though these are not signed. They are among the rarest of all Sicilian coins today: only some half-dozen specimens survive, and it is doubtful if these pieces can have served as ordinary currency. The reverse side has the design of the eagles, and this may be the work of Polyk-(rates). It is however the magnificent chariot—perhaps by Myr(on)—which demands most attention as it is in many ways the most original of all such Sicilian compositions. Here, it seems to have been the artist's intention to display the chariot of Helios the sun-god, as it passes on its daily round through the sky; and this has been conveyed by a simple but brilliant stroke, by omitting altogether the normal ground line so that the horses can appear to be sweeping through the air. The curving movement may of course also have been suggested by the chariot groups which appear on contemporary silverware, such as on the bowl in New York which, as mentioned above (p. 17) has many affinities to coins both in design and technique.

On the Akragas dekadrachm, an extra slant has been given to the wheels to confirm the impression given by the attitude of the horses. Then, as if to restore a point of balance to the composition, the name of the city has been written above across the field, while at the top and bottom there are the vestigial remains of the original Akragantine eagle and crab—the eagle now shown with a captive snake in its claws—and these further enhance the composition by suggesting the setting of sky and sea.

What was the occasion for the minting of this extraordinary coin? The date can be fairly estimated as during the years 412–410 B.C., but since Akragas was neutral in the great war between Syracuse and Athens, we can safely discount any connection with the victory. It seems rather that we must regard it as a coinage celebrating another kind of victory; and this is almost certainly the case, as in the very year 412 B.C. a victory in the Olympic games was indeed won by an Akragantine, Exainetos, an event celebrated in tremendous style on his return to the city in a procession with five hundred white horses. Thus the dekadrachm becomes the most notable of such commemorative coins, of which the Messana mule-chariot was another example.

The style of this dekadrachm exerts some influence on a late tetradrachm of Gela where Nike herself is the charioteer; there is the same predatory eagle above, together with the legend. But the horses here show more affinity to the style of Kimon at Syracuse, and we know of no victorious occasion which could be brought into connection with this piece. Another Gela coin of this period is remarkable for showing a complete figure of the river-god bull, as if standing in the rich plain of corn, for the plant in front seems to symbolize the landscape.

The last decades of the fifth century were brilliant and prolific in the art of coinage in Sicily, but historically also a disturbed and tragic time. Hardly had the Athenian invasion been overcome but the fresh blow of a Carthaginian invasion fell; in 409 B.C. Selinus and Himera were destroyed, then in 406-5 B.C. Akragas and Gela fell in turn. It was probably in connection with this crisis, and for the hire of mercenaries, that these two cities had recourse to the mintage of gold coins, usually a sign of emergency measures, as at Athens during the same period. Akragas minted two issues, the first with her regular eagle and hare and a reverse of crab and fish like the slightly earlier tetradrachm; then a smaller piece with an eagle and snake, and the crab alone, and with the name of the magistrate Silanos added. At Gela the first gold coin shows the regular river-god type but has an obverse of a horseman. At the same moment, it is probable that a gold coin with the head of Athena and reverse olive spray and letter *Ka,* was minted at Kamarina. All these pieces were small, but at the current ratio of value some at least were worth more than a silver tetradrachm. It may well have been the same crisis, during which Dionysios seized power at Syracuse (405 B.C.) that the first gold coins were minted there also; these were pieces with a

small head of Herakles and on the reverse a quartered square with a small head— reminiscent of the archaic tetradrachms— and in fact equivalent to a tetradrachm. Some smaller pieces have the head of Athena and an aegis with Gorgon head. These gold coins have often been assigned to the time of the siege by the Athenians (415–413 B.C.) but may well belong to the first years of Dionysios.

At this same period there probably began to be minted the series of silver dekadrachms by Kimon and Euainetos which are perhaps the most famous of all ancient coins. It seems that both series are somewhat later than the tetradrachms by the same artists. The comparison of the two types afford some enlightening insights into their respective artistic characters.

In both cases the obverse consists of a chariot group with Nike flying above, and below in the exergue is shown a panoply of armour, a cuirass flanked by greaves with a shield on the left seen in end-on view and a crested helmet on the right. Below this is a short legend *athla,* a word that could be taken to mean prizes in an agonistic contest or else trophies of war. The view originated by Sir Arthur Evans was that the dekadrachms themselves constituted prizes awarded at commemorative games held after the defeat of the Athenians in 413 B.C. and others have suggested even earlier dates for the issue of these coins. But it is difficult to substantiate these views. All that is certain is that the dekadrachm issue extends well into the reign of Dionysios and it seems possible that these impressive pieces were in fact one of the main coinages of the tyrant who must have needed vast monetary resources to maintain his autocratic regime.

438 In Kimon's version of the chariot we lack something of the dramatic effect of his tetradrachms and the horses are marked by a supremely elegant and smooth movement, the hooves form a harmonious pattern and the heads are evenly spaced with only a slight 'accent' as the third head is lowered.

440 By contrast the Euainetos type is always easy to distinguish; the 'accent' here falls in the middle between two pairs of horses which are rearing up in a more excited movement, the hooves, all above the ground, forming a jagged broken pattern which certainly gives a greater sense of thrust and vigour.

439 A similar comparison can be made of the heads. Kimon's head, which is signed on the band above the brow, has the hair neatly stacked in a net with innumerable luxuriant locks and yet everything is

441 entirely harmonious. Euainetos, again, seems to show a more restless personality; a crown of reed is woven into the hair, giving it an extra animation as it curls riotously in all directions. Beside the calmer Kimon head, the Euainetos seems to have a greater expressive and emotional force. The signature *Euaine* is clear below the neck.

Such coins could not fail to impress their contemporaries as they have impressed those of later times like Winckelmann who pronounced them to be the ultimate in human concepts of beauty. The Euainetos

416 Syracuse: *Head with corn-wreath, anonymous artist, 410-400 B.C. (tetradrachm, reverse, 17.00 gm., diam. 28 mm., PCG 17.71 ; Tudeer 66)*

417 Syracuse: *Head with hair in sphendone, by Parme..., with dolphins and symbol Silenos head below, 410-400 B.C. (tetradrachm, reverse, 17.15 gm., diam. 24 mm., BMC 219 ; Tudeer 70)*

418 Syracuse: *Facing head of Arethusa, by Kimon, signed on hair-band, 410-400 B.C. (tetradrachm, obverse, 16.50 gm., diam. 28 mm., PCG 17.68 ; RPK ; Tudeer 81), obverse of 420*

419 Syracuse: *Chariot, by Kimon, signed on exergual line, Nike flying above, corn-ear below, 410-400 B.C. (tetradrachm, reverse, 17.26 gm., diam. 27 mm., BMC 208 ; Tudeer 78)*

420 Syracuse: *Chariot, by Kimon, with Nike alighting above, fallen column below, and corn-ear, 410-400 B.C. (tetradrachm, reverse of 418)*

421 Syracuse: *The hero Leukaspis armed, before an altar, 410-400 B.C. (drachm, reverse, 4.11 gm., diam. 19 mm., BMC 226 ; RPK)*

422, 423 Katane: *Chariot cornering with column, crab below, by Euainetos, Nike holding signed tablet/Head of Apollo with fillet and crayfish, c. 412 B.C. (tetradrachm, 17.31 gm., diam. 25 mm., PCG 14.32)*

424 Kamarina: *Facing head of river-god Hipparis, with waves and fishes, by Euainetos, c. 410 B.C. (didrachm, obverse, 7.96 gm., diam. 23 mm., PCG 14.29 ; RPK)*

425 Kamarina: *The nymph Kamarina riding on a swan, with wave pattern, c. 410 B.C. (didrachm, reverse, 8.35 gm., diam. 21 mm., Lloyd 875)*

426 Kamarina: *Head of river-god Hipparis, by Exakestidas, signed on truncation, c. 410 B.C. (didrachm, obverse, 8.38 gm., diam. 20 mm., BM 1952)*

427, 428 Kamarina: *Head of Herakles, probably by Exakestidas, with olive-sprig/Chariot driven by Athena, with flying Nike, and corn-grain below, c. 410 B.C. (tetradrachm, 16.88 gm., diam. 28-27 mm., PCG 14.28)*

416

417

418

419

420

421

422

423

424

425

426

427

428

429

430

431

432

433

434

435

436

437

438

439

440

441

429 Katane: *Facing head of Apollo, by Herakleidas, signed on the right, c. 410 B.C. (tetradrachm, obverse, 16.82 gm., diam. 24 mm., PCG 14.33)*

430, 431 Segesta: *Head of the nymph Segesta, with hair in sphendone, and corn-ear/Pan with hunting dogs, and herm, 410-400 B.C. (tetradrachm, 16.85 gm., diam. 30-27 mm., PCG 16.51)*

432 Eryx: *Aphrodite seated, with Eros, 410-400 B.C. (tetradrachm, reverse, 17.24 gm., diam. 25 mm., Lloyd 943)*

433 Akragas: *Crab, flanked by shells, with large fish, c. 420 B.C. (tetradrachm, reverse, 17.47 gm., diam. 27 mm., BMC 59 ; RPK)*

434 Akragas: *Two eagles, with dead hare, on rock (name, Silanos), c. 410 B.C. (tetradrachm, reverse, 17.24 gm., diam. 27 mm., BMC 55)*

435 Akragas: *Chariot of Helios, with eagle above and crab below, c. 411 B.C. (dekadrachm, obverse, 43.22 gm., diam. 38 mm., Munich)*

436 Gela: *Chariot driven by Nike, eagle with snake above, corn-ear below, 410-405 B.C. (tetradrachm, obverse, 17.04 gm., diam. 24 mm., BMC 58 ; Jenkins 487)*

437 Gela: *The river-god Gelas, with corn-plant, and corn-grain below, 410-405 B.C. (tetradrachm, reverse, 17.25 gm., diam. 24 mm., Lloyd 988 ; Jenkins 485)*

438 Syracuse: *Chariot with flying Nike, panoply of armour below (athla), by Kimon, 405-400 B.C. (dekadrachm, obverse, 43.36 gm., diam. 36 mm., BMC 201 ; Jongkees 2)*

439 Syracuse: *Head of Arethusa with hair in net, by Kimon, signed on hair-band, 405-400 B.C. (dekadrachm, reverse, 42.99 gm., diam. 33 mm., Lloyd 1410 ; Jongkees 7)*

440 Syracuse: *Chariot with flying Nike and panoply of armour below, by Euainetos, c. 390 B.C. (dekadrachm, obverse, 42.15 gm., diam. 36 mm., BMC 177 ; RPK ; Gallatin C XII-R VI)*

441 Syracuse: *Head with corn-wreath in hair, by Euainetos, signed below, c. 390 B.C. (dekadrachm, reverse, 43.37 gm., diam. 37 mm., Lloyd 1413 ; Gallatin D II-R IX)*

type in particular was taken as the prototype copied on a whole range of further coins in other parts of the Greek world notably as we have seen in Lokris and 266 Arkadia, and equally those of the Carthaginians in Sicily later in the fourth century— not to mention imitations in other media.

The dekadrachms do not however quite exhaust the work of Kimon and Euainetos for during the long reign of Dionysios (405-367 B.C.) there were also extensive issues of gold coins and some of these 336*, 337*, were also made by these same two artists. 350-52 The main type of head on these gold coins is similar in a general way to that of the silver, but the hair is always done in a sphendone and the style seems reminiscent of the Kimon dekadrachms. However, the signature of Euainetos is also found, al- 336* though sometimes only the tops of the letters can be seen. The reverse type is a 337*, 350 fine group of Herakles fighting the Nemean lion, in a taut and vigorous composition— perhaps intended to evoke the long struggle of Dionysios against Carthage. This larger gold coin was of the value of one hundred litrai or two dekadrachms, and was accompanied by a half-piece with a youthful head, perhaps the river-god Anapos, and a pranc- 351, 352 ing horse. Such coins were prominent in the important hoards discovered at Avola south of Syracuse, in one case mixed with coins of Lampsakos and of Persia, and very likely representing accumulations made by mercenaries.

Nothing has yet been said of bronze coinage, which did in fact first develop in Sicily on the basis of the litra, originally an indigenous bronze weight-unit. Early in the fifth century strange pyramid-shaped pieces of cast bronze were made at Akragas which may or may not be coins. By about 450 B.C. there are undoubted coins at Himera, of rather primitive aspect, with a Gorgon's head and marks of value representing six onkiai (half-litra). These weighed as much as 23 grammes and although this heavy weight is still found at the end of the century in bronze coins of Akragas, it was found that smaller pieces would serve for the same values, and by the late fifth century a Himera half-litra weighed only 5 grammes. A comparable lightweight coin minted at Piakos on the slopes of Aetna, stylistically influenced by Katane, has a reverse of a dog attacking a fawn. The smallest value represented in the late fifth century bronze was the onkia, but the most usual denomination was the trias, of which Syracuse, Gela and Kamarina provide numerous examples. A specimen from Messana is a particularly choice specimen of a finely preserved bronze coin, showing the head of the local nymph Pelorias and the Messana hare below a trident.

After the death of Dionysios I (367 B.C.), there followed a period of confusion in which civilization almost broke down in Sicily; in these conditions there could be no continuation of the splendid earlier tradition of coinage. When in 344 B.C. Timoleon from Corinth achieved the restoration of Syracuse and other cities, the resumption of coinage seems a comparatively modest affair. The Syracusan mint turned to the production of Pegasos staters almost identical with those of Corinth, and at the same time emitted an important series of heavy bronze coins with a head of Athena which has an equally Corinthian aspect—the wreath on the helmet also sometimes occurred at Corinth. These bronzes, which circulated widely through Sicily and were not infrequently overstruck at other mints, probably represented the value of the litra. The weight soon declined in subsequent issues which have the head of Zeus Eleutherios, 'the liberator'; many of these Zeus heads are of the finest fourth century style and are from the same hand as those on the small gold coins with the Corinthian Pegasos on the reverse. The revival of more continuous Syracusan coinage, however, did not really begin until the time of Agathokles (317–289 B.C.), and only in some isolated instances did it ever again achieve more than an academic echo of its glorious past.

VI. ITALY — FIFTH AND FOURTH CENTURIES

The coinage of the Greek cities in Italy forms yet another homogeneous grouping, distinct from that of the Aegean, and often rivalling the artistic quality of Sicily, though distinguished from that school by a feeling for a more minute delicacy of style. Early in the fifth century the typical archaic coinage of 'incuse' staters had given place to a more normal style of coin with relief on both sides; the incuse form however lingered on longer at some places than at others. The didrachm-stater remained the normal coin, though double-staters were also minted, regularly at Thourioi and occasionally at Metapontion. In any case there is no general historical break after the fifth century, and most of the Italiote series continue in an uninterrupted flow until the early Hellenistic period—with the exception of cities which, like Rhegion and Kaulonia, suffered from the aggression of Dionysios of Syracuse, or else like Terina from that of the Italic tribes, which, later in the fourth century, led to a period of incessant conflict and consequent interventions from abroad on behalf of the Greek cities.

Rhegion, naturally enough from its position on the Straits, is the one city of the Italian mainland which stands out as the exception and whose coinage has more affinity with Sicily. Here, until the end of the tyranny of Anaxilas and his sons in 460 B.C., the same type of coin with the mule-car and hare types was minted as at Messana. At this point the political union between the two cities lapsed, and a new regime at Rhegion was marked by the inception of a new and original style of coin, tetradrachms 455, 456 struck on fine broad flans. On the obverse is a powerfully designed lion's mask, recalling the earlier type of Anaxilas, and on 148 the reverse a virile seated figure, enclosed in a wreath border. He is Iokastos, the mythical founder of the city, and the celebration of the founder is a recurrent theme in the coins of the Italiote cities. By 435 B.C., the date of this specimen, a great degree of sophistication had been achieved in the rendering of the lion mask with its strongly modelled forms and an intriguing detail, small 'warts' above the eyes recalling the 'nose-warts' of the early Lydian lions. 6 The Iokastos figure is tensely seated as if ready for action, and the sculptural quality at once suggests a real statue; there is a suggestion of extra depth conveyed by the foot which overlaps the edge of the plinth. On the right corner of the plinth are to be seen two letters (reversed) K.E whose meaning has been interpreted as the signature of an engraver—if so one of the earliest known; it is conjectured that it stands for *K . . . epoiese* and a suggestion of the possible name is perhaps given by the appearance at this time of a rare name, *Kra . . .*, on a coin of Katane in Sicily. At Rhegion itself there is somewhat later a Kratesippos whose name is given in full, though it would be difficult to link his style with that of the present coin.

Towards the later decades of the fifth century, another change is made in the Rhegion coins. The lion mask remains, but instead of Iokastos there is a head of Apollo, the god who is equally prominent in the coinage of the Chalkidian cities of Sicily, and whose correspondence with the lion head explains the significance of the latter, as the sacred animal of the sun-god. The new style of coin at Rhegion brings a startling change of aspect; the lion mask and the Apollo head display some of the highest relief in any Greek coins of any period. The lion's features are no longer contained within a more or less smooth contour as on the previous coin, but carved deeply into the die, the strong and voluminous forms having an intensity of expression which is well set off by the flame-like mane which rises above. By contrast with the fierce character of the lion, the Apollo head is of a comparatively etherial quality which invites comparison with the Apollos of Katane and Leontinoi. Those of Rhegion are, however, somewhat later, after about 420 B.C., and may be thought to show a greater

refinement and sensibility. Some of the first examples were signed by Kratesippos, whom we have mentioned, but the present coin has behind the head and just above an olive leaf the letters *Py . . . .* In this connection it is difficult to ignore the name of Pythagoras who, earlier in the fifth century, was a well-known sculptor at Rhegion, though we can no more than guess whether this engraver could have been some relative or namesake of his.

The silver of Rhegion terminated in 387 B.C. with the conquest of the city by Dionysios and only momentarily revived in the time of Dionysios II (356–350 B.C.). A later style is however exemplified by bronze coins datable to the later fourth century, the Apollo head in particular coming very close to that of a Syracusan electrum coin of Agathokles' time.

From Rhegion we may turn to coins which are more typical of Italian style as it existed before the full impact of Attic art comes in, later in the fifth century. A didrachm of Kymai, for instance, dating to about 440–420 B.C. has a quiet and restrained character which is appealing, and which seems to hint at a comparable style more exquisitely expressed in the later work of Aristoxenos at Metapontion. This Kymai coin has on the reverse a splendid figure of Skylla, shown here in her more primitive form, fully clothed and with dogs' heads sprouting from her shoulders and below joining on to her fishy tail. The mussel shell below was itself the normal parasemon or emblem of Kymai which has here survived as a subordinate element in the design, in the same way as the eagle and crab on the Akragas dekadrachm.

A similarly quiet and demure style of head is to be seen in many of the attractive didrachms of Terina in the earlier period, but later in the fifth century there appears a richer and more self-confident style reflecting the full strength of Attic influence. The head, which we can only identify as that of the nymph Terina herself, is framed in a circle of olive leaves, the flowing wavy hair with its elaborate band decorated with palmettes. The winged figure on the reverse sits on a large amphora, her feet slightly drawn up, her right hand holding a caduceus, while on her left hand perches a tiny bird at which she is gazing with a sweet and solemn expression. The further wing seems to surround the face like a halo, the gauzy draperies rustle in a light breeze. This figure seems in every way the counterpart and echo of those lightly-clad figures who adorn the Nike balustrade at Athens. We can suppose that she is not simply Nike the goddess of victory but at the same time the local deity Terina whose head we recognized on the obverse, and the amphora seems to symbolize her nature as the source of the local river. The letter Φ placed behind the head on the obverse has been regarded as that of the engraver—perhaps the same as for the next coin.

One of the sources of Attic influence becomes explicit in the next coin which is of Thourioi, the Athenian-led colony established in 445 B.C. near the site of the former city of Sybaris. The bull which had formed the old Sybarite emblem is now prominent in a later guise on the reverse of the Thourian coins; the fish regularly placed below seems to suggest that the bull is now defined as a river-god. The obverse is a masterly head of Athena whose affinity to the art of Athens seems natural and self-evident. Her shallow crested helmet is bound with an olive wreath; the solemn and tranquil expression also has much in common with the head of Terina-Nike, and again we have the letter Φ, and the same problem of its interpretation as at Terina. On some of the Thourioi pieces there is also a small bird below the bull, in one case accompanied by letters *Ph r y*; and some scholars have favoured the interpretation of this as a signature, the shortened name of Phrygillos— possibly the Syracusan artist of that name. The possibility remains an intriguing one, though we cannot be at all sure that this Sicilian was really the author of coins at Terina and Thourioi, as well as perhaps at other Italiote mints; by no means all the examples which have been alleged are even of the same date, and the bare initial letter is certainly quite different from the form in which undoubted artists' signatures are found.

The coin series of Thourioi is one of the most important and extends down to the third century B.C., including not only issues of didrachm-staters but also of doublestaters. The development of the Thourian style is shown by another didrachm of the early fourth century. The bull now shows a fierce disposition and lowers its head in a charging attitude which makes this one of

187

the most impressive animal figures in the whole range of Greek coinage. The Athena is seen now wearing a more elaborate helmet decorated with a large Skylla, of later form than on the previous Kymai coin, naked and with the dogs springing solely from the waist. This impressive type of Athena set the example for other mints, Herakleia and Velia, where the Athena head was equally predominant. Other helmet decorations such as a griffin or sphinx are also known.

A splendid variant of the Athena head, this time in a three-quarter facing position, is displayed on an early fourth century coin of Herakleia, a city in whose foundation, in 433 B.C., Thourioi as well as Tarentum had participated. The solid sculptural mass of the head contrasts effectively with the restless movement of the hair and the helmet-crests. The reverse of the coins of Herakleia invariably depicts the eponymous hero Herakles, usually in combat with the Nemean lion; one version shows him raising the club as if to give the *coup de grâce*, but in a later rendering of about the middle of the fourth century we see the hero locked in a close struggle with the lion, the club left aside. The composition which is at once tense and harmonious conveys the conflict in a manner very similar to that of the gold coins of Syracuse.

Herakles was an important figure not only at Herakleia but also at Kroton where on a coin of the late fifth century he is seen resting from his labours on a rocky seat, on which the lionskin is spread; the bow rests at his side, he holds the club in his left

443▶

442 ▶

444 ▶

445

442 Tarentum: *Poseidon in chariot*, c. *315 B.C. (stater, 8.60 gm., diam. 17 mm., PCG 31.3; RPK), reverse of 452*

443 Tarentum: *The infant Taras appealing to Poseidon*, c. *344-338 B.C. (stater, 8.58 gm., diam. 19 mm., PCG 25.7), obverse of 450*

444 Tarentum: *The Dioskouroi on horseback*, c. *315 B.C. (stater, 8.60 gm., diam. 18 mm., PCG 52.24)*

445 Tarentum: *Alexander of Epeiros: Head of Zeus Dodonaios*, c. *332 B.C. (stater, 8.57 gm., diam. 19 mm., PCG 31.2), obverse of 451*

446

447

448

449

450

451

452

453

454

446 Metapontion: *Head of Leukippos with Skylla on helmet,* c. *330 B.C. (third-stater, 2.86 gm., diam. 12 mm., PCG 25.13)*

447, 448 Metapontion: *Facing head of Nike/ Corn-ear,* c. *330 B.C. (reduced third-stater, 2.58 gm., diam. 14 mm., BM 1961)*

449 Metapontion: *Head of Demeter,* c. *330 B.C. (reduced third-stater, 2.58 gm., diam. 14 mm., PCG 52.25)*

450 Tarentum: *Head of Amphitrite,* c. *344-338 B.C. (stater, 8.58 gm., diam. 19 mm., PCG 25.7), reverse of 443*

451 Tarentum: *Thunderbolt and spearhead,* c. *332 B.C. (stater, 8.57 gm., diam. 19 mm., PCG 31.2), reverse of 445*

452 Tarentum: *Herakles head,* c. *315 B.C. (stater, 8.60 gm., diam. 17 mm., PCG 31.3; RPK, obverse of 442*

453, 454 Tarentum: *Zeus head/Eagle on thunderbolt,* c. *280 B.C. (stater, 8.56 gm., diam. 18 mm., BMC 4 ; RPK)*

hand and in his right hand a lustral branch, above a small altar. The legend in the field proclaims Herakles as *Oikistas,* the founder of the city. A similar type had appeared on the first coin of Herakleia. More remarkable is the other side of the Kroton [472] stater where we see two figures flanking a vast tripod (which was itself the original emblem of Kroton); it is Apollo shooting at the Python, from whose possession he wrested the Delphic sanctuary, a scene unique in the range of Greek coinage: but to regard it as comic relief, as some writers have, seems to underestimate the seriousness of the theme, recalling that of the earlier staters of Kaulonia. Another and rather later coin of Kroton gives another [471] version of Herakles the infant struggling with snakes—a type which had previously occured at Thebes and in Asia Minor; in [282] the Krotonian type the infant seems less dominating and the snakes more ferocious. It was once suggested that the composition reproduced a lost painting by Zeuxis, but this is pure conjecture.

The question of the identification of artists on the Italiote coins has been mentioned already, and in view of the numerous names which have been claimed as such it is well to recall that in fact remarkably few can be distinguished with certainty. One example from the middle of the fourth century comes from Velia; it is a three- [473] quarter view Athena head of considerable charm, with the name *Kleudorou* clearly legible across the front of the helmet like that of Eukleidas at Syracuse. The reverse of this head is an extremely lively lion devour- [484]

ing its prey, a theme which since the earliest
Phokaian-style coins of Velia had been
characteristic of this mint. Sometimes the
485 lion is shown as part of a group, attacking
a stag.

Another artist we can identify with con-
fidence is Aristoxenos, who placed his name
on coins not only of Herakleia but also of
Metapontion where his earlier head of
487 Demeter has the same attractively modest
aspect which seems to have marked the
Italiote style of coin-engraving and to owe
little to extraneous influences, Athenian or
otherwise. Aristoxenos worked during the
first part of the fourth century, and another
and perhaps more mature head from his
486 hand is again Demeter, but richer and more
expressive, showing how his art developed.

The Metapontion coin series provides a
long series of heads of gods and heroes—
Zeus, Nike, Karneios, Apollo, Herakles and
others—in which we can follow the artistic
development of the mint step by step.
Later in the fourth century there is a rare
double-stater with the magnificent head of
488, 489 a bearded warrior, wearing a Corinthian
helmet the bowl of which is decorated with
a racing chariot driven by Nike, while below
this at the side is a small hippocamp; behind
the head is a lion symbol and a magistrate's
name. The reverse is the corn ear traditional for Metapontion, with a magistrate's
symbol, a club, balancing on the leaf. The
identity of this warrior is revealed by a
446 comparison with a gold coin where a very
similar head (though with a different helmet, having a Skylla device) is named as
Leukippos. He was the legendary founder

455, 456 Rhegion: *Lion mask/Iokastos seated,
within wreath border, letters* k.e., *c. 435 B.C.
(tetradrachm, 17.01 gm., diam. 29 mm., Lloyd
679 ; Herzfelder 42)*

457, 458 Rhegion: *Lion mask/Head of Apollo,
with bay-leaf and letters* Pu, *410-400 B.C.
(tetradrachm, 17.37 gm., diam. 23 mm., Lloyd
695 ; Herzfelder 79)*

459, 460 Kymai: *Head of nymph/Skylla with shell
below, c. 430 B.C. (stater, 7.61 gm., diam.
21-20 mm., BM 1841)*

461 462 Terina: *Head of Terina-Nike within
wreath/Terina-Nike seated on amphora holding
caduceus and bird, c. 420 B.C. (stater, 7.74
gm., diam. 20 mm., PCG 14.23 ; Regling 30)*

455

456

457

458

459

460

461

462

463

464

465

466

467

468

469

470

471

472

473

463, 464 Thourioi: *Head of Athena with wreathed helmet/Bull, with small bird and fish below*, c. 420 B.C. *(stater, 7.72 gm., diam. 22 mm., PCG 13.12)*

465, 466 Thourioi: *Head of Athena with Skylla on helmet/Butting bull with fish below*, 400-380 B.C. *(stater, 7.85 gm., diam. 22 mm., Lloyd 472)*

467, 468 Herakleia: *Facing head of Athena/Herakles clubbing lion*, 410-400 B.C. *(stater, 7.27 gm., diam. 24 mm., Lloyd 270; Work 22)*

469 Herakleia: *Herakles fighting lion, club in field, owl below*, c. 350 B.C. *(stater, reverse, 7.77 gm., diam. 22 mm., PCG 25.12; RPK; Work 39)*

470, 471 Kroton: *Herakles seated/Apollo shooting Pytho, with tripod*, c. 400 B.C. *(stater, 7.62 gm., diam. 22-21 mm., PCG 14.18; RPK)*

472 Kroton: *The infant Herakles with snakes*, c. 340 B.C. *(stater, reverse, 7.69 gm., diam. 20 mm., Lloyd 617)*

473 Velia: *Facing Athena by Kleidoros*, 360-350 B.C. *(stater, 7.29 gm., diam. 19 mm., BMC 71)*

of Metapontion, though there is some uncertainty about his precise identity as a figure of mythology. But the honouring of founders—Iokastos, Herakles, Taras—is a prevalent practice on the coins of the Italian cities.

The occasion for gold coins, whose issue was in Italy as elsewhere an isolated phenomenon in classical times, has been sought, rightly, in the period of the later fourth century when foreign powers were constantly being called in to assist the Italiote cities against repeated attacks by barbarians. Thus the small gold pieces of Metapontion all seem to belong to the period of intervention by Alexander of Epeiros (334-330 B.C.). The coin with the Leukippos head 446 had a reverse of two corn ears: other types, of lighter weight, have the single corn ear reverse and either a head of Hera in profile 449 or of Demeter or Nike facing. The last-mentioned is an exquisite piece of work 447, 448 which finds some parallel in the contemporary coinage of Kroton. These gold issues were in any case of short duration; but at this same period a more regular issue of gold was started, as we shall see, at the more important mint of Tarentum.

First we should recapitulate briefly the development of the Tarentine coinage since the early fifth century. The silver staters bore the regular type of the dolphin-rider, which for half a century had as reverse a seated male figure, generally recognized as Taras in his guise as founder, and strictly analogous to the similar figure of Iokastos at Rhegion. Towards the end of the fifth century the founder is replaced by a horseman who is sometimes a peaceful agonistic type and sometimes an armed cavalryman. The dolphin-rider remains the constant counterpart of this horseman, and in both subjects there is a rich and brilliant variety of detail and style that makes the Tarentine coins one of the most attractive series in all Greek coinage. From coins of the period when Tarentum was ruled by the dominating character of Archytas (380–345 B.C.), a Pythagorean philosopher and friend of

490 Plato, we see for example a horseman who is performing in an athletic contest, dismounting in full career with a shield on his

491 arm; corresponding to this is a serene Taras holding out a wine cup, while in another

492 version he holds a trident across his shoulder, Poseidon-like, as he skims along on the dolphin's back with a pattern of waves lightly indicated below as on the coins of Sicilian Kamarina. Another at-

493 tractive horseman composition has a boy-jockey mounted while an attendant kneels below to clean the horse's hoof. Slightly later is a fine stater with an armed horse-man thrusting with his spear and equipped

494 with a shield and extra spears on his left

495 side. Here the corresponding Taras holds in his hands a crested helmet and the scene is flanked by two stars, which have been seen as an allusion to the Dioskouroi and so to Sparta. The coin has been associated with the ill-fated expedition of the Spartan Archidamos who came over to assist the Tarentines in 344 B.C. in response to their appeal for help against the barbarians, and the dolphin-rider may perhaps be thought of as mourning for Archidamos who was killed in battle in 338.

474 ▶

475 ▶

476 ▶

474 Etruria: *Marine deity with dolphin cap (value-mark 50), fourth century B.C. (bronze coin, 26.45 gm., diam. 33 mm., BM 1889), obverse of 483*

475 Etruria: *Lion head (with value-mark 25), fifth-fourth century B.C. (gold coin, 1.37 gm., diam. 13 mm., Lloyd 10)*

476 Etruria: *Gorgon (with value-mark 50), fifth-fourth century B.C. (gold coin, 2.73 gm., diam. 14 mm., BM 1963)*

477

478

479

480

481

482

483

477 Etruria: *Female head (with value-mark 50), fourth century B.C. (gold coin, 2.70 gm., diam. 14 mm., Lloyd 11)*

478 Etruria: *Reverse with X-marks, fourth-third century B.C. (silver coin, 6.95 gm., diam. 23 mm., Lloyd 9)*

479 Etruria: *Lion-serpent monster, fifth century B.C. (silver coin, 10.87 gm., diam. 23 mm., BM 1956)*

480, 481 Etruria: *Gorgon (with value-mark 20)/ Crescent and stars with name of Populonia, fourth-third century B.C. (silver coin, 7.60 gm., diam. 21 mm., BM 1958)*

482 Etruria: *Athena head (with value-mark 20), fourth-third century B.C. (silver coin, 7.89 gm., diam. 19 mm., Lloyd 8)*

483 Etruria: *Hippocamp intaglio with wave-pattern, fourth century B.C. (bronze coin, 26.45 gm., diam. 33 mm., BM 1889), reverse of 474*

It was this same Spartan intervention which initiated the period of gold coinage at Tarentum. A fine stater shows the appeal 443• of the infant Taras to his father Poseidon. Whether the meaning is the contemporary one, the appeal to send help against barbarians, or something of a more historical nature—Taras asking to be granted a city to found in his father's honour—is difficult to be sure. Generally the idiom of Greek coinage prefers the oblique and mythological allusion to the directly factual. In any case the composition has considerable charm as a *genre* scene and is brilliantly engraved. The obverse of the coin 450 shows the head of a goddess wearing a stephane and a light veil, and we can discern something of the influence of earlier Syracusan prototypes on Italian style. She is usually called Hera, but the small dolphin in front would rather suggest Amphitrite, consort of Poseidon the father of Taras.

After this point, the history of Tarentum is one of repeated interventions each of which is marked by a fresh issue of gold staters struck on the international Attic weight and designed largely no doubt for the pay of the mercenary armies involved. Alexander of Epeiros who arrived in Italy in 334 B.C. and was killed in 330, did in fact strike extremely fine coins in his own 445•, 451 name at the Tarentine mint. These have the head of Zeus, the god of the great sanctuary at Dodona in Epeiros, depicted with his wreath of oak leaves; executed in an impeccable and sensitive style that reflects the art of the Praxitelean school, this coin is one of the masterpieces of the fourth century. The reverse by contrast is austere, the thunderbolt and spearhead (the emblem of Alexander) and his name 'Alexander the son of Neoptolemos'. Later, about 315 B.C., renewed threats of barbarian aggression compelled the Tarentines to appeal once more to Sparta, and help arrived under the leadership of a certain Akrotatos. On this occasion the Spartan sentiment was **444*** expressed by a design of the Dioskouroi on horseback, naked youths carrying wreaths and palm branches in emblem of victory; a gem-like miniature which ranks, beside the 'appeal to Poseidon', as one of the high points of numismatic art of Taren- **442*, 452** tum, or indeed of Italy. A second issue, perhaps also of Akrotatos' time, has the obverse of a youthful Herakles wearing his lionskin, and on the reverse Poseidon makes his appearance leaping into a two-horse chariot and grasping the reins, at the same time still carrying his trident, while a symbolic dolphin appears below.

453, 454 As a final contrast, a stater from the Tarentine mint, which chronologically takes us well into the Hellenistic period, since it was minted during the most famous intervention of all, that of Pyrrhos (281 B.C.). It is an interesting coin to compare with that of the previous generation of the Epirote Alexander, and is in any case a fine example of early Hellenistic style; the eagle perched on the thunderbolt is quite the equal of the lordly Ptolemaic eagle, and where the helmet symbol appears to the right, on some specimens there appears instead a small Athena Alkidemos, a figure

which from its use elsewhere by Pyrrhos serves to connect this stater with him. Another sign of his presence was the small elephant symbol which now occurs on some of the silver coins at Tarentum; these, like those of other cities at this juncture, underwent a devaluation and their weight was drastically reduced. Eventually all the major coinage of the Greek cities of Italy was superseded by the new coins of the Roman Republic, apart from isolated revivals during the Hannibalic occupation.

One region of Italy has not been mentioned—Etruria, whose coinage followed in general the Greek model but remains, like so many other aspects of Etruscan life, somewhat enigmatic. It would be a great advance if it were possible to settle the chronology of Etruscan coinage, but this remains, for lack of evidence, its most intractable feature. In addition, there were several different weight systems in use and there must have been several different minting centres though these are not always identifiable and intelligible inscriptions are a rarity. Two of the mints which can be identified are the coastal towns of Populonia and Vetulonia; another town, apparently called Thezi or Thezle, cannot at present be convincingly linked with any known location.

Many of the coins, at least in the earlier phases, have a curious one-sided form, the reverse being smooth and blank; the only analogy for this is in some of the archaic coins of Cyprus, but any significant connection seems quite lacking. In any case the earliest gold coins are of that form, with the type of a lion's head, a Gorgon or a human head. These coins, whose actual gold content fluctuates widely, are marked with numerals expressing the value in terms of 50, 25 or 12 ½ units, which may be related to similar markings on some of the silver coins. Some of the gold may have been minted as early as the fifth century—the lion head at least looks quite archaic; other types could be of the fourth century or even later.

Silver coins, which at first also had blank reverses, display some types suggesting Greek models, such as a running Gorgon or a calf's head, but other types are stranger, as for instance the lion-headed and snake-tailed monster which is quite distinct from a Greek chimaera. The main series of silver coins are of didrachm weight and marked X (= 10 units), though the same coin was later revalued and marked XX (20 units); these have the type of a Gorgon head which is never truly archaic and cannot be before the late fifth century. The blank reverse of this type became gradually diversified with some elements of design, a caduceus or a series of strange X-marks which, here at least, have no reference to value. The mint

of this series is later revealed, with the adoption of a more regular type of reverse, on which appear stars and crescent and the inscription *pupluna*, giving the name of Populonia. Other obverse types also occur, such as a facing Herakles head or an attractive Athena whose style is very distinctive and could not be mistaken for that of a regular Greek coin.

There is an extremely curious bronze series which incorporates features of the early Italiote incuse coins, having a reverse type which appears in intaglio and not in relief, and even a similar kind of border. The reverse is here a hippocamp, as distinct from the head on the obverse which seems to be that of some local sea-deity wearing a strange head-dress formed of a dolphin. Neither the date nor the mint can be determined, though we see here the same mark of value for 50 which occurs on the gold. There are also bronze coins of normal two-sided form: one of these, of Populonia, shows a head of Herakles clearly copied from Roman coins of the mid-third century, from which it may be deduced that the gold and silver issues of typically Etruscan style must at least be before that date.

484 Velia: *Lion, 360-350 B.C. (stater, 7.50 gm., diam. 20 mm., RPK)*

485 Velia: *Lion attacking stag, c. 380 B.C. (stater, reverse, 7.72 gm., diam. 20 mm., PCG 13.15)*

486 Metapontion: *Head of Demeter wearing corn-wreath, by Aristoxenos, signature off flan, c. 380 B.C. (stater, obverse, 7.72 gm., diam. 20 mm., BMC 83 ; Noe 439)*

487 Metapontion: *Head of Demeter, by Aristo-xenos, signed on the neck, c. 400 B.C. (stater, obverse, 7.93 gm., diam. 21 mm., Lloyd 341 ; Noe 422 ; from the Carosino hoard)*

488, 489 Metapontion: *Head of Leukippos, in helmet with chariot decoration, lion symbol/Corn-ear, symbol club, c. 330 B.C. (double-stater, 15.79 gm., diam. 27 mm., Lloyd 376)*

490 Tarentum: *Horseman with shield jumping from horse, 380-345 B.C. (stater, obverse, 7.76 gm., diam. 20 mm., Lloyd 166 ; Evans III.L)*

491 Tarentum: *Taras riding dolphin, with kan-tharos, 380-345 B.C. (stater, reverse, 7.78 gm., diam. 20 mm., Lloyd 154 ; Evans III. A.4)*

492 Tarentum: *Taras riding dolphin, with trident, 380-345 B.C. (stater, reverse, 7.80 gm., diam. 20 mm., BMC 193 ; Evans III.M)*

493 Tarentum: *Horseman with attendant, 344-334 B.C. (stater, obverse, 7.82 gm., diam. 21 mm., PCG 25.9)*

494, 495 Tarentum: *Horseman armed with spears and shield/Taras on dolphin holding helmet, 344-334 B.C. (stater, 7.72 gm., diam. 22 mm., PCG 25.10 ; RPK)*

496, 497 Alexander the Great: *Head of Herakles/Zeus enthroned ; Amphipolis mint, 336-323 B.C. (tetradrachm, 17.10 gm., diam. 26 mm., BM 1841)*

498, 499 Alexander the Great: *Head of Herakles/Zeus enthroned ; Babylon mint, 336-323 B.C. (tetradrachm, 17.20 gm., diam. 25 mm., BM 1922)*

500, 501 Alexander the Great: *Head of Herakles/Zeus enthroned ; Alexandria mint, c. 326-318 B.C. (tetradrachm, 17.19 gm., diam. 26 mm., BM 1911)*

502 Ptolemy I: *Head of Alexander wearing ele-phant-scalp ; Alexandria mint, c. 318-315 B.C. (tetradrachm, 17.40 gm., diam. 27 mm., BM 1949)*

503 Ptolemy I: *Athena Alkidemos ; Alexandria mint, c. 310-305 B.C. (tetradrachm, reverse, 15.68 gm., diam. 29 mm., BMC 46)*

504, 505 Medallion of Alexander: *Alexander on horseback attacking Porus on elephant/Alexan-der deified, holding thunderbolt, c. 323-300 B.C. (dekadrachm, obverse: 42.20 gm., diam. 36 mm., BMC 61 ; found in Bokhara, 1887 ; reverse: 39.65 gm., diam. 33 mm., PCG 27.4 ; found in Iraq, 1926)*

484

485

486

487

488

489

490

491

492

493

494

495

496

497

498

499

500

501

502

503

504

505

VII. THE HELLENISTIC PERIOD

ALEXANDER, MACEDONIA AND GREECE

The conquests made by Alexander the Great in the course of his short life produced the most fundamental changes both in the geographical extent of the Greek world and in the character of its civilization. That world had previously consisted of city-states and their colonies, each an intense centre of cultural and political life; it now became a vast empire, still based on Macedonia and Greece but including the whole of the area previously controlled by the Achaemenids as far as Egypt in the south and India in the east. This huge expansion was consolidated by the settlement of Greek communities each forming a new focus of Hellenism, in centres such as Babylon and Susa and newly founded cities of which Alexandria became the most famous. The generation after Alexander's death saw the whole of this vast empire convulsed with struggles between his various successors, which resulted in the emergence of three principal monarchies, Macedonia, the Seleukid empire and Ptolemaic Egypt, as well as others such as Pergamon and Baktria. But centrifugal tendencies continued unabated and finally enabled the rising Roman Republic to swallow the Greek world piecemeal, while the Parthians accounted

for the rest. Yet the Hellenistic Age, though far from peaceful, has many brilliant achievements to its credit in the spheres of art and science and brought a degree of economic unity to an area wider than ever before. Its coinage is of no less interest than that of classical Greece, and branched out in new directions.

We must look first at the coinage which Alexander created for his great new empire. His main mints, like those of his father Philip II, were in Macedonia itself and Amphipolis, close to the important silver mines, remained the chief source. But the coinage now had to be designed to provide a universal currency for a far vaster area than ever before, and this was gradually achieved by the establishment of numerous further minting centres in each new area as it was conquered. Thus in Asia Minor mints were opened at such cities as Lampsakos, Miletos, Sardes, Side, Tarsos, and several in Cyprus; new mints at Damascus in Syria, on the Phoenician coast at Sidon and Akko, in Egypt at Alexandria, and after the decisive victory of Gaugamela in 331 B.C. at Babylon. Babylon remained the most easterly mint during Alexander's lifetime, though later under the Seleukids the system was extended into Iran. The output of all these centres was enormous, and the raw material was provided largely by the huge treasures captured from the Persians.

The full range of this new universal currency consisted of gold, silver and bronze coins of identical form, design and weight from all the mints. Philip II had already minted gold on the Attic standard, and now Alexander used the same standard also for silver, not only in order to harmonize with the current relative values of the metals, but also because the previous currency which had approximated to a universal medium of circulation had been that of Athens, and the Attic standard became the normal one for nearly all the important international currencies of the Hellenistic age. In an economic sense, the unity of Alexander's empire survived his death and subsequent political upheals, and during the first generation of his successors the identical coins, still in the name of Alexander, continued to be minted without change in every part of the empire, often by different authorities who were actually at war with each other.

The types of Alexander's coinage were evidently designed to make the widest appeal to Greeks everywhere, and accordingly we find the dominating figures of Athena, Zeus and Herakles. Athena was the deity of the gold coins, on whose obverse we see her head, wearing a Corinthian helmet with flowing crests; while on the reverse appears the figure of Nike, her wings spread, holding out a wreath and a stylis, normally the emblem of naval victory. The suitabil-

507 ▶

508▶▶

506 ▶

506, 507 Alexander the Great: *Athena head, snake on helmet/Nike with wreath and stylis; Amphipolis mint, 336-323 B.C. (double-stater, 17.16 gm., diam. 21 mm., RPK)*

508 Lysimachos: *Athena seated with Nike; Alexandria Troas mint, 297-281 B.C. (stater, 8.45 gm., diam. 18 mm., BM 1924), reverse of 517*

509

510

511

512

513

514

515

516

517

518

519

520

521

ity of displaying the goddess of victory is obvious, but there has been much discussion whether there may be more specific reasons for this type—possibly, it has been suggested, the Nike is copied from an actual monument set up at Athens. The normal denomination is the stater weighing 8.6 grammes; and early in the reign there are also some double-staters from the mint of Amphipolis. Fractions were also minted —the half, quarter and eighth; on the smaller pieces the reverse displays either the club and bow of Herakles or the thunderbolt of Zeus. Many variations are to be seen between the styles of different mints according to the capacity of the engravers. The Amphipolis double-stater gives the goddess a curious and rather archaizing arrangement of corkscrew curls, a feature which may suggest or recall some statuery prototype; her helmet is decorated with a coiled snake, as is seen again on a much later coin of Tyre. A stater of Sidon has similar curls but the helmet decoration is a winged griffin of the Persian type, the significance of which is far from certain. Another variant is exemplified from the mint of Babylon where the archaizing curls give place to more naturalistic renderings and there is now a sphinx on the helmet; at the same time there is a considerably freer version of the Nike reverse.

Gold coin was not struck at every mint however, and the bulk of Alexander's coinage as we know it consists of silver tetradrachms; in addition there were occasional issues of other denominations, dekadrachm, didrachm, drachm and smaller fractions,

509 Alexander the Great: *Athena head, griffin on helmet ; Sidon mint*, c. *331-327 B.C. (stater, obverse, 8.59 gm., diam. 18 mm., BM 1878 ; Newell 13)*

510, 511 Alexander the Great: *Athena head, sphinx on helmet/Nike ; Babylon mint, 330-323 B.C. (stater, 8.61 gm., diam. 17 mm., PCG 27.2)*

512 Alexander the Great: *Athena head, snake on helmet ; Tyre mint*, c. *306 B.C. (stater, obverse, 8.61 gm., diam. 18 mm., BM 1872)*

513, 514 Alexander the Great: *Athena head/ Thunderbolt, bow and club ; Amphipolis mint, 336-323 B.C. (quarter-stater, 2.12 gm., diam. 11 mm.)*

515, 516 Alexander the Great: *Athena head/ Thunderbolt ; Amphipolis mint, 336-323 B.C. (eighth-stater, 1.08 gm., diam. 9 mm., BM 1853)*

517 Lysimachos: *Head of Alexander deified ; Alexandria Troas mint, 297-281 B.C. (stater, 8.45 gm., diam. 18 mm., BM 1924), obverse of 508*

518, 519 Demetrios Poliorketes: *Portrait head/ The king on horseback ; Pella mint, 288-283 B.C. (stater, 8.87 gm., diam. 18 mm., BM 1892 ; Newell 137)*

520, 521 Philip V: *Head of Perseus/Club ; Amphipolis mint, 221-179 B.C. (stater, 8.50 gm., diam. 18 mm., in private possession ; photo from electrotype)*

though the smallest values were catered for in bronze. On silver coins the obverse type is the head of the young Herakles dressed in his lion's scalp, honouring him as the legendary ancestor of the Macedonian royal house; as such the Herakles type had already appeared on the coins of several preceding Macedonian kings. Over and above, this, the type aptly expresses the heroic tasks which Alexander spent his life accomplishing, and indeed to the eyes of many in the ancient world it really seemed that this Herakles was the very portrait of the king himself. He is represented in the guise of Herakles on the Sidon sarcophagus; and the possibility that the coins sometimes at least feature Alexander in this form has been much discussed. However, it can only be said that there is no certainty about this, and that a recognizable portrait can only be identified on coins of another type minted after Alexander's death. As the counterpart to the Herakles head there is the reverse showing the principal Greek god, Zeus, enthroned and holding sceptre and eagle. The early version of this type at the Amphipolis mint has a somewhat artless aspect which gives place to a figure of greater majesty and freedom in some of the eastern versions, such as those from Babylon and Alexandria.

The considerable variety of style and detail on these coins enables us to distinguish the coins of different mints and also those minted in Alexander's lifetime from those of the next generation. It is, however, rarely that the name of the mint is explicitly marked on the coin, as it is for instance at

Damascus, or in Phoenicia at Sidon and Akko, where we have in addition a series of dates according to local eras which are of crucial importance for the whole chronology of these coins. The possibility of reconstructing the various mint series depends upon the detailed study of a large number of specimens and the interconnections of the dies. The scheme of the lifetime issues now generally accepted is the achievement of the American scholar E. T. Newell, whose studies of the great hoard of Alexander coins found at Demanhur in Egypt in 1905 laid the foundations for present-day knowledge of the whole subject.

It was a few years after Alexander's death, and on coins of the Alexandria mint, that the first true portrait is found. By contrast with the many variations of the Herakles head which had appeared on the lifetime tetradrachms, we find here a distinct individuality of feature which is as marked as the symbolism which accompanies it. For as Herakles had appeared with the lion-skin on his head, so here Alexander seems to be depicted as the conqueror of India, his head covered with the skin of an elephant with the tusks and trunk protruding above and the ears hanging behind the neck. This particular iconography was used again on a gold coin minted by Seleukos I at Ekbatana and another Indian conqueror, Demetrios of Baktria, imitated the type at a later date; it may perhaps go back to some cult-statue at Alexandria, where the king was buried in a great mausoleum. His association with elephants is again emphasized on some of the early gold coins of Ptolemy I.

The series of Alexandrian coins with the elephant-clad portrait continued with a re-
503 verse showing an archaistic figure which is Athena Alkidemos, tutelary goddess of Pella in Macedonia, the home of Alexander's dynasty, and a type which is used on the coins of more than one of his successors in token of their attachment, however theoretical, to Macedonia. This emblem was used not only as here by Ptolemy I but later in Macedonia by Antigonos Gonatas, in the west by Pyrrhos, and again in remote Baktria by Menander.

Another representation of Alexander himself occurs on a rare dekadrachm or medallion struck perhaps at Babylon not
504 long after his death. There is a scene showing Alexander on horseback attacking an Indian king riding an elephant; and on the
505 reverse a standing figure of Alexander wearing an elaborately plumed helmet and holding a thunderbolt, so by implication venturing to identify him with Zeus. Such concepts of the deified Alexander probably go back to works of the court artists such as Apelles and Pyrgoteles, as also probably does the most famous of all the coin por-
34, 535 traits which makes its first appearance in 297 B.C. on the tetradrachm of Lysimachos. Here we see Alexander wearing on his head the ram's horns of Zeus Ammon, proclaiming his divine nature of which the god at the Siwa oasis had allegedly spoken during the king's visit to that oracle in 331 B.C. It is certainly no accident that the first stages of Hellenistic royal portraiture are those showing Alexander as a god, since it was an age when people were very ready to

think of powerful kings as divine saviour-figures and to say, in the words of a hymn once addressed by the people of Athens to Demetrios Poliorketes: 'The other gods are not, or are far away; they hear us not or heed us not; but thou art here, and we can see thee, not in wood or stone but in very truth.' Many of the subsequent royal portraits give much emphasis to this idealized and quasi-divine character, though it is equally the fascination of such portraits that they give such well-observed and vivid individual features and such insight into character.

Lysimachos himself, whose Alexander coins have been mentioned, was one of the most successful of the successors in his day, starting as satrap of Thrace and gradually building a great empire covering much of the Black Sea and of Asia Minor, and rivalling almost the power of Seleukos until defeated by him at Korupedion in 281 B.C. Though his empire vanished, his coins, which were extremely profuse and minted in gold and silver at many mints, remained very influential and a number of cities continued to mint them centuries afterwards. During Lysimachos' lifetime were minted the gold stater of Alexandria Troas and the 508*, 517 tetradrachm of Pergamon; the particularly 534, 535 splendid style of the latter is appropriate to a city which was so prominent in the art of Hellenistic times.

Another of the successors whose power vanished with him was Demetrios Poliorketes; together with his father Antigonos Monophthalmos, he controlled a fluctuating realm which at different times consisted of

large parts of Asia Minor (later lost to Lysimachos), a great empire at sea, where
Demetrios was especially in conflict with
Ptolemy, and even for a time Macedonia
itself. It was his victory over Ptolemy and
subsequent occupation of Cyprus which
was celebrated by the issue, from the mint
536, 537 of Salamis, of a magnificent tetradrachm
displaying Nike alighting on the prow of
a war galley—the same motif expressed a
century later in the famous Nike of Samothrake now in the Louvre. Similar monu-
ments must already have existed, and one
of them may be the prototype of Demetrios' coin. The reverse shows the king's
patron god Poseidon wielding his trident—
a commanding figure whose body is rendered in purely Hellenistic style though the
hanging drapery is archaistic like that of the
Athena Alkidemos at Alexandria. Demetrios' coins are of an exceptional historical
interest, since those minted in Macedonia
and elsewhere in Greece are in fact the first
portrait coins to be minted in Europe. A
518, 519 gold stater from the mint of Pella, with a
reverse of the king riding on horseback, has
a somewhat idealized head, once more as in
the case of Alexander with divine attributes,
here a bull's horn as if to emphasize the
kinship with Poseidon. Other of Demetrios' portraits, such as that on a tetra-
538 drachm of the mint of Thebes, give a more
realistic representation and suggest something of his ardent yet somewhat unbridled
character.

In view of the fact that portraiture was
now becoming the dominant mode, it is
rather surprising that, after Demetrios, it

522 Antiochos II: *Apollo seated on omphalos;
Baktra mint, 261-246 B.C. (stater, 8.41 gm.,
diam. 18 mm., BMC; Hierax 2; Newell 709),
reverse of 529*

523 Antiochos III: *Portrait of Antiochos III;
Antioch mint, 208-200 B.C. (octodrachm,
obverse 33.87 gm., diam. 29 mm., BMC 1;
RPK; Newell 1907)*

524 Diodotos of Baktria: *Zeus with thunderbolt,
wreath and eagle below, c. 230 B.C. (stater,
8.44 gm., diam. 19 mm., BMC 1), reverse of
530*

525

526

527

528

529

530

531

532

533

was not adopted again in Macedonia itself until towards the end of the dynasty. Some few years after Demetrios had lost the throne it was gained by his son Antigonos Gonatas; his opportunity came in 279 B.C. when Greece suffered an invasion of the Gauls, upon whom Antigonos managed to inflict a crushing defeat at Lysimachia. In this battle, it was said, panic had been spread among the Gauls by the god Pan, and it is he who was honoured with pride of place 539 on Antigonos' coins, a splendidly powerful head set in the centre of a Macedonian shield. It is, however, idle to conjecture, as some have, that some versions of this Pan head may represent Antigonos himself. The reverse bears a type showing the Athena Alkidemos of Pella.

The coins of the next Macedonian king, Antigonos Doson, were likewise based on a theme of victory, commemorating the battle of Andros in 227. His tetradrachms 540, 541 bear a head of Poseidon which can rank as one of the really grand and imaginative concepts among the coin types of the Hellenistic age. The reverse shows Apollo seated on the prow of a warship.

Among the later kings of Macedonia, Philip V is well known for his designs against Rome and his shattering defeat at Kynoskephalai in 197 B.C. This was not yet the end of the kingdom and Philip's coinage is as impressive and profuse in his later years as earlier. Occasionally it carries his portrait but regularly the design is reminiscent of that of Antigonos Gonatas, a Macedonian shield with a head as centre- 542 piece; here a head of Perseus wearing a winged helmet surmounted by a griffin's head, and his weapon, the harpa, placed behind the neck. The cult of Perseus, the Argive hero, was in consequence of Philip's marriage with an Argive woman. It seems possible that in the case of this Perseus head we may in fact have a quasi-portrait, as the features are reasonably similar to those of Philip as we know them from other coins. The Perseus head appears beardless on an-

520, 521 other coin, a gold stater which may date to the earlier part of Philip's reign; while on the reverse, as on the tetradrachms, there is the club of Herakles, ancestor of the Macedonian dynasty.

It is only in the final reign, that of Perseus, Philip's son, that we have finally

543, 544 a whole series of true portrait coins with a brilliant likeness of the young, lightly-bearded king wearing the royal diadem, and with a reverse of an eagle standing on a thunderbolt. The portrait is one of the finest of the middle Hellenistic period, restrained and full of careful realism without pretension to represent a god or hero—in this perhaps aptly depicting a character seems to have lacked the ultimate courage which might have enabled him to resist the Romans, and so to avoid the defeat at Pydna in 168 B.C. which brought the history of the Macedonian kingdom to an end.

Even while the Macedonian kingdom flourished, it was not by any means master of the whole of Greece. While great cities such as Athens were kept under close control, other new centres of power were coming into existence in rivalry with Macedonia.

One of these was the league of Aitolia, a comparatively backward people whose greatness, like that of Antigonos Gonatas, stemmed from a triumphant resistance to the Gallic invasion, which at one moment had reached as far as Delphi. The victory was commemorated by a monument which the Aitolians set up at Delphi representing Aitolia personified. A redoubtable female warrior, she is duly depicted on the coins **546** holding a sheathed sword and seated in a defiant posture upon a heap of shields left behind by the enemy; some of the shields look Macedonian, but others are definitely Gallic, and below a Gallic carnyx lies at her feet. As a further assertive gesture the obverse of the Aitolian tetradrachms borrows the head of Herakles from the coinage **545** of Alexander.

In other parts of Greece there arose similar leagues, a new form of political organization typical of the Hellenistic period. One of these was the Epirote league which succeeded to the local monarchy and issued **547, 548** coins showing the jugate heads of Zeus of Dodona with Dione, and the reverse of a charging bull, encircled by an oak wreath. The other important confederation was the Achaean league, a powerful political entity whose coinage, however, is hardly impressive save in quantity and which was struck on identical pattern at the numerous cities which formed the league.

The Achaean league had a local rival in the shape of Sparta, whose kings at this period seem sometimes to have been ambitious enough to emulate the great monarchs by striking coins—the first ever minted at Sparta, whose old traditions had forbidden it. It is unfortunate that some of these cannot be more closely dated, for during the third century was minted a coin with a royal portrait which might almost be that of some Seleukid king. In fact it must be either Areos or else Kleomenes III of Sparta; but no name is given and the legend on the reverse merely reads *La* (for Lakedaimon). The type of the reverse is an interesting one, as it depicts the famous archaic image of the Apollo of Amyklai, with helmeted head, holding a spear and bow; other Spartan coins show only a helmeted head, which is probably that of this same god.

THE SELEUKIDS AND ASIA

The greatest of Alexander's marshals and successors was Seleukos. His tenacious and heroic character, and the vast extent of his domains which before his death consisted of the greater part of Alexander's heritage, from Ionia to the Hindu Kush, give him a place in history which is not far inferior to that of Alexander himself. Moreover Seleukos and his dynasty can claim credit for the extent to which Hellenism took root in Asia. Firmly established at Babylon, after some vicissitudes, in 312 B.C.—the date from which the Seleukid dynasty thereafter reckoned its era—Seleukos was further strengthened by the victory of Ipsos in 301 over Antigonos, and by that of Korupedion in 281 over Lysimachos.

The coinage of Seleukos' empire remained at first, as in other regions, a pure continuation of Alexander's type, with the change to his own name occurring when he, like Ptolemy and others, took the royal title in 305 B.C. New mints were established at Ekbatana, Susa and Persepolis in Iran, and that of Babylon transferred to the new capital at Seleukia-on-the-Tigris. At Ekbatana was issued a gold coin of the weight of a double-daric (a denomination which had continued to be minted at Babylon in Alexander's time) showing the head of Alexander as conqueror of India dressed in an elephant scalp—the type created at Alexandria—and with the Nike of Alexander's gold coins on the reverse. The various eastern mints inaugurated a new type after Seleukos' successful Indian campaign of 305 B.C., when he took an indemnity of five hundred war elephants from Chandragupta Maurya. The reverse consists of an elephant-drawn chariot driven by Athena and with the head of Zeus on the obverse, for the silver coins; these types remained the principal mintage for the last decades of Seleukos' reign. On a rare gold issue from the mint of Susa the chariot is driven by Artemis and the head on the obverse is that of Apollo, the patron deity of the Seleukid dynasty.

The victory of Ipsos in 301 B.C., was the special occasion for the issue of another type, minted almost exclusively at the old Achaemenid capital, Persepolis. Here we see the head of a king wearing a helmet, complete with cheek-pieces, covered with panther skin and further adorned with the

horns and ear of a bull; there is a further
suggestion of an animal skin knotted round
the throat, like the lionskin on the Herakles
552 type of Alexander. The reverse is a clear
victory type, Nike with open wings just
alighting to place a wreath on a trophy of
arms—a design which recalls, if only by
296 contrast, the very different treatment of the
590 same theme at Lampsakos and in Sicily. The
royal helmeted head has generally been
regarded as that of Seleukos himself, which
would be in many ways the most natural
interpretation; and if so it would be virtually the only occurrence of his portrait on
coins of his own lifetime. It is, however,
hard to be sure that the features are really
those of Seleukos, and the alternative
suggestion has been made that it is really
an idealized head of Alexander, though the
attributes—the bull's horn, and the panther-
skin which seems to be connected with
Dionysos and allude to conquests in India—
would suit either interpretation. For an
553 authentic portrait of Seleukos, and one of
the highest quality, we have an example
dating from the period immediately after
his death, from the mint of Pergamon; the
bold simplicity of its presentation only
enhances the powerful impression of Seleukos' personality.

It is only in the time of Seleukos' son and
successor Antiochos I (280–261 B.C.) that
the definitive coinage appears, bearing the
554 regular portrait of the king and the dynastic
555 god Apollo as the reverse, usually shown
seated on the omphalos with the bow at
his side and an arrow poised in his hand.
This Apollo—possibly derived from some

534, 535 Lysimachos: *Head of Alexander with
horn of Ammon/Athena enthroned, with Nike
on hand crowning the King's name; Pergamon
mint, c. 297-281 B.C. (tetradrachm, 17.22
gm., diam. 31 mm., BM 1919)*

536, 537 Demetrios Poliorketes: *Prow of galley
with Nike alighting/Poseidon brandishing trident; Salamis mint, 306-295 B.C. (tetradrachm, 17.24 gm., diam. 28 mm., PCG 27.15;
Newell 23)*

538 Demetrios Poliorketes: *Portrait of Demetrios with bull's horns; Thebes mint, 289-287
B.C. (tetradrachm, obverse, 16.87 gm., diam.
28 mm., RPK; Newell 141)*

539 Antigonos Gonatas: *Macedonian shield with
head of Pan, 277-239 B.C. (tetradrachm,
obverse, 17.18 gm., diam. 30 mm., RPK)*

540, 541 Antigonos Doson: *Head of Poseidon/
Apollo on prow, 229-220 B.C. (tetradrachm,
obverse: 17.08 gm., diam. 31 mm., George III
collection; reverse: 16.85 gm., diam. 31 mm.,
PCG 35.41)*

542 Philip V: *Macedonian shield with Perseus head,
220-179 B.C. (tetradrachm, obverse, 16.87
gm., diam. 32 mm., PCG 35.5)*

543, 544 Perseus: *Diademed portrait of Perseus/
Eagle on thunderbolt within wreath, 179-168
B.C. (tetradrachm, 16.77 gm., diam. 31-30
mm., BM 1866)*

534

535

536

537

538

539

540   541

542

543   544

545

546

547

548

549

550

551

552

553

554

555

sculptural prototype—remained the main theme of the Seleukid coins, with only a few variations, during the whole period when the empire was at its most powerful. In many ways however it is the portraits which have the deepest claim on our attention; their deeply-felt realism brings us very close to the living originals.

The head of Antiochos I as we see it on 554 the obverse of his coins is a very moving study of a man whose energy and splendour of will seem to have called deeply on all his strength to enable him and his empire to survive intact. This tetradrachm comes from the mint of Seleukia-on-the-Tigris, which was still at this time the pivotal centre of the empire. Further east at Baktra (Balkh) there is sometimes another reverse type, the head of Alexander's fa- 572 mous horse Bukephalos wearing, like the kings, the horns which were often the typical marks of royalty and even divinity, surmounted by a splendid flame-like mane.

In subsequent reigns, it was Antioch rather than Seleukia which gradually became the nerve-centre and this is clearly reflected in the great increase of output from its mint. Moreover signs of disintegration already began to appear, for during the reign of Antiochos II (261–246 B.C.)—whose character, for all we can deduce from a gold stater of Baktra, was perhaps less in the 529 heroic mould than that of his father—the province of Baktria broke away to form a new and independent kingdom, under Diodotos. At one moment Babylonia, the 524*, 530 heart of the Seleukid empire, had to suffer invasion by Ptolemy III of Egypt; then

545, 546 Aitolian league: *Head of Herakles, as on Alexander's coins/Aitolia as an armed Amazon seated on shield,* c. *250 B.C.* (*tetradrachm, 16.78 gm., diam. 30 mm., PCG 36.14; RPK*)

547, 548 Epirote league: *Heads of Dodonean Zeus with Dione/Charging bull within wreath,* c. *234 B.C.* (*didrachm, 9.98 gm., diam. 27 mm., PCG 35.10; Franke; Koinon 1*)

549, 550 Sparta: *Diademed portrait of King/Cult-statue of the Apollo of Amyklai, third century B.C.* (*tetradrachm, 16.56 gm., diam. 26 mm., PCG 29.14*)

551, 552 Seleukos I: *Head of king wearing helmet with bull's horn and ear, panther skin/Nike crowning trophy; Persepolis mint, 300-280 B.C.* (*tetradrachm, 16.87 gm., diam. 26-25 mm., BM 1969; Newell 420; from the Pasargadae excavations*)

553 Philetairos of Pergamon: *Head of Seleukos I, 274-263 B.C.* (*tetradrachm, obverse, 16.98 gm., diam. 28 mm., BMC 29*)

554, 555 Antiochos I: *Diademed portrait of Antiochos/Apollo seated on the omphalos; Seleu-keia-on-Tigris mint, 280-261 B.C.* (*tetradrachm, 17.19 gm., diam. 30-29 mm., BM 1947; Newell 177*)

Seleukos II was compelled to acquiesce in the rival reign of his brother Hierax based at Sardis in Asia Minor, as well as facing attacks from the Parthians in the east. Seleukos II's coins of Antioch give us the portrait of a young man with refined and amiable features; and also an interesting variant of the Apollo type, here shown not in the traditional posture seated on the omphalos but standing and reclining in what seems a somewhat languorous attitude against a large tripod and looking down at the arrow held in his hand. The pose seems to recall irresistibly some of the sculpture of the school of Praxiteles; and the Seleukid Apollo figures form an interesting comparison to the Apollo coin of Antigonos Doson in Macedonia, with the emphasis on grace rather than strength.

The period of comparative confusion in the Seleukid empire was terminated by the advent of Antiochos III (223–187 B.C.), who with determination set about consolidating his heritage once more, regaining control of Asia Minor and making an important expedition to recover the east, where his success was limited by the formidably increased power of Euthydemos of Baktria. However, Antiochos conquered Phoenicia and Palestine from the Ptolemies and even invaded Greece. But he was finally confronted with the Romans and defeated by them at the battle of Magnesia in 190 B.C., after which the Seleukid empire was never the same again. There was an impressive output of coinage during Antiochos' reign, and among the coins of Antioch were some large gold octodrachms weighing

34 grammes; these have the reverse type of Apollo seated on the omphalos, and a portrait of the king, wearing the royal diadem; his features still belong to a fairly youthful phase, though as the series of coins progresses at several mints we can follow through many variations the gradual effects of increasing age. During the eastern campaign, Antiochos found it necessary to impound the temple treasures to assure his supply of money, and this is reflected in enormous issues from the Iranian mints such as Ekbatana, where was minted an exceptional tetradrachm with a somewhat older portrait and a powerful Indian elephant on the reverse.

Even at the height of their power, the Seleukids were not the undisputed masters of all Asia, and one of their great rivals in Asia Minor was the kingdom of Pergamon, established by one Philetairos, an erstwhile officer of Lysimachos, before the death of Seleukos I. The splendid portrait of Seleukos which has already been mentioned formed the first type of Philetairos' coins. The latter's portrait, which gives a vivid impression of this rugged and realistically ambitious man, did not appear during his lifetime but during the reign of his successor Eumenes I (263–241 B.C.); and the coins continued in the name of Philetairos and with a reverse type adapted from the seated Athena of Lysimachos. At Pergamon the portrait and name of the dynastic founder remained, as in Ptolemaic Egypt, unchanged apart from a considerable development of style and detail, for several generations. We may regret that this was so, and that such a major school of Hellenistic art as Pergamon had not the opportunity to leave portraits of the other rulers who succeeded in building up Pergamon both as a power and a cultural centre. Only in one case, that of Eumenes II (197–160 B.C.) on a unique and somewhat corroded tetradrachm with a reverse showing standing figures of the Kabeiroi, do we find a portrait where there can nevertheless be perceived something of the same sculptural quality previously realized in the heads of Philetairos, of Seleukos and of Lysimachos' Alexander.

Asia in the Hellenistic period is not however exclusively the history of the great empires. A number of Greek cities managed to enjoy a certain degree of independence and even local sovereignty, though few could emulate Rhodes, whose sea power in the later third century made her the rival of the kingdoms. The freedom of the cities, however intermittent, can often be traced from the coins: for these took the unexpected form of a new mintage of the older types of Alexander or Lysimachos (or even in a few isolated cases, of Philip II)—an interesting phenomenon, as a reaction against the royal coinage of the time which could nevertheless hardly be construed as a sign of overt hostility. Thus we find a late form of the Herakles head and Zeus of the Alexander coinage used for purely civic issues such as those of Alexandria Troas, Chios, Priene and Miletos. Such coins were invariably marked with the name or symbol of the city; sometimes, as at Aspendos, they bear the dates of a local era and at Rhodes, which produced a specially important issue, the names of local magistrates appear. Some tetradrachms of a specially vigorous and 'baroque' style were produced at Sardis during a period when the control of the Seleukid kings was in abeyance. These issues were not in fact confined to Asia Minor—others appeared in Phoenicia, at Arados, and in the Black Sea area at Odessos and Mesembria; though in that region it was the late versions of the Lysimachos coin which were the most important, and were the main currency of the cities of Byzantion and Kalchedon for two hundred years. Sinope, on the southern shore of the Black Sea, had issued the Alexander type during the third century, but towards 200 B.C. emitted some individual tetradrachms with a fine head of the city goddess wearing a mural crown representing the city wall, and for the reverse an Apollo seated on the omphalos which strongly recalls the Seleukid type, except that Apollo here holds a lyre instead of bow and arrows.

Finally there is an important development of a purely Greek style of coinage in several of the lesser kingdoms of Asia—Pontus, Bithynia, Kappadokia—which though not Greek by origin were deeply infused with Greek culture and art; and some of the portrait coins produced for these kingdoms are among the finest of the Hellenistic age. In Pontus, for example, where the royal line was of partly Persian descent, we have a head of Mithradates III (246–190 B.C.) which is an example of the most brilliantly conceived realistic portraiture coupled with an insight into character,

and which can only be due to a Greek
artist of the highest calibre.   Similar qual-
ities can be found in the portrait of his
successor Pharnakes (190–169 B.C.), whose
586 very striking and individual features convey
a definite suggestion of his non-Greek
origins.   The reverses of these coins bear
figures of Zeus or of Hermes, with the
characteristic Pontic emblem of star and
crescent which recurs on the coins of
Mithradates VI at a later date.

The portrait coins of the Bithynian kings
scarcely attain the noble quality of the
Pontic, though that of Prusias I has a
considerable elegance.   His son Prusias II
was, according to the tradition, a coarse and
degenerate person, an impression which is
587 not contradicted by his coins where we see
a portrait which rather startlingly anticipates some of the later Seleukids in its
formality and vacuity.   The wing attached
to the diadem alludes to the descent of
this dynasty from Perseus.   The Bithynian
reverse shows a Zeus figure probably
copied from a cult statue at Nikomedia by
Doidalsas.   By contrast, another extremely
fine portrait, a late example of the realistic
style is that of the Kappadokian Orophernes
(158–157 B.C.); untypical for that kingdom,
588 it is uncertain where this was executed and
it may be Ionian work.   A group of these
coins was found in 1870 below the pedestal
of the cult-statue of Athena Polias at
Priene, where it is known that Orophernes
had deposited his treasure.   This portrait is,
however, fully worthy to be compared with
its contemporaries among the later Seleukids, many of which it surpasses in quality.

556 ▶

557 ▶

558 ▶

556 Ptolemy I Soter: *Portrait of Ptolemy, 300-*
285 B.C. (pentadrachm, 17.79 gm., diam.
23 mm., BMC Ptolemy I, 89), obverse of 561

557, 558 Ptolemy III Euergetes: *Busts of Ptolemy*
II Philadelphos and Arsinoe II/Busts of
Ptolemy I Soter and Berenike I, 246-221 B.C.
(octodrachm, 27.77 gm., diam. 28 mm., PCG
33.21 ; RPK)

559

560

561

562

563

564

565

The coinage of the Ptolemies has great historical importance as being the first regular monetary currency ever made in Egypt in antiquity. Before Alexander's conquest Egypt had formed part of the Persian empire and during that period absorbed large quantities of Greek silver coins as bullion. During the fourth century B.C. the last Egyptian kings had a relative independence, expressed by the issue of some isolated coinages, one of which as we 334 have seen, bore a demotic legend. Another, probably minted during the very last reign, that of Nektanebo II, was a gold stater one 559, 560 side of which shows a horse of Greek style and the other hieroglyphic characters meaning 'good gold'.

The foundation of Alexandria was followed in a few years by the establishment of a regular Greek mint where the portrait of Alexander was placed on the coins shortly 502 after his death. In the later phases of that coinage, the policy of Ptolemy, as satrap of Egypt, became apparent with the adoption, about 310 B.C., of a new weight standard lighter than the Attic standard which was so far universal in the empire of Alexander—a move apparently designed deliberately to isolate Egypt from the rest of the Hellenistic world and to build up an autarchic economy within Egypt. Ptolemy I Soter took the royal title in 305 B.C. and from that moment his own portrait appears on the gold coins, 562, 563 the reverse of which shows a chariot drawn by elephants, bearing a deified figure of 502 Alexander; as on the medallion of Babylon,

559, 560 Nektanebo II: *Prancing horse/Hieroglyphic signs (bead collar, heart and wind-pipe) nefr nub = 'good gold', 359-343 B.C. (stater 8.18 gm., diam. 17 mm., PCG 51.12)*

561 Ptolemy I Soter: *Eagle on thunderbolt, 300-285 B.C. (pentadrachm, 17.79 gm., diam. 23 mm., BMC Ptolemy I, 89), reverse of 556*

562, 563 Ptolemy I Soter: *Portrait of Ptolemy/Alexander in elephant-drawn chariot, 305-300 B.C. (stater, 7.10 gm., diam. 19 mm., BM 1897)*

564, 565 Arsinoe II: *Portrait of Arsinoe with veil and sceptre/Double cornucopiae, 270-250 B.C. (octodrachm, 27.81 gm., diam. 27 mm., BMC 9 ; RPK)*

he is shown holding a thunderbolt. The portrait of Ptolemy is at once arresting in its realism, capturing the extraordinary jagged physiognomy of the king and at the same time endowing him with divine attributes, for round his neck he wears the aegis of Zeus. This portrait has the same fundamental importance for the whole coinage of the dynasty as that of Philetairos at Pergamon; throughout the entire duration of the dynasty it was this image, with variations of style, that dominated the coinage, not only of gold but also of silver, and at the various mints not only at Alexandria but in Phoenicia and Cyprus, though fortunately portraits of many of the other Ptolemies also occur. The Soter head is normally accompanied by a reverse showing the eagle of Zeus standing on a thunderbolt, as for instance in the gold pentadrachm; it is this same type that persists through nearly all the silver coinage also, which down to the reign of Ptolemy III Euergetes was very abundant.

It is characteristic of the Ptolemaic dynasty that gold coinage plays a far more important role than in any of the other Hellenistic kingdoms, and it has survived in great quantities. One very striking series of large gold pieces to the weight of eight Ptolemaic drachms were contemporaneously known as 'mnaieia', as being the equivalent of one hundred drachms (= 1 mina) of silver. Some of these were minted after the death, in 270 B.C., of Arsinoe II the brilliant and capable sister-wife of Ptolemy II Philadelphos (285–246 B.C.); she was instantly proclaimed a goddess and as part of

567 ▶▶

566 ▶

569 ▶

568 ▶

566 Ptolemy III Euergetes: *Portrait of Euergetes wearing radiate crown and aegis, with trident; posthumous mintage,* c. *221-204 B.C. (octodrachm, 26.83 gm., diam. 27 mm., PCG 34.24; BM 1841)*

567 Arsinoe III: *Bust of Arsinoe III, 221-204 B.C. (octodrachm, 27.73 gm., diam. 26 mm., PCG 34.28)*

568 Berenike II: *Veiled portrait; minted at Ephesos, 246-221 B.C. (octodrachm, 27.73 gm., diam. 26 mm., PCG 33.23)*

569 Ptolemy IV Philopator: *Bust of Ptolemy IV, 221-204 B.C. (octodrachm, 27.88 gm., diam. 26 mm., BMC 34)*

556*, 561

570

571

her cult these gold mnaieia, together with **564, 565** silver dekadrachms and tetradrachms, were struck. Her portrait is impressively beautiful; and divine attributes are present, for she is depicted wearing a stephane and veil with the lotus tip of a sceptre visible above, and with a small horn of Ammon (recalling the deified Alexander) by the ear. The reverse of these coins sets a new style with the composition of two cornucopiae brimming with fruits and tied with a royal diadem. These gold coins were issued over a long period and even revived, in far inferior style, at much later dates.

A new type of gold coin was inaugurated **557*, 558*** by Ptolemy III Euergetes (246–221 B.C.); here remarkably there is a pair of heads on both sides and, as they are respectively labelled 'Adelphon' and 'Theon', it is clear that the first pair represents Philadelphos and Arsinoe, and the second pair Soter and Berenike I. The vast quantity of this issue, made both as the mnaieion and the half-piece, gives it a great importance in the scheme of Ptolemaic currency, though it must be admitted that the style has deteriorated, as can be seen by comparing the formalized Ptolemy Soter head with that of his own coins, and that of Arsinoe from the 'Adelphon' pair with hers. Yet the 'Adelphon' type is valuable for giving us a close idea of the features of Philadelphos which are not so easy to pin down from other coins. At the same time, the reign of Euergetes was not without some coins of extremely high quality, the best of which however were minted outside Egypt; there is, for instance, the fine coin of Berenike II, **568***

570, 571 Ptolemy V Epiphanes: *Bust of Ptolemy V with radiate crown/Radiate cornucopiae, bound with fillet, between two stars, 204-180 B.C. (octodrachm, 27.77 gm., diam. 27 mm., BMC 51)* a portrait rendered with subtlety and intimacy of feeling such as are quite lacking in the 'Adelphon-Theon' coins. The Berenike was a product of the mint of Ephesos, which at that time formed a part of the wide-ranging Ptolemaic dominions in the Aegean, and this is indicated by the bee symbol beside the cornucopiae.

However, the Alexandria mint was still capable of splendid work among the portraits of the later third century. One of these, posthumously struck in the time of Ptolemy IV Philopator (221–203 B.C.), 566* depicts Euergetes, under whom Egypt had been at the height of its power. A clear suggestion of corpulence does not detract from his lofty assurance and he is invested with a whole range of divine attributes, the aegis of Zeus thrown around the shoulders, the trident of Poseidon behind, and the rayed crown of Helios on his head. It is a noteworthy feature of Ptolemaic portraiture to include the shoulder and drapery as shown here, instead of terminating the head in a neck truncation.

Other fine examples are to be seen in the 569*, 567* portraits of Philopator and his wife Arsinoe III. As in the case of Philadelphos and Arsinoe II, it seems that he was the weak character and she the strong one—it was she who rallied the army at the battle of Raphia in 217 B.C. Their respective personalities are well differentiated on the coins. He is shown without any divine attributes, whereas Arsinoe's portrait includes the stephane and the sceptre like Arsinoe Philadelphos; the detail and expression

572 Antiochos I: *Head of horned horse ; Baktra mint, 280-261 B.C. (tetradrachm, reverse, 16.83 gm., diam. 25 mm., PCG 32.9 ; from the Oxus Treasure, 1877)*

573, 574 Seleukos II: *Portrait/Apollo standing against tripod ; Antioch mint, 246-226 B.C. (tetradrachm, obverse: 16.93 gm., diam. 32 mm., BM 1885, Newell 1000 ; reverse: 16.97 gm., diam. 28 mm., PCG 32.10 ; Newell 991)*

575, 576 Antiochos III: *Portrait within reel-and-bead border/Elephant ; Ekbatana mint, 221-187 B.C. (tetradrachm, obverse: 16.97 gm., diam. 28 mm., PCG 33.13 ; reverse: 17.23 gm., diam. 25 mm., BMC 29 ; Newell 627-8)*

577, 578 Eumenes I of Pergamon: *Portrait of Philetairos with combined diadem and laurel wreath/Athena enthroned holding shield, 262-241 B.C. (tetradrachm, 16.99 gm., diam. 30 mm., PCG 32.4 ; Westermark V.XXII)*

579, 580 Eumenes II of Pergamon: *Portrait diademed/Kabeiroi within wreath, as on coins of Syros, 197-159 B.C. (tetradrachm, 15.24 gm., diam. 34 mm., BMC 47)*

581, 582 Sardes: *Head of Herakles/Zeus, as on the Alexander coins, c. 225 B.C. (tetradrachm, 16.85 gm., diam. 30 mm., BM 1910)*

240

572

573

574

575

576

577

578

579

580

581

582

583

584

585

586

587

588

589

590

591

592

593

594

alike make this one of the most attractive of all Hellenistic portrait coins.

Philopator and Arsinoe apparently were murdered by a court cabal and were succeeded by their young son Ptolemy V Epiphanes (204-181 B.C.); it was for his Egyptian coronation that the Rosetta stone was inscribed. His portrait, in which he 570, 571 wears the crown of Helios, shows clear features and an alert air which contrast strongly with the looks of his father. The cornucopia on the reverse is also invested with solar rays and flanked by stars. We can be sure that the portraits of Epiphanes, at least, are contemporary and not posthumous, since some of them already appear on coins of the Phoenician mints which were lost to Antiochos III in 200 B.C.

After the time of Epiphanes it is clear enough that decline sets in in every aspect of the Ptolemaic coinage. Portraits become rarer, and it is exceptional to find them as on some rare silver coins of Ptolemy VI Philometor (181-145 B.C.) and of later kings such as Euergetes II and Auletes. The stereotyped quality of the coinage becomes more and more apparent, gold becomes infrequent and silver debased. After the loss of Phoenicia, provincial mints in Cyprus began to issue a long series of tetradrachms, usually of poor metal and, like those of Alexandria, usually marked with the regnal year dates of each king. The shortage of silver—a metal not obtainable within Ptolemaic territory—had begun already well before the end of the third century, and partly as a response to this situation there had been instituted an important coinage in bronze, perhaps from the time of Philadelphos and certainly during the succeeding reigns. The sizes and probable values of this bronze coinage were unusual in the Greek world, and the largest pieces sometimes weigh as much as 100 grammes, though there are many smaller pieces as well. The best of this bronze belongs to the later third century, and typically shows the head of Zeus Ammon on the obverse, with the eagle and thunderbolt on the reverse as on the silver. The precise dates and denominations of many of these coins are difficult to determine: some definitely belong to Ptolemy III Euergetes. By the end of the third century, bronze had become the main currency in Egypt, virtually replacing silver, and the drachm of bronze became henceforth the unit of reckoning for all purposes, even after the resumption of silver coinage in the second century.

595, 600

On the whole, the later bronze currency remains as stereotyped as the silver, until in the time of Kleopatra VII (51–30 B.C.) there is an exceptional issue with a portrait. It is of the greatest value and interest as one of the most authentic surviving likenesses, emanating from Alexandria itself, in comparison with which some of the images of the famous queen in conjunction with Antony, which occur on coins of the other parts of her dominions, seem mere caricatures. The coin is also interesting from the purely monetary point of view, as the value is, for once, explicitly stated; the letter Π behind the eagle is the numeral 80, and so the coin was worth 80 bronze drachmai which, as we know from the documentary

601, 602

evidence of papyri, would be about one-sixth of a silver drachm at the current valuation (silver drachm = 480 bronze drachms).

THE WEST

The western Mediterranean was comparatively remote from events in Asia and from the new world that came into being after Alexander. In the west, the Hellenistic period saw the culmination of the age-long struggle between the Greeks and Carthage and the final absorption of both into the domain of Rome. The coinage of this period lacks the sustained aesthetic interest and development of the classical period and sometimes seems by comparison merely imitative and perfunctory, though it is always of great historical value and in some cases, at least, rises to considerable heights.

The restoration of Sicilian affairs by Timoleon in 344 B.C. was followed by a period of comparative calm until the establishment of Agathokles as tyrant of Syracuse (317–289 B.C.) opened up a fresh phase of struggle and conflict. Numismatically his reign is noteworthy for the re-introduction of a regular and copious issue of silver tetradrachms, the first since the time of Dionysios. The first type was simply an imitation, in later style, of the older types such as those of the Euainetos dekadrachms, and probably only after Agathokles' sensational invasion of Africa was there created a new type, which has considerable quality. A

589

head of Kore in an elaborate style with hair flowing down across the neck and even appearing on the far side, and a crown of corn ears on her head—all this owes something to the classical prototypes, though we can at once sense the gulf in time which has elapsed and the quality of expression is 590 something new. The reverse also is a fine one; Nike, naked to the waist, is erecting a trophy of arms, like the earlier type at Lampsakos, but imbued with a new and dramatic sense in the virtuosity of the execution that are typical of the early Hellenistic style. On the right is seen the triskelis, the symbol of Agathokles' claim to the domination of all Sicily.

At some date during his reign, there was minted at Syracuse a series of coins in electrum, a metal which the Carthaginians were also using at this time, and which may have influenced Syracuse in the use of this unusual metal. The smaller pieces, of which 27*, 629 there is a long series, show a long-haired head of Apollo with the tripod on the reverse while on a larger piece we find, as a somewhat unusual practice, the head of a 632, 633 deity on each side of the coin. The obverse is Apollo and the reverse is Artemis Soteira, with a quiver indicated behind her neck, of a style which can be paralleled from bronze coins of Agathokles. His name, however, is nowhere mentioned on these electrum coins, which we could hardly assign to this period but for the consistent evidence of several coin hoards. Eventually Agathokles set himself on a par with other Hellenistic monarchs and openly took the title of king; on a unique gold piece he imitated the Alexandrian head of Alexander in the elephant scalp, and the kingly title finally appears on the gold coins of the last phase where the Athena head is exactly copied from gold staters of Alexander with a griffin on the helmet, and the reverse is 630, 631 a winged thunderbolt. As we shall see, the coinage of Alexander was not without influence even on the types of Carthaginian coins at this time.

It was only some years after Agathokles, namely in 280 B.C., that Pyrrhos the king of Epeiros made his meteoric irruption into the affairs of Italy and Sicily, in the conduct of his costly campaigns against Rome on the one hand and Carthage on the other. In Italy, his main headquarters was at Tarentum, where the local coins already men- 453, 454 tioned carry allusions to his presence. Coins in his name however seem to have been minted at Lokroi Epizephyrioi. It is at 591-4 once apparent that in one important respect Pyrrhos' practice is closely akin to that of the Macedonian kings of this time, in that nowhere does his portrait appear. Much as we may regret this, the splendid and exuberant types of Pyrrhos' Lokrian coins go far to compensate for it. The tetradrachm has for the obverse the head of Dodonean Zeus, whose sanctuary lay in 591 Pyrrhos' homeland; this head, crowned with oak leaves and with restless flowing hair and beard, makes a strong contrast with the restrained and classical head of the same god minted for Alexander of Epeiros at 445* Tarentum, and even with the more concentrated style of Antigonos Doson's Pos- 540 eidon, but the Pyrrhos coin is masterly in

its different way. Its exciting and dynamic
quality is well matched by the calm majesty
592 of the reverse type, Dione seated on a high-
backed throne and swathed in the complex
drapery so typical of Hellenistic sculpture.
593 The didrachm has a helmeted head which
in its intensity and idealistic gaze recalls the
style of the Alexander and Seleukos heads
from the mint of Pergamon; it is, however,
the head of Achilles which we see here, and
594 the reverse shows the goddess Thetis, his
mother, reclining on a seahorse and ad-
miring the shield which Hephaistos has
prepared for her son. The suggestion is
clearly conveyed that Pyrrhos was destined
to rival the Homeric hero whose son was
indeed the king's namesake. The impressive style of these coins is quite different
from anything we might have expected at
an Italian mint at this time, and it may well
be that the artist responsible was not a
local one, but may have come from mainland Greece or Macedonia.

The other coinage of Pyrrhos was minted
at Syracuse, and seems more in harmony
with the established traditions of that mint,
giving what are in any case the finest of its
products at this period. There is not only
an important series of Syracusan bronze
coins with the head of Herakles and the
figure of Athena Alkidemos (which recurs
on Pyrrhos' silver, as if to emphasize his
links with Macedonia) but coins minted in
his own name, gold staters and half-staters.
635 On the stater is the head of Athena with the
griffin-decorated helmet, harking back not
merely to Agathokles but to Alexander; it
is here rendered with unparalleled grace, and

*ties to Achilles,
a's favorite hero.*

595 ▶

596 ▶

595 Egypt, Ptolemy III Euergetes: *Head of
Zeus-Ammon, 246-221 B.C. (36.04 gm.,
diam. 35 mm., BMC 90), obverse of 600*

596 Hieron II of Syracuse: *Armed horseman
265-215 B.C. (19.45 gm., diam. 28 mm.,
BM 1931), reverse of 597*

597

598

600

599

601

602

behind the head is a small symbol, an owl with open wings. For the half-stater there is a head of Artemis with an elaborate and artificial coiffure frequently met with in Hellenistic sculpture but rarely elsewhere in coinage except for a head of Berenike I in Cyrenaica. Both the Pyrrhos gold coins have the same reverse, one of the most splendid Nike figures in Greek coinage, miraculously light-footed, carrying in her left hand a trophy and a wreath held out in front, with drapery swirling about her feet.

634
628*

Pyrrhos withdrew from the west in 276 B.C. having achieved comparatively little, and Syracuse settled down to the long reign of Hieron II (275–215 B.C.) during which stability and calm were maintained in his part of Sicily by means of friendship with Rome. To this time belongs a vast quantity of coinage whose precise system still remains to be determined and whose character in general seems lacking in originality or imagination. There are gold half-staters in Hieron's name but without any royal title, which seem to belong to the earlier part of this long period; the head, Persephone or Kore, is a merely academic derivative of the Agathokles' Kore, and the reverse, following the long tradition of the Syracusan mint depicts a racing chariot but here a comparatively lifeless one. More interesting are the bronze coins which form an enormous issue and have the merit of presenting a portrait of Hieron, with a horseman on the reverse which may also be intended to depict the king. The portrait seems to express a benevolent if unexciting personality, and it hardly appears on the

636, 637
596*, 597

597 Hieron II of Syracuse: *Diademed portrait, 265-215 B.C. (19.45 gm., diam. 28 mm., BM 1931), obverse of 596*

598, 599 Brettian league: *Head of Ares, griffin stars and scorpion on helmet/Hera Hoplosmia armed, c. 210 B.C. (13.46 gm., diam. 27 mm., BM 1921)*

600 Egypt, Ptolemy III Euergetes: *Eagle on thunderbolt, cornucopiae symbol, 246-221 B.C. (36.04 gm., diam. 35 mm., BMC 90), reverse of 595*

601, 602 Egypt, Kleopatra VII: *Portrait bust of Kleopatra/Eagle, with cornucopiae and mark of value = 80, 51-30 B.C. (18.40 gm., diam. 27 mm., 80-drachma piece; BM 5)*

silver coins, which are dominated by the queen Philistis and her son, Gelon II. The

603, 604

Philistis coins were the most numerous of all, and her head shown wearing a royal diadem below the veil must inevitably recall the Arsinoe II at Alexandria, though it lacks the vitality of the Alexandrian art with which Hieron's Syracuse must have been in contact. The reverse showing a chariot drawn by horses at the walk has a somewhat perfunctory air when compared with the chariots of the really creative period of numismatic art in Sicily. The coinages of the short reign of Hieronymos (215-214 B.C.) and of the subsequent republic which lasted only until the Roman conquest in 212 B.C., are on the whole aridly academic.

The cities of Italy had since the time of Pyrrhos increasingly fallen under the control of Rome, and there are few enough signs of creative activity in the coins of those cities which remained independent, except for a brief interlude at the time of the Hannibalic occupation, when a newly formed league of the Brettii, based perhaps on Lokroi, became the close ally of the Carthaginians. This league within a few years issued a large and complex series of coin-

626*, 638

ages in all metals, of which the finest are gold half-staters. The head of Poseidon, identified by the trident half-concealed in his hair and a small dolphin below his neck, has a rare grace and vitality which is hard to parallel at this period, while the design of the reverse seems to recall the Thetis of Pyrrhos' coins at Lokroi. The goddess of the Brettian coins is not so easy to identify, as instead of the armour of Achilles there is

a small Eros shooting with his bow which would be more suitable to Aphrodite. The bronze coins of the Brettii were extremely numerous; one of the best types has a head

598, 599

of Ares with a finely-decorated helmet and on the reverse a warlike goddess. Close connections between the Brettii and the Carthaginians seem to be indicated by certain details such as the presence of a Punic letter on some of the bronze coins, and a small *gamma* on some of the silver which re-appears on coins of Hannibal; this seems to imply the use of the same mint or engravers.

CARTHAGE

Carthage, the great historical opponent both of the western Greeks and of Rome, was a Semitic city founded from Tyre as early as the eighth century B.C., or even before, and long commanded a widespread maritime empire which included parts of Spain, Sardinia and western Sicily. Slow to adopt coinage, she had eventually become receptive to Greek custom by about 400 B.C. and the earliest coins were those minted in Sicily for the payment of mercenaries during the wars against Dionysios. By the late fourth century these issues had become prolific, and were to a large extent Greek in style and no doubt made by Greeks. An exceptional tetradrachm of the

605

late fourth century shows a female head wearing an oriental tiara: she was once rather fancifully identified as Dido the foundress of Carthage but in fact is almost certainly a goddess, whose attributes were the lion and the palm tree on the reverse, as in the case of the Greek Artemis. Below the lion in Punic script is the legend *ommachanat*, signifying 'in the camp', or army headquarters; this legend occurs also on a more regular series of tetradrachms below the national emblem of the horse's head, usually accompanied by a palm tree. The obverse, so clearly adapted from the Syracusan Arethusa, complete with encircling dolphins, is probably here intended to represent the Punic goddess Tanit pene Baal; in this head we may see a Punic copyist at work, subtly transforming the Greek style. Such coins as these were being minted contemporaneously with Agathokles at Syracuse; but after about 300 B.C. the head of Tanit was replaced by a fine copy from the coins of Alexander the Great, the Greek Herakles here standing for his Punic counterpart Melqart.

While the main silver coinage was minted for military purposes by the Carthaginians in Sicily, a mint was also opened during the later fourth century at Carthage itself for the production of a prodigious gold coinage whose extent seems almost to rival that of the Greek kingdoms. It has been conjectured that the supply of gold may have been procured from West Africa, to which the Carthaginians had their sea routes. In these coins, which consisted mainly of staters weighing 9.5 grammes, the style of the 'Tanit' head shows a less marked Greek influence than in the silver of Sicily, and it is characteristic that the wreath of corn ears

is always worn, together with an elaborate pendant necklace. The standing horse, the regular type of the reverse, has the same significance as the horse's head on the silver, alluding to the foundation legend of Carthage, where the discovery of a horse's head in the ground was the omen provided by Juno (the Latin equivalent for Tanit). There were also smaller divisions of the stater, half, quarter, fifth, tenth, of which the half has a palm tree behind the horse and the tenth merely the palm tree and horse's head. Supplies of gold were evidently not inexhaustible for in the subsequent phases of this coinage, lasting into the third century, the weight was reduced to that of a shekel (7.6 grammes) and the metal increasingly alloyed, a debasement into electrum which is visible by the time of the wars against Agathokles from the paler colour of the metal, corresponding to that of the Syracusan electrum.

At the time of the first Punic war against Rome (264–241 B.C.) there were minted, probably in Sicily, a series of large Carthaginian coins, mainly in silver but also including large electrum three-stater pieces. These have the usual head of Tanit, but the reverse has a welcome variant in the shape of a prancing horse and palm tree, and a legend which reads *bearzat*—interpreted as meaning 'in the land', that is in the dominions outside Carthage, and this, as various coin hoards indicate, must mean Sicily. Apart from this legend and those which occurred on the previous Sicilian-minted coins, it is a peculiarity of Carthaginian coins that they bear no inscription, apart from individual letters and other control marks. This feature, coupled with the great uniformity of type and theme in the Carthaginian coinage as a whole, has made it only gradually possible, with the aid of all the methods now used in numismatic study, to disentangle the various components of this coinage, both chronologically and otherwise. It is still difficult to define the characteristics of a 'Carthaginian' style though the following coins are perhaps the best examples of it, and it is clearly distinct from a purely Greek style. This at least has some importance in view of the comparative lack of a Punic art in other forms.

640*, 648 At about the time of the first Punic war, a further series of rather spectacular gold coins was minted at Carthage itself; these were virtually unknown before the discovery of a large hoard in Tunisia in 1948. Here it is possible to perceive that the style of the Tanit head has moved further away from any Greek prototype, although the basic elements are unchanged. Another 639*, 649 subtle change is seen in the next important type, an electrum coinage minted during the first Punic war in vast quantities; its distinguishing feature is that above the standing horse there is the Egyptian solar emblem of the sun-disk flanked by uraeus-cobras. Both here and in the preceding issue there are sometimes small dots placed on the exergual line, no doubt as control marks.

After her defeat by Rome in 241 B.C., Carthage was able to produce coins only on a much reduced scale, with debased silver and bronze mainly replacing the more prec-

603, 604 Syracuse, Philistis: *Veiled portrait/ Chariot driven by Nike, 265-216 B.C. (tetradrachm, 13.50 gm., diam. 28 mm., Lloyd 1545)*

605, 606 Carthage: *Head of goddess wearing tiara/ Lion walking before palm-tree; Sicilian mint, 320-300 B.C. (tetradrachm, 17.18 gm., diam. 26 mm., BM 1841)*

607, 608 Carthage: *Head of Tanit with dolphins/ Horse's head, Punic inscription; Sicilian mint, 320-300 B.C. (tetradrachm, obverse: 17.03 gm., diam. 25 mm., BM 1846; reverse: 17.09 gm., diam. 25 mm., BM 1875)*

609 Carthage: *Head of Melqart; Sicilian mint, 300-280 B.C. (tetradrachm, obverse, 16.91 gm., diam. 24 mm., BM 1910)*

610, 611 Carthage, the Barcids in Spain: *Bearded head of Melqart, with club/Elephant with mahout, 237-218 B.C. (double-shekel, 14.61 gm., diam. 25 mm., PCG 37.1; from the Mogente hoard, 1910)*

612 Carthage, the Barcids in Spain: *Beardless head of Melqart, 237-218 B.C. (triple-shekel, 22.05 gm., diam. 28 mm., PCG 52.35)*

603

604

605

606

607

608

609

610

611

612

613

614

615

616

617

618

619

620

621

622

623

624

625

613, 614 Euthydemos I: *Diademed portrait/Herakles seated*, c. *200-190 B.C. (tetradrachm, 16.45 gm., diam. 32 mm., BM 1888)*

615 Demetrios I: *Portrait of king in elephant scalp*, c. *190 B.C. (tetradrachm, obverse, 16.73 gm., diam. 32 mm., BMC 3)*

616, 617 Antimachos: *Portrait of king wearing kausia/Poseidon with trident and palm branch*, c. *180 B.C. (tetradrachm, 17.00 gm., diam. 33 mm., PCG 33.20)*

618, 619 Demetrios II: *Portrait of king wearing kausia, Greek inscription/Zeus, Kharoshthi inscription*, c. *170 B.C. (tetradrachm, 9.05 gm., diam. 25 mm., BM 1922)*

620, 621 Eukratides: *Portrait of king wearing helmet/The Dioskouroi riding*, c. *160 B.C. (tetradrachm, 16.82 gm., diam. 35 mm., BM)*

622 Menander: *Diademed portrait*, c. *150 B.C. (tetradrachm, 16.31 gm., diam. 30 mm., BM 1966; found in Iran)*

623, 624 Archebios: *Helmeted spear-thruster portrait/Zeus with thunderbolt*, c. *120-100 B.C. (tetradrachm, 16.72 gm., diam. 32 mm., BM 1959)*

625 Theophilos: *Diademed portrait*, c. *120-100 B.C. (tetradrachm, 16.78 gm., diam. 33 mm., BM 1965)*

ious metals. But the semi-independent dominion established in Spain by Hamilcar Barca and his family in 237 B.C. enabled the rich mineral resources of the Peninsula to be used in building up a new base of power eventually to become a springboard for Hannibal's invasion of Italy. In this context must be placed some of the most remarkable of all Carthaginian coins, many of them representing a considerable departure from the traditional scheme. Along with a number of gold coins, we find large and impressive pieces in silver, the highest value being of three shekels (or in Greek terms, a hexadrachm). Some of these maintain the traditional horse and palm, but others display a diademed head of royal aspect with a warship on the reverse, or in place of the horse an African war-elephant 611 complete with its mahout. In place of Tanit, there is a bearded head of Melqart with 610 a massive club behind the neck; other versions of the Melqart are beardless. It is at 612 once apparent that these powerfully modelled heads are of a purely Greek style, which at once makes a strong contrast to the regular Carthaginian coins, and the artists must have been drawn from the Hellenistic world. Are these heads also, as has been suggested, intended as portraits? The idea that the bearded head could be Hasdrubal Barca and the beardless head Hannibal, is undeniably attractive, but can hardly be regarded as demonstrable. In any case these examples are no mean contribution to the repertoire of Hellenistic coinage.

Otherwise the Carthaginian coinages continued on traditional lines; during the Han-

nibalic war, issues of small silver and of electrum were made even at mints in Italy such as Lokroi, showing, as we have seen, points of contact with the local Brettian coins. In the remaining half-century of her existence after the Roman victory at Zama in 202 B.C., Carthage made a remarkable economic recovery (of which the elder Cato so complained) and this is borne out by her coins of the period, which include tetra-
650-53 drachms of good silver, and even some gold on a restricted scale, whose style seems to owe more than usual to Greek models.

BAKTRIA

The Baktrian kingdom which broke away from the Seleukid empire in the time of Antiochos II (261-246 B.C.) remained for nearly two centuries the easternmost outpost of the Greek world. Its coins are of exceptional quality and interest giving us evidence of a long and powerful dynasty which has otherwise almost vanished from the historical record. Since the archaeological exploration of the region has not yet yielded many tangible remains of the Greek period, the coins still form the only continuous historical documents and are in any case among the finest works of art surviving from the Hellenistic age.

It was, as we have seen, Diodotos the governor of Baktria who broke away from the Seleukid empire during the third century. In the first phase, he substituted his own portrait for that of Antiochos II while

retaining the name of the latter, but later he took the royal title himself and placed it beside a new reverse type of a thundering 524*, 53 Zeus. Diodotos was apparently succeeded by his son, of the same name, and among the extant Diodotos coins there are some wide variations in the portrait which may well include the image of both kings.

The new kingdom consisted at first of the northern part of modern Afghanistan, and was stabilized in alliance with the Parthians, a nomad people who at the same time founded a state in northern Iran which was eventually to absorb much of the Seleukid east. It was not until about 208 B.C. that there was a significant reaction from the Seleukid side, when Antiochos III made his eastern expedition. By then the Baktrian kingdom had become too powerful to be reconquered, as Antiochos realized when he met the Baktrian king Euthydemos. A glance at the portrait of the latter in his 613 old age soon makes it clear that he was indeed one of the most formidable characters of the time. Equally evident is the detailed realism which an artist of the highest calibre has deployed in order to convey this impression. The reverse draws on the 614 theme of Herakles, here shown seated on a rock.

The long series of Euthydemos' coins showing considerable development in the portrait seems sure evidence of a prolonged reign during which the king consolidated and extended his dominions, though apparently without crossing the Hindu Kush into India. This step seems to have been taken by his son Demetrios, who on his 615 coins appropriately wears the elephant scalp like Alexander the Great, as if claiming to be his successor. Something of the lost tradition seems to have filtered through deviously to medieval Europe, as we gather from Chaucer's mention of the 'grete Emetrius king of Inde'. But reconstructions of the conquests made by him and his successors have to be made very cautiously, and the coins in any case attest the existence at this period of several other important rulers, a second Euthydemos, Agathokles, Pantaleon—of whom the last two are notable for having first minted coins with legends in the Indian Brahmi script.

There was also one Antimachos who, like the others, is totally unknown apart from
616 his coins; but these preserve for us a portrait which is startling in its actuality, and a masterpiece of characterization. In this shoulder-length head he wears the kausia, a traditional Macedonian head-dress, with the royal diadem beneath. We have not only a vivid and accurate record of Antimachos' personal appearance but also an unequalled suggestion of a personality in which strength of character is combined with a civilized scepticism and sense of humour—such is the immediacy and impact
617 of this superb head. The reverse is likewise of great interest; a standing figure of Poseidon, carrying his trident and a palm branch, which would in another context suggest naval victory. In a land-locked kingdom this poses problems unless, as has been suggested, there may have been victories gained on the Oxus river against invaders from the north.

It is remarkable to see how the Baktrian kingdom, at least from the time when it spread into India, seems to have aimed at having something of the dual character of a Graeco-Indian state; in the same way that Alexander had aimed to include the Iranians as equals in his empire. This, at least, seems to be the explanation for the development of a bilingual coinage, minted at Alexandria on the south of the Hindu Kush, at Pushkalavati and at Taxila, proclaiming the dual nature of the realm by including the names and titles of the king in Greek on one side and in the Kharosthi script on the other. Apart from this, the general aspect of the coins remained basically Greek in their art and in the figuring of Greek deities, except that some were square in shape, conforming to Indian custom, instead of round. An early example of the bilingual coin is a unique tetradrachm 618, 619 of a Demetrios who must, as his excellent portrait makes clear, be distinct from Demetrios I. The quality of portraiture which was maintained here and in the subsequent coinage is of the greatest value in itself as a documentary fact, and also because it enables us to determine whether kings of the same name can or cannot be identified.

Alongside the bilingual coins, however, most of the Baktrian kings also produced some purely Greek tetradrachms and it is these which are mainly considered here. An important figure towards the middle of the second century was Eukratides, who in addition to a long series of tetradrachms has also left a magnificent gold medallion of which a single specimen survives. In his

620 regular portrait, of which there are many varieties, he wears a crested helmet with the emblems of quasi-divine royalty, the bull's horn and ear, which we have already seen

551 on the Seleukos I tetradrachms from Persepolis. Among the numerous varieties of Eukratides' coins some are comparatively formalized, but at best they are finely ob-

621 served and full of character. The reverse type is a group of the Dioskouroi on horseback, which has a vigorous sense of movement and is well framed by the disposition of the lettering in an arc above. Eukratides is not quite unknown to the ancient sources, but the theory that this king was acting in concert with the Seleukid Antiochos IV against Parthia and that he was himself a Seleukid by birth, are conjectures that go far beyond the evidence.

There seems little doubt however that of all the Baktrian kings the one who made the most lasting impression in Indian tradition was Menander. His coins, mostly bilingual, are the most numerous of all and have been found over the widest area. The main seat of his power must have been Alexandria, south of the Hindu Kush, and there is no doubt of his control over at least the northern Punjab, though it is less certain that he ever extended his realm as far as the Ganges Basin. It seems that he was sympathetically inclined towards the Buddhists in India, and was claimed by them as an adherent. His coins, however, give little hint of such possibilities, and their regular emblem is the characteristically Macedonian image of the Athena Alkidemos

622 of Pella. His portrait as preserved on a

626 Brettian league: *Thetis ? riding on hippocamp, with Eros*, c. 210 B.C. (*gold drachm, 4.21 gm., diam. 16 mm., Lloyd 539*)

627 Syracuse, Agathokles ?: *Tripod*, c. 315-305 B.C. (*electrum 50-litra, 3.66 gm., diam. 15 mm., BM 1937), reverse of 629*

628 Syracuse, Pyrrhos: *Nike with wreath and trophy*, 278-276 B.C. (*gold stater, 8.59 gm., diam. 20 mm., PCG 37.15 ; RPK), reverse of 635*

629

630

631

632

633

634

635

636

637

638

unique Greek style tetradrachm has a vigorous and bold relief without reaching the artistic heights of the Antimachos, and it is repeated more or less faithfully over the great range of his coinage.

The successors of Menander have left a rich series of coins, the study of which strongly suggests that the Graeco-Baktrian realm was all too familiar with the vicissitudes and rivalries that afflicted other Hellenistic states. In some cases it seems possible to surmise the dynastic affinites of the various kings from the types of their coins, and conquests of one by another are sometimes attested by overstrikings of the coins of a conquered rival. The art of portraiture gradually became more formalized, as it did elsewhere in the Hellenistic world, though it must be said that nevertheless the individuality of the various rulers is generally well maintained.

A very remarkable type of portrait, first appearing on some rare coins of Eukratides, is adopted on a tetradrachm of Archebios 623 (probably about 100 B.C.), in which the attitude is one of thrusting with a spear, held in the right hand, and the shoulders are seen from behind. The helmet is similar to that of Eukratides, and across the left shoulder is the aegis of Zeus. The scheme of this portrait with its highly dramatic quality is something which occurs more than once among the Baktrians, though never on any other series of Hellenistic coins; the scheme was, however, not unknown elsewhere, and it is to be found, for instance, on a gem representing Philip V of Macedonia. The reverse of the Archebios 624 coin seems to show an equal sense of the dramatic in the figure of Zeus seen from the front, holding a long sceptre and brandishing his thunderbolt. Another tetradrachm, 625 of Theophilos, again gives a great feeling of actuality which makes a most vivid impression, as well as showing the tenacity with which Greek art survived in these remote regions, probably until *c*. 100 B.C. and after. Similar coins of purely Greek style, of which a few were minted in each reign down to the time of the last king, Hermaios, are great rarities today; they can hardly have been normal currency, and were more probably made for presentations and other special purposes. Few of them were known before the discovery in 1947 of the great hoard from Qunduz in northern Afghanistan.

THE LATER SELEUKIDS

The coinage of the later Seleukid empire, after the death of Antiochos III (187 B.C.) has a rather different complexion from that of the previous period; still of great historical interest, it gives a vivid picture of the decline of this vast realm to the status of a local Syrian kingdom. The fact that the coins, at least from the middle of the second century onwards, can be closely dated, not merely to the reign but to the year, also provides a valuable chronological framework for an understanding of Hellenistic art as it developed in the later phases. The heroic and realistic portraiture typical of

the third century was gradually succeeded by a phase of more classicizing and academic style, which has its counterpart elsewhere in the revived coinage of Athens and other cities, and later still by a kind of semi-abstract formalism.

After Antiochos III, the kingdom of Pergamon became established as the main power in western Asia Minor, leaving only Cilicia to the Seleukids, whose domain, however, still extended eastwards as far as Iran. After a period of retrenchment by Seleukos IV (187–175 B.C.) there came the reign of Antiochos IV Epiphanes (175–164 B.C.) who still showed an ambitious spirit— not only campaigning in the east and founding or re-founding cities, but also in the attempt to augment his still considerable empire by the conquest of Egypt. This was however foiled by Roman intervention. Also, as is well known, his attempt to impose the worship of the Greek Zeus at Jerusalem earned him the implacable hostility of the Jews. Yet his personal cult of Zeus was intended as a unifying factor in his empire; as such his coins display an image of the god enthroned which can be related to the reconstruction of the Olympian Zeus of Pheidias at Daphnai near Antioch. A unique gold stater exemplifies 532*, 53 the style of his coins, with a grandiose row of titles; the small Nike held by Zeus places a crown upon the title of the king as 'God manifest'. Special issues were made for the celebrations at Daphnai in 166 B.C. some of which depicted Apollo (with a reverse showing the famous statue by Bryaxis) and others with a fine head of 654

Zeus which may partly reflect the classical quality of the Pheidian Zeus but in any case has features which, save for the beard, would pass as a portrait of Antiochos. The same celebrations marked Antiochos' 'conquest' of Egypt by the issue, from the mint of Antioch, of a set of large bronze coins of purely propaganda value, exactly on the model of the Ptolemaic bronzes but with the name of Antiochos.

After the death of Epiphanes (164 B.C.) it seemed for a moment that the Iranian provinces would break away under the satrap Timarchos—possibly acting in concert with Eukratides of Baktria, as the coins suggest. Timarchos' coins are however rare survivals, since they were mostly reminted after his defeat at the hands of Demetrios I. This Seleukid who returned from exile in Rome to claim the throne in 162 B.C. did, by his energy, preserve the empire intact for his own time, though within a decade of his death in 150 B.C. Iran and Babylonia were conquered by the Parthians. The portrait of Demetrios as we see it on his coins of the Antioch mint is strongly modelled and expressive of a resolute character, though somewhat idealized and hardly equalling the meticulous realism of his contemporary and ally Oropherles; the reverse type shows Tyche seated on an elaborate throne decorated with winged Nereids. It is interesting to note that here, and henceforth in subsequent reigns, the date is inscribed on the coin, in this case year 161 of the Seleukid era, equivalent to October 152–October 151 B.C.

Demetrios I was finally defeated by a coalition headed by Ptolemy VI of Egypt, who now proceeded to regain his lost influence in Syria and Phoenicia; the throne of Antioch was obtained for his protégé Alexander Balas (150–145 B.C.) and consolidated by the marriage of the latter with the Ptolemaic princess Kleopatra Thea. A special coin was minted for the occasion, showing the heads of Alexander and Kleopatra side by side, though it is the queen who, in the guise of Isis and with a cornucopia as emblem, is given precedence; she exercised a powerful influence over the state during the following generation, as the queen of three Seleukid kings and ultimately, for a time, sole ruler herself. A further sign of renewed influence by the Ptolemies was that, from this time, in parallel with the normal Seleukid coins on the Attic standard, Tyre, Sidon and other cities revived a semi-Ptolemaic type of coinage on the Egyptian standard and displaying the Ptolemaic eagle (though with the portrait and name of the Seleukid kings); later the city coins of Tyre still conformed to the same model.

There followed a succession of Seleukid rulers who clearly lacked force and capacity and who, often at war amongst themselves, achieved only the decline of their kingdom. One of these was the boy-king Antiochos VI (145–142 B.C.) who on his coins wears the rayed crown of the sun-god like Ptolemy Euergetes, but in whose portrait the 'classicizing' style of his predecessors seems to be turning to a sort of academic mannerism; the modelling is comparatively

weak and the elaborate curling hair lacks
659 vitality. The reverse, showing the galloping
Dioskouroi, has an equal air of artificiality
—especially if compared with the similar
621 group on the coins of Eukratides—which
is not diminished by the wealth of detail,
the wreath border, the royal titles and
the date (equivalent to 144–143 B.C.)
and as an addition the name, added
above, of Tryphon, the scheming general for whom Antiochos VI was a mere
figurehead, to be put out of the way in
due course.

Antiochos VI had reigned only at
Antioch, meanwhile Demetrios II (146–
140 B.C.) controlled the rest of the kingdom
and succeeded merely in losing Babylonia
and Media to the Parthians and himself
becoming their prisoner. His brother
Antiochos VII Sidetes (139–129 B.C.) was
the outstanding figure of this time and did
much to restore the kingdom, though his
heroic attempt to regain the east was
doomed to failure, while the Parthians
cunningly released their royal prisoner to
make a bid for the throne of Antioch
behind his brother's back. During Demetrios' second reign (129–125 B.C.), the
660 coins show him wearing a beard, commonly
supposed to be a sign that he had adopted
Parthian usage during his captivity. Whereas
the reverse types at Antioch are usually figures of Zeus or Athena, other mints used
661 types of local significance; on a tetradrachm
minted at Tarsos we see an interesting mon-
umental type, the altar of Sandan, on which
the deity, probably of Hittite origin, is
seen according to the conventions of Near

639 Carthage: *Horse, with sun-disk above, 260-240
B.C. (electrum stater, 10.88 gm., diam. 21 mm.,
BM 1925; Jenkins-Lewis 408; found in
Sardinia), reverse of 649*

640 Carthage: *Horse looking back, 270-260 B.C.
(gold one-and-a-half-stater, 12.48 gm., diam.
23 mm., PCG 52.34; Jenkins-Lewis 377;
from the Tunis hoard, 1948), reverse of 648*

641 Carthage: *Prancing horse with palm-tree and
Punic inscription (Be)arzt; Sicilian mint, 270-
260 B.C. (electrum triple stater, reverse, 22.64
gm., diam. 29 mm., PCG 38.28; Jenkins-
Lewis 372; from the 'Porto Empedocle' hoard,
1897)*

642

643

644

645

646

647

648

649

650

651

652

653

Eastern iconography, standing on the back of a griffin-like animal.

A rival king, Alexander Zebina (128–123 B.C.) minted at Antioch some rare gold 531 staters, perhaps using the precious metal obtained from melting down the Nike held by the statue of Zeus set up by Antiochos Epiphanes; the reverse, ironically, copies that statue from Epiphanes' gold stater, and the portrait maintains a certain liveliness within the current style.

An increasing degree of formalization in the coin portraiture does not prevent us from being able to recognize and distinguish the individual members of the declining dynasty, who are also differentiated by their types and titles. The coins of the various mints—principally Antioch, Tarsos, Ptolemais, Askalon and Damascus—continue to give a vivid documentation of the confused course of events. This is specially valuable, for instance, for the years during which Antiochos VIII Grypos and his brother Antiochos IX Kyzikenos were virtually at war and the various regions of the kingdom were for ever changing hands. A good and typical portrait from this time is that of Antiochos IX, distinguishable by 662 his lightly bearded image, from the mint of Damascus. Towards the last days of the foundering dynasty the coins become more and more stereotyped. Finally the Seleukids were swept away altogether when the people of Antioch called in the Armenian Tigranes as their deliverer, in 83 B.C.

The Antiochene coins of Tigranes seem 663, 664 to call into play much of what was best in the existing traditions of Greek art; his

642, 643 Carthage: *Head of Tanit with corn-wreath and pendant necklace/Horse, 350-320 B.C. (gold stater, 9.36 gm., diam. 19 mm., PCG 31.18; RPK; Jenkins-Lewis 114)*

644, 645 Carthage: *Palm-tree/Horse's head, 350-320 B.C. (gold tenth-stater, 0.86 gm., diam. 8 mm., BM 1841; Jenkins-Lewis 159)*

646, 647 Carthage: *Head of Tanit/Horse with palm-tree, 350-320 B.C. (gold half-stater, 4.72 gm., diam. 13 mm., Jenkins-Lewis 52)*

648 Carthage: *Head of Tanit, 270-260 B.C. (gold one-and-a-half-stater, 12.48 gm., diam. 23 mm., PCG 52.34; Jenkins-Lewis 377; from the Tunis hoard, 1948), obverse of 640*

649 Carthage: *Head of Tanit, 260-240 B.C. (electrum stater, 10.88 gm., diam. 21 mm., BM 1925; Jenkins-Lewis 408; found in Sardinia), obverse of 639*

650, 651 Carthage:*Head of Tanit/Stepping horse, 200-146 B.C. (gold, 2.99 gm., diam. 13 mm., RPK); Jenkins-Lewis 496)*

652, 653 Carthage: *Head of Tanit/Horse's head, 200-146 B.C. (gold 1.51 gm., diam. 10 mm., BM 1938; Jenkins-Lewis 500)*

portrait, in some ways entirely hieratic and 'oriental' with the high decorated tiara, has an almost classical firmness in the modelling of the features, superior to what is normal among the later Seleukids. In Greek style, he wears no beard. The reverse has a special interest as being a representation of a famous Greek statue, the Tyche of Antioch by Eutychides, a pupil of Lysippos, which had been erected in the time of Seleukos I. The female figure in her mural crown is seated on a rock, holding a palm branch with a personification of the river Orontes shown swimming below at her feet.

Of the fragments into which the erstwhile Seleukid empire had disintegrated, it is interesting to note the way in which the powerful commercial cities of the Phoenician coast profited by the convulsions of the later Seleukid dynasty to establish their own autonomy. Aradus, for instance, was more or less independent since the third century and in the second century began issuing autonomous tetradrachms. In 125 B.C., Tyre became independent, followed by Sidon in 111 B.C. In each case the visible proof of independence is to be found in the issue of coinage, mainly in silver but also, on occasion, in gold; and the dating by the years of the local era is regularly proclaimed on these coins. The great deity of Tyre was Melqart, whose head was accordingly given 665, 666 prominence on the new series of tetradrachms. The reverse shows the persistent type of the Ptolemaic eagle here, however, poised not on a thunderbolt but on a galley, while the city name is accompanied by the titles 'Sacred and inviolable' (*hiera kai asylos*) which were the formula of autonomy. These coins flowed on without interruption and maintained the quality of their metal well into the period of the Roman empire as the most important coinage of the whole area of Phoenicia and Palestine.

In the eastern regions, the Seleukid empire had been taken over by the Parthians who had, under Mithradates I (171–137 B.C.), overrun the whole of Media and Babylonia by 141 B.C. Under Parthian rule, much of the Hellenic heritage was in fact retained, notably the coinage which developed quite naturally from that of the Seleukids and continued to bear inscriptions in the Greek language and even to be dated by the years of the Seleukid era. There is, however, a perceptible change of style even by the time of Mithradates II (123–91 B.C.) as we can see in his portrait, 667 very far removed from the decadent formalism of Antioch, displaying the king in an atmosphere of hieratic solemnity, bearded, elaborately robed and wearing a torque round his neck. The same may be said of another portrait, that of Orodes II 668 (57–37 B.C.) famous for his victory over Crassus and the Roman army at Carrhae. These are typical early examples of a style of coinage which, in later phases, while continuing to distinguish the features of individual kings, seems increasingly to shed any Greek characteristics and even at times to hark back to older traditions of Assyrian and Babylonian art.

THE GREEK CITIES AND MITHRADATES

The assertion or re-assertion of independence by the Greek cities during the later Hellenistic period is to be correlated naturally enough with the decline in the power of the kingdoms. Allusion has been made to the rise of cities such as Tyre in the wake of the declining Seleukids; the comparable revival of cities and their coinages in the Aegean area took place somewhat earlier in the second century B.C.

In Greece itself this phase was initiated by the Roman conqueror Flamininus after his victory over Philip V at Kynoskephalai and his proclamation of the freedom of the Greeks at Corinth in 196 B.C. It was perhaps soon after this that a radically new coinage made its appearance at Athens. The so-called 'New Style' coins were minted on the fine broad flans which had become universal in this phase of Hellenistic minting technique; like many other contemporary coins, they are also characterized by the presence of a prominent wreath border on the reverse, and they are referred to, for instance, in inventories from Delos as *stephanephoroi*. The basic elements, the head of Athena and the owl, are still present as in older Athenian types, but it is difficult to imagine a greater contrast. The new head of Athena clearly looks back to the Parthenos of Pheidias as its prototype, though the coins present not so much an exact copy as a classicizing re-creation; the elaborate helmet is shown with its triple crests, a Pegasos above the cheek-

669, 670

pieces and a row of horses' heads along the vizor. The traditional owl on the reverse is shown standing on an amphora and within the border is seen not only the city name but signs of an elaborate control system—there are three names—in this case *Mened(emos)*, *Epigono(s)* and *Alexa(...)*; there is also a symbol, here a standing figure of Asklepios on the left. Each year's coins were signed in this way: two of the names are constant for the year—probably those of prominent men honoured for undertaking the 'liturgy' of providing or organizing the coinage of the year, the third name, which changes more often, being that of a junior colleague. On the amphora, a letter denotes the month of issue. Other letters below probably refer to the source of the metal. This meticulous system, though hardly aesthetically advantageous, enables the whole scheme of the coinage to be followed year by year and month by month, and the precise sequence of the coins has been established by the identification of the obverse dies used from one year to the next. The series lasted for a century or more and furnishes striking evidence of Athens' regained prosperity, stimulated by the possession of the newly constituted free port of Delos from 166 B.C. onwards. The immense prestige and importance of these coins are amply attested by their prominence in widely scattered finds, as by the numerous imitations of them made in Crete (and, even more distantly, in southern Arabia). There is, however, still considerable controversy over the absolute chronology of the series.

At about the same date as the first of the Athenian 'New Style' tetradrachms, early in the second century B.C., coins of similar character were also minted in Euboia, and 671, 672 of them the most prominent were those of Eretria. These show an attractive bust of Artemis complete with her bow and quiver, and on the reverse the traditional Euboian cow, with garlanded horns as if ready for sacrifice; below is the name of a magistrate, and the wreath border is similar to that of Athens. The effect is simpler and less cluttered than that of the Athenian coin. Comparable issues were made at other Euboian cities, for instance at Chalkis whose tetradrachms show Hera in her chariot, linking to the theme of the archaic coins, and at Karystos where some small gold coins were minted. Another coinage issued in great quantity in Greece was that of the Thessalian league, bearing the type 503 of Athena recalling the Athena Alkidemos of Ptolemy and other Hellenistic rulers: and the island of Thasos produced an important issue of tetradrachms from the middle of the second century.

Roughly contemporary with the new coinage of Athens, and belonging to the same artistic phase, came an outburst of autonomous coins from numerous cities in Asia Minor. Many of these had, as already noted, intermittently struck coins of the Alexander type in the third century, but in the second century the emphasis is on purely autonomous types. Tetradrachms of impressive quality were now minted by cities in the Hellespontine region, Kyzikos, Abydos, Lampsakos, Ilion, Alexandria

654 Antiochos IV Epiphanes: *Head of Zeus; minted at Antioch, 175-164 B.C. (tetradrachm, 16.83 gm., diam. 33 mm., BMC 22; Mørkholm 14)*

655, 656 Demetrios I: *Diademed portrait/Tyche seated with cornucopiae; minted at Antioch, 152-1 B.C. (tetradrachm, 16.82 gm., diam. 32 mm., BMC 17)*

657 Kleopatra Thea and Alexander Balas: *Jugate heads; minted at Seleukia Pieria, 150-146 B.C. (tetradrachm, 14.96 gm., diam. 29 mm., BM 1903)*

658, 659 Antiochos VI: *Portrait with radiate diadem/Dioskouroi riding, within wreath; minted at Antioch, 144-3 B.C. (tetradrachm, obverse: 16.53 gm., diam. 32 mm., PCG 40.25; reverse: 16.89 gm., diam. 31 mm., BMC 4)*

660, 661 Demetrios II Nikator (second reign): *Bearded portrait/Monument of Sandon; Tarsos mint, 129-125 B.C. (tetradrachm, 16.65 gm., diam. 31-30 mm., PCG 41.27)*

662 Antiochos IX Kyzikenos: *Portrait with light beard; Damascus mint, reverse dated year 200 = 112 B.C. (tetradrachm, 16.35 gm., diam. 30 mm., BM 1924; from the Mandali hoard)*

663, 664 Tigranes of Armenia: *Portrait of king in tiara/Statue of the Tyche of Antioch; Antioch mint, 84-69 B.C. (tetradrachm, 16.45 gm., diam. 30 mm., PCG 44.15; RPK)*

665, 666 Tyre: *Head of Melqart/Eagle on prow, dated year 19 = 107 B.C. (tetradrachm, 14.40 gm., diam. 29 mm., BMC 89)*

667 Mithradates II of Parthia: *Portrait; Seleukeia-on-Tigris mint, 123-91 B.C. (tetradrachm, 15.48 gm., diam. 32 mm., BMC 1)*

668 Orodes II of Parthia: *Portrait; Seleukeia-on-Tigris mint, c. 57-38 B.C. (tetradrachm, 15.32 gm., diam. 30 mm., BMC 33)*

654

655

656

657

658

659

660

661

662

664

663

665

666

667

668

669

670

671

672

673

674

675

676

677

678

679

Troas. From the island of Tenedos is a curious tetradrachm with a double head which at first sight recalls the Roman Janus but in fact one head is male and the other female; it remains uncertain whether these should be regarded as Zeus and Hera or whether some more recondite mythological allusion is intended. The double-axe on the reverse is perhaps the symbol of Dionysos, as suggested by the bunch of grapes which is regularly associated with it. Further south there is a similar series of coins minted at Kolophon, Kyme, Magnesia and Smyrna; one or two mints such as Herakleia and Lebedos imitate the Athena head of the New Style Athenian coins, but in most cases each city was minting distinctive types of its own, as in earlier times. As an example, Myrina has a fine Apollo head with a standing Apollo on the reverse; this head has a sure and sculptural feeling which we scarcely find at Athens and which is fully equal to the quality of many of the royal portraits of this time.

There are two exceptions and contrasts to this array of autonomous tetradrachm coinages. Firstly, the so-called 'cistophoric' coins of the cities in the Pergamene kingdom, which started in the time of Eumenes II and which are distinguished only by the most uninspiring of all Greek coin designs (the cista mystica and a bow-case with writhing snakes). This coinage, which marked a move away from the prevailing Attic weight system, became the normal currency of the eventual Roman province of Asia. Secondly, at the important cities of the Bosphoros, Byzantion and Kalchedon,

669, 670 Athens: *Head of Athena Parthenos/Owl on amphora, 167-6 B.C. or later (tetradrachm, 16.89 gm., diam. 30 mm., PCG 36.17; Thompson 355; from the Salonika hoard)*

671, 672 Eretria: *Bust of Artemis/Cow within wreath, c. 196-190 B.C. (tetradrachm, 16.92 gm., diam. 31 mm., BM 1959; ex. Lockett)*

673, 674 Tenedos: *Double head, male and female/Double-axe with grapes, symbol Dioskouroi caps, c. 150 B.C. (tetradrachm, 16.71 gm., diam. 30 mm., PCG 39.8)*

675, 676 Myrina: *Head of Apollo/Standing Apollo within wreath, c. 150 B.C. (tetradrachm, 16.65 gm., diam. 33 mm., PCG 39.10)*

677, 678 Byzantion: *Head of Alexander/Athena; types of Lysimachos, BY on throne, c. 125-100 B.C. (tetradrachm, 17.02 gm., diam. 34 mm., BM 1923)*

679 Mithradates VI Dionysos Eupator of Pontos: *Diademed portrait, reverse dated month 9 of year 222 = 75 B.C. (tetradrachm, obverse, 16.80 gm., diam. 33 mm., PCG 44.2)*

a coinage bearing the old type of Lysimachos
677, 678 with the idealized head of Alexander and
the mint name unobtrusively placed under
Athena's throne, had continued without
interruption—except for a short time in the
third century when both cities temporarily
abandoned the Attic standard with some
coins of autonomous type. The long series
of Byzantion shows many fluctuations of
style, reflecting various phases of Hellenistic art; and the series undoubtedly continues until the first century B.C. In any case
there is an evident distance between a
comparatively late specimen of Byzantion,
with its rather formalistic and stylized
534 treatment, and the third century original.

Among the cities of Asia Minor another
coinage phenomenon which belongs to the
later Hellenistic period is the minting of
gold. This is in its way as impressive as the
great series of autonomous tetradrachms,
and perhaps less easy to define, owing to
the fact that gold coins tend to survive more
erratically than silver—thus making it more
difficult to be sure to what extent surviving
specimens really represent the original
issues. Some of these certainly were quite
extensive, as for instance at Rhodes, from
about the middle second century onwards.
Large silver coins had been profusely
minted at Rhodes, both Attic tetradrachms
of Alexander type, and also autonomous
type coins of Rhodian weight, at the end of
the third century; but there is at Rhodes no
counterpart to the important second century tetradrachm issues of other cities
mentioned above. Instead, there were gold
coins, both staters (equivalent to twenty

Attic drachms, or five silver tetradrachms)
and fractions. The larger pieces are of the   684, 68
same type as the earlier Rhodian coins, with
a facing head of Helios, whose style is often
not much inferior to that of the fourth
century staters. Smaller coins, such as the   686, 68
quarter-stater (equivalent of five Attic
drachms) show a profile Helios. These
issues, as can be established from their
correspondence with the complex silver
issues, of drachms and hemidrachms,
extend roughly from 150 to 100 B.C.

At other cities, the issues of gold were
probably more spasmodic and ephemeral.
From Smyrna we have a stater with a head   682*, 6
of Tyche and an interesting reverse of
Aphrodite supporting her left hand on a
column and holding Nike; this reverse is
signed by the 'Prytaneis', the board of city
magistrates, in contrast to the individual
names we should expect. At Miletos there
are staters with a head of Artemis and on   688, 68
the reverse a lion looking back at a star, the
traditional Milesian type. Ephesos has
another but very different head of Artemis,   692, 69
coupled with a reverse which is of great
interest as it shows the primitive cult-image
of the Ephesian goddess, wearing a tall
polos on her head, with garlands hanging
from her hands and a suggestion of her
many breasts. Apart from these examples,
there are also surviving gold staters from
Abydos and from Tralles, and smaller coins
from Kyzikos, Erythrai and Teos, the
last-mentioned being a comparatively new   690, 69
discovery on which we see an attractive
springing griffin, the regular emblem of
Teos, with a lyre on the reverse.

Many of these gold coins are extremely difficult to date precisely, and they may well have been short-lived issues; some survive only as single specimens. The theory has often been advanced that the outburst of gold coinage in Asia Minor is basically an emergency one, and that the occasion for it is the great rising against the Romans which took place in 89 B.C. at the instigation of Mithradates VI of Pontus (120–63 B.C.). This may indeed apply in some cases, but we cannot be sure that all the gold coins which survive are necessarily of identical date; and the example of Rhodes, where the gold is earlier than Mithradates, enforces some caution in accepting the theory too readily.

The reign of Mithradates, and his dramatic intervention in Asia Minor as the champion of Hellenism against the Romans, was in any case the occasion for some of the most remarkable of late Hellenistic coins. The king had spent the earlier part of his reign consolidating his power and preparing for an eventual conflict with Rome. The coinage of his own kingdom began only in 96 B.C., bearing the type of Pegasos in allusion to his claimed descent from Perseus; and a portrait whose style though realistic is not altogether immune from late Hellenistic academicism. At the moment of the revolt against Rome, Mithradates installed himself at Pergamon and simultaneously invaded Greece. At the mint now 694 opened at Pergamon a new portrait style was created whose impact is comparable with the high points of Pergamene art, and rivals the earlier coin portraits of Alexan-

der, Seleukos, Philetairos and Eumenes II. The drama of the Mithradates head with its floating hair and diadem-ends and the air of excitement and ardour, well convey his aspirations to be thought of as a Dionysos —whose name he adopted and which is emphasized by the ivy wreath on the coin reverse—or even, as some have suggested, a second Alexander. The reverse type was 680* at the same time changed from the Pegasos to a stag, possibly to evoke the Greek Artemis. There also appears, on the reverse of the gold stater, the star and crescent of Pontus, and the monogram of Pergamon accompanied by the year-letter 4, dating from the new era of Asia Minor which Mithradates was attempting to inaugurate. The idealistic Pergamene portrait survived the failure of Mithradates' crusade against Rome, and a later version of it is to be seen on a tetradrachm of the Pontic mint, dated 679 to year 222 of the local era, which is 75 B.C. This portrait remains one of the most striking of later Hellenistic coins.

The history of Mithradates however brings us back to Athens, and the problems of its coinage. In 87–86 B.C., a certain Aristion, a partisan of the Pontic king, brought Athens over to his cause and for a short time ruled the city as virtual dictator in Mithradates' interest. A gold stater whose issue was quite exceptional among 681*, 695 the New Style coins of Athens, bears the name of King Mithradates and of Aristion as the 'first magistrates' of the year, and the symbol is the Pontic star and crescents. So clearly does all this fit the situation of 87–86 B.C. that this coin has long been regarded as the cornerstone of the Athenian chronology. But it is one of the serious paradoxes of modern numismatic research that, as a result of the detailed reconstruction of the Athenian New Style series, we are now faced with the challenging theory that this stater should be placed more than thirty years earlier, representing a benefaction by the previous Pontic king, Mithradates V. It seems hard to believe, however, that a coin, which appears to proclaim its origin so clearly, can be shifted to another context by reason of indirect arguments, especially when other indirect arguments, notably those based on hoard evidence and on the prosopographical study of the names appearing on other Athenian coins, still tend to give strong support to the date of 87–86 B.C. The controversy about this coin, and by implication the whole chronology of the Athenian New Style coinage, as well as of many other related coinages, is still going on, and the problem—one of the most intractable historical questions relating to the coinage of the Hellenistic period—remains to tax the resources of historians and numismatists.

This short survey of Greek coins has attempted to display some of the fascination which they can afford, alike to the mind and to the eye. It may be of interest to conclude by quoting the impressions recorded, after a first sight of such coins, by a sensitive and well-informed observer in the eighteenth century. Goethe, in the course of his famous visit to Italy during 1786–88, visited

680 ▶

681 ▶

682▶▶

680 Mithradates VI Eupator Dionysos of Pontos: *Feeding stag, with star and crescent, within ivy-wreath border, monogram of Pergamon; Pergamon mint, date year 4 = 86-85 B.C. (stater, 8.49 gm., diam. 20 mm., PCG 44.1; RPK), reverse of 694*

681 Athens: *Head of Athena Parthenos, 87-86 B.C. (?) (stater, 8.23 gm., diam. 21 mm., PCG 46.8; Thompson; 121 B.C.), obverse of 695*

682 Smyrna: *Head of Tyche in mural crown, second-first century B.C. (stater, 8.31 gm., diam. 20 mm., BM 1934)*

ΒΑΣΙΛΕΩΣ
ΠΕ
ΜΙΘΡΑΔΑΤΟΥ
ΕΥΠΑΤΟΡΟΣ

683

684

685

686

688

689

687

692

693

690

691

694

695

683 Smyrna: *Standing Aphrodite leaning on column and holding Nike, in the name of the 'Prytaneis'*, second-first century B.C. *(stater, 8.31 gm., diam. 20 mm., BM 1934), reverse of 682*

684, 685 Rhodes: *Helios head facing/Rose, with name of Antaios, 150-100 B.C. (half-stater, 4.25 gm., diam. 17 mm., BMC 230a)*

686, 687 Rhodes: *Helios head in profile/Rose, with symbol aphlaston and name of Alexandros, 150-100 B.C. (quarter-stater, 2.05 gm., diam. 13 mm., BM 1927)*

688, 689 Miletos: *Artemis head/Lion looking back at star, with the name of Bion, second-first century B.C. (stater, 8.44 gm., diam. 19 mm., PCG 44.11)*

690, 691 Teos: *Springing griffin/Lyre, with name of Polythrous, second-first century B.C. (third-stater, 2.85 gm., diam. 11 mm., BM 1964)*

692, 693 Ephesos: *Artemis head/Cult-statue of Artemis Ephesia, with tripod, second-first century B.C. (stater, 692: 8.42 gm., diam. 18 mm., BM 1896; 693: 8.46 gm., diam. 20 mm., PCG 44.9)*

694 Mithradates VI Eupator Dionysos of Pontos: *Portrait head; Pergamon mint, date year 4 = 86-85 B.C. (stater, 8.49 gm., diam. 20 mm., PCG 44.1; RPK), obverse of 680*

695 Athens: *Owl on amphora, with symbol star and crescents and the names of King Mithradates and Aristion, 87-86 B.C. (?) (stater, 8.23 gm., diam. 21 mm., PCG 46.8; Thompson; 121 B.C.), reverse of 681*

Prince Torremuzza at Palermo to view his collection, and afterwards wrote:

'I went there almost reluctantly. I understand too little about this field, and a merely inquisitive tourist is the bane of the true connoisseur. But after all, one has to begin somewhere, so I relented and derived great pleasure and some profit from our visit.

'The ancient world was dotted with cities and even the smallest of them has left us, in its precious coins, a record, if not of the whole course of art history, at least of some epochs of it. An eternal spring of art's immortal fruits and flowers smiled up at us out of these drawers, telling of a craftsmanship perfected and practised over a lifetime, and of much else besides.

'Alas, we others possessed in our youth nothing but family medals which say nothing and coins bearing the portraits of emperors in which the same profile is repeated ad nauseam, of overlords who cannot be regarded as paragons of humanity. It makes me sad to think that in my youth my historical knowledge was limited to Palestine, which had no images at all, and Rome, which had far too many. Sicily and Magna Graecia have given me hope of a new life.'

SELECT BIBLIOGRAPHY

GENERAL

Kraay, C. M. and Hirmer, M. *Greek Coins.* London, 1966.

Franke, P. R. and Hirmer, M. *Die griechische Münze.* Munich, 1964.

Kraay, C. M. *Greek coins and history.* London, 1969.

Seltman, C. T. *Greek Coins.* (2nd ed.) London, 1955.

Seltman, C. T. *Masterpieces of Greek Coinage.* Oxford, 1949.

Regling, K. *Die antike Münze als Kunstwerk.* Berlin, 1924.

Cahn, H. A. *Griechische Münzen archaischer Zeit.* Basel, 1947.

Newell, E. T. *Royal Greek Portrait Coins.* New York, 1937.

Head, B.V. *Historia Numorum.* Oxford, 1911.

Babelon, J. *Traité des monnaies grecques et romaines.* Paris, 1901–33.

Macdonald, G. *Coin types.* Glasgow, 1905.

Noe, S. P. *Bibliography of Greek Coin Hoards.* (2nd ed.) New York, 1937. (3rd ed. in preparation).

Essays in Greek coinage presented to Stanley Robinson, edited by C. M. Kraay and G. K. Jenkins. Oxford, 1968.

Literaturüberblicke der griechischen Numismatik, *Jahrbuch für Numismatik und Geldgeschichte,* 1954–5 onwards.

Reports and Proceedings of International Numismatic Congresses – London, 1936; Paris, 1953; Rome, 1961; Jerusalem, 1963; Copenhagen, 1967.

Centennial Publication of the American Numismatic Society. New York, 1958.

British Museum Catalogues of Greek Coins (29 vols.). London.

Guide to the Principal Coins of the Greeks. British Museum, London, 1932; 2nd ed. 1959.

Sylloge Nummorum Graecorum : Great Britain (1931 onwards) incl. vol. II, Lloyd collection, vol. III Lockett collection, vol. IV Cambridge, vol. V Oxford ; U.S.A., American Numismatic Society (in progress) ; Germany, incl. H. von Aulock collection, Munich collection (in progress) ; Denmark, Copenhagen collection (in progress) ; Austria, Klagenfurt collection (in progress) ; Greece, Evelpides collection (in progress).

Catalogues of collections : Boston (1955); Jameson (1913–32); McClean, Cambridge (1923–9); Weber (1922–9); de Hirsch, Brussels (1959); de Luynes, Paris (1924–36).

TECHNIQUE

Hill, G. G. Ancient methods of coining, *Numismatic Chronicle* 1922.

Le Rider, G. Sur la fabrication des coins monétaires, *Schweizer Münzblätter* 1958.

Schwabacher, W. Zu der Herstellungs-methode der griechischen Münzstempel, *Schweizer Münzblätter* 1958.

Sellwood, D. G. Some experiments in Greek minting technique, *Numismatic Chronicle* 1963.

SPECIAL STUDIES

ABDERA

May, J. M. F. *The Coinage of Abdera.* London, 1966.

AIGINA

Brown, W. L. Pheidon's alleged Aeginetan coinage, *Numismatic Chronicle* 1950.

AINOS

May, J. M. F. *Ainos, its history and coinage 474–341 B.C.* Oxford, 1950.

AITNA

Boehringer, C. Hierons Aitna und das Hieroneion, *Jahrbuch für Numismatik und Geldgeschichte* 1968.

AKANTHOS

Desneux, J. *Les Tetradrachmes d'Akanthos.* Brussels, 1949.

AKRAGAS

Seltman, C. T. The engravers of the Akragantine decadrachms, *Numismatic Chronicle* 1948.

ALEXANDER THE GREAT

Newell, E. T. *Alexander hoards, Demanhur 1905.* New York, 1923.

Newell, E. T. *Dated Alexander coinage of Sidon and Ake.* New Haven-London, 1916.

AMBRAKIA

Ravel, O. *The "Colts" of Ambracia.* New York, 1928.

ARKADIA

Williams, R. T. *The confederate coinage of the Arcadians in the fifth century B.C.* New York, 1965.

ATHENS

Seltman, C. T. *Athens: its history and coinage before the Persian invasions.* Cambridge, 1924.

Cahn, H. A. Zur frühattischen Münzprägung, *Museum Helveticum* 1946.

Kraay, C. M. The archaic owls of Athens, *Numismatic Chronicle* 1956.

Kraay, C. M. *Coins of ancient Athens.* Newcastle, 1968.

Starr, C. G. *Athenian Coinage 480–449 B.C.* Oxford, 1970.

Robinson, E. S. G. The Athenian currency decree and the coinages of the allies, *Hesperia* suppl. VIII, 1949.

Thompson, M. *The New Style silver coinage of Athens.* New York, 1961.

Lewis, D. M. The chronology of the Athenian New Style coinage, *Numismatic Chronicle* 1962.

BAKTRIA

Curiel, R. and Fussmann, G. *Le trésor monétaire de Qunduz.* Paris, 1965.

CARTHAGE

Jenkins, G. K. and Lewis, R. B. *Carthaginian gold and electrum coins.* London, 1963.

CHALKIDIAN LEAGUE

Robinson, D. M. and Clement, P. *The Chalkidic mint.* Baltimore, 1938.

CORINTH

Ravel, O. *Les poulains de Corinthe.* Basel, 1936; London, 1948.

CRETE

Le Rider, G. *Monnaies crétoises du Ve au Ier siècle av. J.-C.* Paris, 1966.

CYPRUS

See below Persia, Robinson 1948.

DELPHI

Raven, E. J. P. Amphictyonic coinage of Delphi, *Numismatic Chronicle* 1950.

ELIS

Seltman, C. T. *Temple coins of Olympia,* Cambridge, 1921.

EPHESOS AND THE BEGINNINGS OF COINAGE

Head, B. V. *in* Hogarth, D. G. *Excavations at Ephesus.* London, 1908.

Robinson, E. S. G. Coins from the Ephesian Artemision, *Journal of Hellenic Studies,* 1951.

Robinson, E. S. G. The date of the earliest coins, *Numismatic Chronicle* 1956.

EPIROS

Franke, P. R. *Die antiken Münzen von Epirus.* Wiesbaden, 1961.

EUBOIA

Wallace, W. *The Euboian league and its coinage.* New York, 1956.

GELA

Jenkins, G. K. *The coinage of Gela.* Berlin, 1970.

HERAKLEIA

Work, E. *The earlier staters of Heracleia Lucaniae.* New York, 1940.

HIMERA

Gutmann, F. and Schwabacher, W. *Die Tetradrachmen- und Didrachmenprägung von Himera.* Munich, 1929.

KAULONIA

Noe, S. P. *Coinage of Caulonia.* New York, 1958.

KNIDOS

Cahn, H. A. *Knidos.* Berlin, 1970.

KYRENE

Naville, L. *Les monnaies d'or de la Cyrénaïque.* Geneva, 1951.

KYZIKOS

von Fritze, H. Die Elektronprägung von Kyzikos, *Nomisma* 1912.

LAMPSAKOS

Baldwin, A. *Gold staters of Lampsacus.* New York, 1924.

LYKIA

Mørkholm, O. Coin hoard from Podalia, *Numismatic Chronicle* 1971.

MACEDONIA

Raymond, D. *Macedonian regal coinage to 413 B.C.* New York, 1953.
Newell, E. T. *The coinages of Demetrius Poliorcetes.* Oxford, 1926.

MENDE

Noe, S. P. *The Mende (Kaliandra) hoard.* New York, 1926.

METAPONTION

Noe, S. P. *The coinage of Metapontum.* New York, 1927, 1931.

NAXOS

Cahn, H. A. *Die Münzen der sizilischen Stadt Naxos.* Basel, 1946.

PERGAMON

Westermark, U. *Das Bildnis des Philetairos von Pergamon.* Stockholm, 1961.

PERSIA

Robinson, E. S. G. The beginnings of Achaemenid coinage, *Numismatic Chronicle* 1958.
Robinson, E. S. G. Greek coins acquired by the British Museum, *Numismatic Chronicle* 1948.
Schlumberger, D. *L'argent grec dans l'empire achéménide*. Paris, 1953.

PTOLEMAIC EGYPT

Svoronos, J. *Ta nomismata tou kratous ton Ptolemaion*. (in Greek) Athens, 1904–1908.

RHEGION

Robinson, E. S. G. Rhegion, Zankle-Messana and the Samians, *Journal of Hellenic Studies* 1946.
Herzfelder, H. *Les monnaies d'argent de Rhegion*. Paris, 1957.

SAMOS

Barron, J. P. *The silver coins of Samos*. London, 1966.

SELEUKID EMPIRE

Newell, E. T. *The coinage of the Eastern Seleucid mints*. New York, 1938.
Newell, E. T. *The coinage of the Western Seleucid mints*. New York, 1941.

Mørkholm, O. *Studies in the coinage of Antiochus IV of Syria*. Copenhagen, 1963.
Le Rider, G. *Suse sous les Séleucides et les Parthes*. Paris, 1965.

SEGESTA

Lederer, P. *Tetradrachmenprägung von Segesta*. Munich, 1910.

SELINUS

Schwabacher, W. *Die Tetradrachmenprägung von Selinunt*. Munich, 1925.

SICILY–ITALY

Rizzo, G. E. *Monete greche della Sicilia antica*. Rome, 1946.
Lacroix, L. *Monnaies et colonisation dans l'occident grec*. Brussels, 1965.
Ashmole, B. Late archaic and early classical sculpture in Sicily and Italy, *Proceedings of the British Academy* 1934.
Vermeule, C. C. Chariot groups in fifth-century Greek sculpture, *Journal of Hellenic Studies* 1955.

SIDE

Atlan, S. *Untersuchungen über die sidetischen Münzen*. Ankara, 1967.

SYBARIS

Kraay, C. M. Coins of Sybaris after 510 B.C., *Numismatic Chronicle* 1958.

SYRACUSE (*see also* Aitna, Boehringer 1968)

Boehringer, E. *Die Münzen von Syrakus*. Berlin, 1929.

Tudeer, L. *Die Tetradrachmenprägung von Syrakus in der Periode der signierenden Künstler*. Berlin, 1913.

Gallatin, A. *Syracusan decadrachms of the Euainetos type*. Cambridge, Mass., 1930.

Jongkees, J. H. *The Kimonian decadrachms*. Utrecht, 1941.

Evans, A. J. *Syracusan medallions*. London, 1892.

Schwabacher, W. *Das Demareteion*. Bremen, 1958.

Liegle, J. *Euainetos*. Berlin, 1941.

TARENTUM

Evans, A. J. The "horsemen" of Tarentum, *Numismatic Chronicle* 1889.

TERINA

Regling, K. *Terina*. Berlin, 1906.

THASOS

West, A. B. *Fifth and fourth century gold coins from the Thracian coast*. New York, 1929.

GLOSSARY

AMPHORA
a jar for storing wine.

AMPYX
the part of a hair-band which appears above the forehead.

BILLON
an alloy of base silver.

CARNYX
a Gallic war-trumpet.

CISTA MYSTICA
a sacred basket used in Dionysiac rites, invariably shown as being of wickerwork and with the sacred serpent emerging or entwined around it.

CORNUCOPIAE
the horn of plenty, filled with various fruits.

DARIC
the standard gold coin of the Persian empire, perhaps so named after Darius I.

DEKADRACHM
the ten-drachma coin.

DIDRACHM
the two-drachma coin.

DIE
tool for striking coins, engraved with the design in negative.

DILITRON
the two-litra coin.

DIOBOL
the two-obol coin.

DODEKADRACHM
the twelve-drachma coin.

DRACHM(A)
a coin of the normal unit of weight, usually divided into six obols. The name is supposed to be derived from a 'handful' (*drax*) of six iron spits (*obeloi*) formerly used as primitive currency.

ELECTRUM
an alloy of gold and silver, either natural or artificial.

EXERGUE
the separate area of a coin design below the ground line.

HARPA
the hooked sword used by Perseus.

HEMIDRACHM
the half-drachm coin.

HEMILITRON
bronze coin with the value of a half-litra.

HEMIOBOL
the half-obol coin.

INCUSE
the reverse of a coin without design. But the so-called 'incuse' coins of South Italy show a design which is concave corresponding to the type of the obverse in relief.

KAUSIA
a Macedonian flat-topped hat.

KHAROSHTHI SCRIPT
an Indian script, derivative from Aramaic, used in bilingual inscriptions on Baktrian coins.

LITRA
a weight originally used for bronze in Sicily; the silver coin of corresponding value formed a fifth of the drachma in Sicily (instead of the obol elsewhere).

MINA
unit of one hundred drachmae.

NIKE
the winged goddess of victory.

OBVERSE
the front and principal side of a coin (e.g. that on which the main design, generally the portrait, is placed), struck from the anvil die.

OCTODRACHM
the eight-drachma coin.

OMPHALOS
the sacred 'navel-stone' of Apollo at Delphi, so called as Delphi was thought to be the centre of earth.

ONKIA
the ounce, one-twelfth of the Sicilian bronze litra.

OVERSTRIKING
the use of an older or foreign coin as the blank for striking with new types.

PENTADRACHM
the five-drachma coin.

PETASOS
a hat with wide curving brim.

QUADRIGA
chariot drawn by a team of four horses.

REVERSE
the back side of a coin, struck from the punch die.

SHEKEL
unit of coinage in the Near East, comparable with the drachm in Greece.

SIGLOS
Greek word for shekel, usually used as the name of the standard Persian silver coin.

SPHENDONE
literally a 'sling'; usually used of the rear portion of a hair-band, often decorated.

STATER
the principal denomination of a coinage either in gold, electrum or silver.

STYLIS
naval standard in the form of a pole with crossbar.

TALENT
unit of sixty minae, thus of 6,000 drachmae.

TETARTEMORION
a quarter-obol coin.

TETRADRACHM
a four-drachma coin.

TETROBOL
a four-obol coin.

TRIAS
a three-onkia bronze coin.

TRIDRACHM
a three-drachma coin.

TRIHEMIOBOL
a three-hemiobol coin (viz. $^1/_4$-drachm).

TRIHEMITETARTEMORION
a one-and-a-half tetartemorion (viz. $^3/_8$-obol).

TRIOBOL
a three-obol coin.

TRIPOD
bronze three-legged stand supporting a bowl; the sacred emblem of Apollo.

TRITARTEMORION
a three-tetartemorion coin (viz. $^3/_4$-obol).

TYCHE
the goddess of Fortune, usually identified with the goddess of a city.

WAPPENMÜNZEN
literally 'heraldic coins', used of the early Athenian didrachms.

INDEX

The text of this book, the four-colour offset illustrations and the jacket were printed by the Imprimerie Paul Attinger S.A., Neuchâtel.—The heliogravure reproductions were executed by Roto-Sadag S.A., Geneva.—Photolithos by Atesa, Geneva. —The binding is by Clerc & C^{le} S.A., Lausanne.—Layout and design by André Rosselet.—Editorial: Suzanne Meister.

Printed in Switzerland